GRIMSARGH:

THE STORY OF A LANCASHIRE VILLAGE

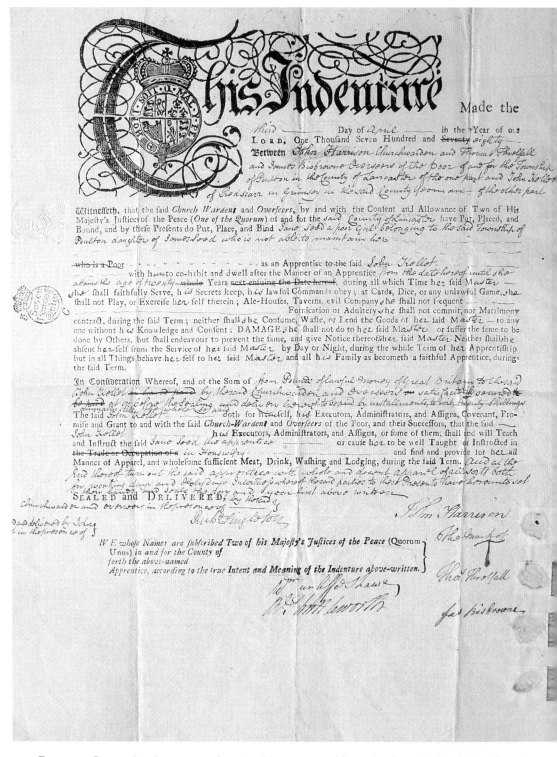

Frontispiece. Grimsargh indenture, 1780. *Reproduced by permission of Lancashire Record Office, LRO, PR 2027/30*

Grimsargh

THE STORY OF
A LANCASHIRE VILLAGE

David Hindle

Carnegie Publishing, 2002

Published by Carnegie Publishing Ltd
Carnegie House, Chatsworth Road
Lancaster LA1 4SL
publishing website: www.carnegiepub.co.uk
book production website: www.wooof.net

British Library Cataloguing-in-Publication data
A CIP record for this book is available from the British Library

ISBN 1-85936-094-7

Typeset by Carnegie Publishing
Printed and bound in the UK by
The Cromwell Press, Trowbridge, Wilts

Front cover painting of Red Scar by Albert Woods,
reproduced by kind permission of Mrs E. Woods

Contents

Grimsargh

THE STORY OF A
LANCASHIRE VILLAGE

Dedicated to my wife, Dorothy,
for her patience and constant support

Foreword

By the author of 'Memories of a Preston Childhood', Wing Commander Alan Wilding (RAF Retd)

*I*N THIS EXCELLENT BOOK, David Hindle, the author of the classic book *Twice Nightly: An Illustrated History of Entertainment in Preston*, has used more of his considerable detective and research skills to unearth an astonishing amount of detail on the origins of Grimsargh. I know he has gone to enormous lengths to produce a very readable book encapsulating the life and work of the people over the centuries. The evocative writings of Katherine Ellen Cross of Red Scar and the vanished Grimsargh farm of Moss Nook make compelling reading; and railway enthusiasts will wish they had caught the 'Little Annie' train from Grimsargh to Whittingham, as I did in the 1930s.

The author has once again successfully combined local history with a good proportion of anecdotal material and a touch of nostalgia. Indeed, it is due to David's unstinting effort that much of the material has never before appeared in print. His concern for Grimsargh, and his anxiety to retain what was, and still is, best about it, shines throughout the book. In putting his work into print, before the historic village and surrounding countryside he loves is obliterated by urban development, the author has performed a service in social history for which future generations of readers, scholars, and academics alike will surely be grateful. This is probably the finest definitive history of Grimsargh, in very readable story form, ever written, or ever likely to be written; and I commend it most sincerely.

Alan Wilding, May 2002

Miss Nellie Carbis, 1904–1999. 'It was in 1935 that I was appointed to the leadership of a village school, not far from Preston. I had never heard of the place before – Grimsargh!' (from *Nellie Carbis Looks Back*)

Introduction

*T*HIS BOOK is intended to perpetuate the memory of a remarkable lady and stalwart member of the local community, Miss Nellie Carbis.

It is a permanent tribute to a Lancashire friend and character who possessed a natural sense of humour, a sharp wit and who always expressed human kindness. Nellie was born, the seventh child of a working-class family, in Newton-le-Willows, Lancashire. For twenty-nine years she was the headmistress of the old Grimsargh Parochial School until her retirement in 1964. Sadly, Nellie died just a few weeks before the millennium, on Saturday 20 November 1999, at the age of ninety-five.

Many of Grimsargh's senior citizens were taught by her and can remember the formation of what is now the Nellie Carbis Millennium Woodland. It was a testament to her role in the local community and village life when on Tuesday, 30 November 1999, a full congregation gathered at her funeral service in Grimsargh Church to pay their last respects. I felt humbled to read the lesson on that sad occasion. I could empathise with her views and share her humour and I hope that in some respects we shared a similar view on life. High on the joint agenda would be the enhancement of the quality of life by an interest in all things natural and an appreciation of local history. Before the onset of the electronic age, it was old trains and buses, ancient farmsteads, colourful Lancashire characters and traditions that helped characterise small villages like Grimsargh. During my visits to see Nellie Carbis, over a glass or two of apricot wine and anecdotes, which got better by the minute, I was given the impetus to research the Grimsargh area. Armed with my cherished signed copies of her booklets on local history I have found that many years of research have been both stimulating and pleasurable.

Grimsargh village lies five miles to the north-east of the ancient Borough of Preston – which gained city status in 2002 – and three miles from the expanding small town of Longridge. The village

2

OPPOSITE
The riverine landscape of
Grimsargh in winter.
Author's collection

Introduction

is familiar to many motorists and walkers who pass through it whilst en route to discover the delights of the Trough of Bowland and the picturesque villages nestling in the Ribble and Hodder Valleys. Grimsargh might be described as the gateway to the Ribble Valley for the view from Elston Lane reveals a picturesque river valley still largely unspoilt and rich in wildlife. Down below the Ribble flows with increased momentum as its serpent-like course takes it onwards towards Preston and the estuarine mud flats, marshes, and sand dune sequences so characteristic of Southport and Lytham. This book is, however, mainly concerned with the former township of Grimsargh-with-Brockholes, which includes the present-day civil parish of Grimsargh.

Grimsargh-with-Brockholes originates from a Norse settlement

The Ribble at Alston Wood.

Snowdrops on the banks of
the Ribble at Alston.
Author's collection

and has a fascinating history. There was even a mention in the Domesday Book for Grimsargh. I have aimed to provide for a range of interests as well as producing an historical and social account of the parish. Records generated by the ecclesiastical and civil parish administrations are held at the Lancashire County Record Office and many documents are relevant to Grimsargh including the census returns, maps, wills and probate, Quarter Sessions records, and a comprehensive local history library. The language and spelling of original documents have been reproduced as written. I am pleased that during the course of my research some valuable documents, privately held, have been passed into the safe custody of the Record Office.

I could never have completed this book without the generous support of others. Shared conversations have unlocked storehouses of reminiscences. I acknowledge the encouragement and help of Alan Wilding for his contribution to the final chapter and writing the Foreword, to the late Nellie Carbis, and to Preston historian, Marian Roberts, for stimulation and inspiration. I would also like to thank leading academic historian, Dr Andrew Gritt of the University of Central Lancashire for reading the proof and making helpful comments. I am grateful for the generous level of sponsorship provided by local industries which has helped to make the book affordable for people. I thank all contributors, some of whom have played a part in Grimsargh's history, for sharing their memories and allowing me to use their valued documents and photographs and for expertise in other areas. I apologise if I have unknowingly breached copyright in the use of any photograph. Illustrations for which copyright still exists or for which special permission has been granted have accordingly been credited. Finally, I would like to thank Directors Alistair Hodge and Anna Goddard and the staff of Carnegie Publishing for their professionalism in producing this book.

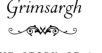

Grimsargh

THE STORY OF A
LANCASHIRE VILLAGE

Grimsargh on the Map

An introductory historical and topographical perspective

*T*HE sixteenth-century north-west administrative areas were known as townships or vills. Lancashire is known for having very extensive ecclesiastical parishes that were subdivided into many townships or civil parishes. This reflects the very low density of population in Amounderness during the medieval period, where single township parishes were unusual. The ecclesiastical boundary covered by St Michael's Church overlaps today's civil parish boundary, which is governed by Grimsargh Parish Council.

The establishment of certain ecclesiastical boundaries such as Preston may have their origins in the boundaries of pre-Conquest estates. Indeed, the history of the parish church of St John the Divine at Preston goes back since at least this far. At the time of the Domesday Book in 1085, the church occupying the site of Preston Parish Church was dedicated to St Wilfrid. Several thou-

Townships in the lower Ribble Valley, 1835.
By courtesy of Dr A. Crosby and the Friends of Lancashire Archives

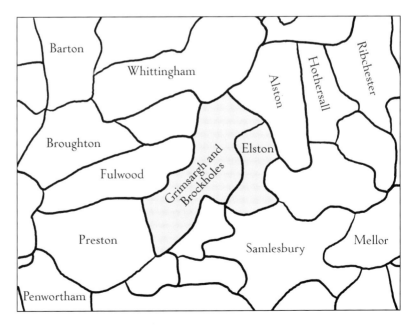

sand parish churches had been built by the time of the Norman Conquest and between 1150 and 1250 the division of England into ecclesiastical parishes had been completed. Between 1350 and 1500 a great number of new buildings were added to the English landscape.

Grimsargh was originally the township of Grimsargh-with-Brock-holes, being composed of the hamlets of Grimsargh and Brockholes, and within the Parish of Preston. The neighbouring time-worn Saxon settlements of Alston and Elston each had their own township authorities. With the advent of local government reform in 1894, Grimsargh gained its own parish council and later absorbed the area covered by Elston. The geographical area covered by the hamlet of Brockholes was subsequently lost by legislative procedures to the Borough of Preston.

Within the current political structure of local government a parish is one of the smallest governmental units. Grimsargh is one of eight parishes within the City of Preston. To the north and east of Grimsargh the boundary is partly flanked by Savick Brook and the Parish of Haighton. Old Boundary Stone Cottage on Preston Road, a few hundred metres short of Alston Lane Roman Catholic Church, represents the approximate boundary separating Grimsargh from Alston and Longridge. At the time of writing the western boundary on the north side of Preston Road is likely to be extended to incorporate a new residential development at The Hills, built on the site of the former St John Southworth School. Due east, the River Ribble flowing between ancient woodlands is a natural and historical boundary between the parishes of Grimsargh and Samlesbury.

Grimsargh's St Michael's Church was built on the western outskirts of the village to serve a wider community in 1716. Alston Lane Roman Catholic Parish was established during the same century to the east of Grimsargh provoking clichéd questions from curious villagers, 'Do you go up or down the road?'

The passenger railway station on the Longridge branch line has been closed for over seventy years, and nowadays it seems beyond the bounds of credibility that Grimsargh once had two railway stations on separate lines and even had junction status for the long-gone Whittingham Hospital line.

Grimsargh developed significantly in the nineteenth century with more houses built along the side of the main Preston Road and Whittingham Lane ,and additional newly constructed or

Grimsargh

THE STORY OF A
LANCASHIRE VILLAGE

The Parish of Grimsargh in 2001. The outlined area shows the extent of the parish boundary.
This map contains Ordnance Survey-based mapping on behalf of © Crown Copyright 2002. All rights reserved. Licence No. LA07 9014. Also courtesy of Preston City Council.

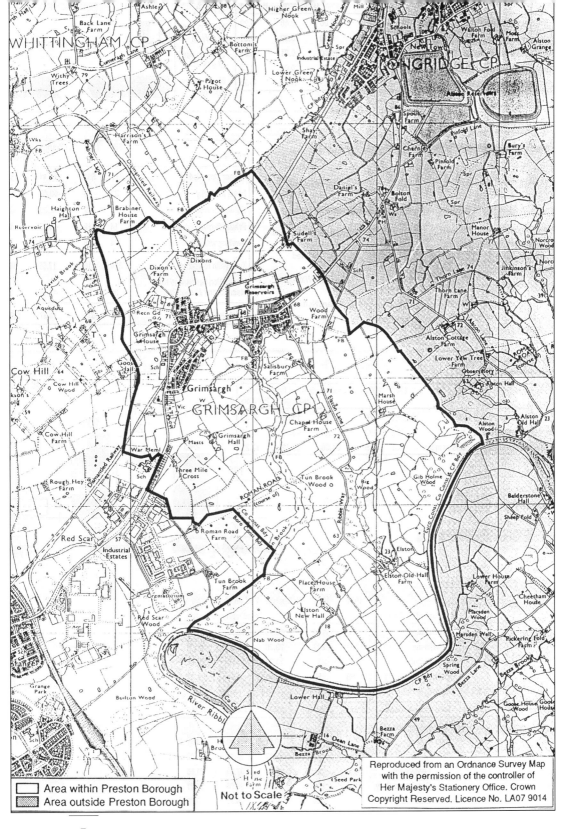

Area within Preston Borough
Area outside Preston Borough

Not to Scale

Reproduced from an Ordnance Survey Map
with the permission of the controller of
Her Majesty's Stationery Office. Crown
Copyright Reserved. Licence No. LA07 9014

7

Do you go up the road (to church)? ABOVE Grimsargh St Michael's Church School and School House looking east towards the railway bridge (who had ever heard of traffic calming measures when this photo was taken around 1912?); or BELOW down the road (to church)?: looking west along the main road towards St Michael's Church and School with one classic period car.

Photographs courtesy of Mrs V. Raby

rebuilt farms dispersed throughout the countryside of both Elston and Grimsargh. As the village grew it transformed from agricultural hamlet to a 'T' shaped or cruciform village. Grimsargh has long been recognised as a pleasant linear village with Victorian, Edwardian and more recent houses, extending at least a mile along the main Preston to Longridge Road. Along Whittingham Lane, more houses overlook the largest green in the county. The traditional village green is a typical and important characteristic of the English rural scene, and the 'icing on the cake' came when the land was acquired by Preston Rural District Council in 1938. The green was subsequently transferred by Preston RDC to the present ownership of Preston Borough Council.

Complementing the village green is a fine Georgian mansion called Grimsargh House, which nestles in woodland alongside

Grimsargh village green is one of the largest in the county and is situated next to Grimsargh House.
N. Carbis collection

Grimsargh's amenity area. The style of architecture has changed little since Grimsargh House was occupied by the families of James Blanchard in 1840 and Edward Sidgreaves in 1860.

Grimsargh House was the residence of Mr and Mrs H. Mallott

LEFT
Today, Grimsargh House is a
care home for the elderly.
N. Carbis collection

BELOW
An engraving of Grimsargh
House as it appeared in 1845.
N. Carbis collection

during the Second World War. The house had a part to play in wartime Grimsargh when many of the voluntary services were based there. The Mallotts were both managers of Grimsargh School and in 1943, they leased a piece of land at a peppercorn rent which became the School Garden and the present Nellie Carbis Millennium Woodland. Long after the war, the Mallotts were still in residence, ensuring that the period rooms, with family treasures and Regency furnishings, maintained the atmosphere of a fine country house. Margaret Mallott's many activities on behalf of the community included being President of the local Women's Institute and West Lancashire Guides County Commissioner.

In 1965 Mr and Mrs Richard Anthony Jackson and family moved from St Annes on Sea to Grimsargh House, to be nearer to Stonyhurst College where their two boys boarded between 1962 and 1970. Captain Richard 'Tony' Jackson was commissioned at Sandhurst during the Second World War. He was mentioned in despatches on account of saving the lives of personnel on a blazing ammunition train in Scotland During the advance of the allies in Europe, Captain Jackson, of the Royal Armoured Corps (Tanks) was billeted in Holland where he met Therese de Wit, who became his wife. Therese, despite her youth, bravely assisted the resistance during the German occupation of her country and at one stage was interviewed by the Gestapo. The Jacksons became the last family to occupy Grimsargh House as a private residence. In 1982 it was converted into a nursing home and shortly thereafter became a rest home for the care of the elderly. Tony and Therese Jackson's four children, Michael, Josephine, Richard and Louise, are today directors of Grimsargh House Residential Care Home.

Close to Tun Brook two or three copper beeches still dominate the woodland plateau that was the site of an historic mansion overlooking one of the most beautiful stretches of the Ribble Valley at Horse Shoe Bend. The romantic history of Red Scar is fascinating. From 1803 to 1898 the building was occupied by three generations of the Cross family, who as principal landowners became Squires of Grimsargh. The Cross family and their tenant farmers played an important part in the development of agriculture in Grimsargh. The name of their home, Red Scar lives on as the site of an industrial estate and is now within the Borough of Preston. The authorities are planning more urban expansion in the designated areas of countryside of 'Preston East'.

Throughout history, the River Ribble has helped to preserve

the relatively unspoilt Ribblesdale landscape and every house, farm, earthwork, woodland and field boundary has its own story to tell, reflecting human activity over many centuries. There are no road bridges between Preston and Ribchester and there was little incentive to build important roads alongside the northern course of the meandering river with its propensity for flooding. Consequently there are few major roads or railways, and industrialisation has not impacted too heavily on the landscape. King Cotton was mainly confined to the towns and cities of Lancashire and locally only a few mills were built in Longridge and Ribchester. The river has seen environmental improvements in levels of pollution including the principal tributaries of the Rivers Calder and Darwen and in ecological, geomorphological, and visual terms it is still a fine river.

The history of Grimsargh-with-Brockholes is described in the invaluable *Victoria County History of Lancashire* (Farrer and Brownbill, vol. 1 1906, vol. 2 1908 and vol. 7 1912). Volume 7 describes the features of the old township.

> The township consists of two distinct parts connected by a narrow strip of ground beside the Ribble. Grimsargh, the northern half, has an area of 1,184 acres, stretching from the Ribble to Savick Brook. It is divided from Elston on the east by a wooded clough. In the southern corner the land rises steeply from the river, and here is Red Scar, a mansion commanding fine views over the valley. The surface of Grimsargh is comparatively level, but mostly above 200 feet over sea level. The principal road is that from Preston to Longridge, going north and then east. The railway between these towns crosses this part of the township in a north-easterly direction and has a station named Grimsargh, from which a branch line runs north-west to the asylum at Whittingham.
>
> Brockholes lies in a bend of the Ribble, its boundary on the east and south being closed in by Ribbleton on the other sides. The greater part of it is low-lying level ground, but on the border of Ribbleton the surface rapidly rises for nearly 100 feet. Lower Brockholes and Higher Brockholes are in the south-west and north-east respectively. There are very few houses in this part of the township, which has an area of 753 and a half acres. The Township is governed by a Parish Council. The area of the original Township of Grimsargh-with-Brockholes was 1,937 acres and in 1901 there was a population of 453. The line of a Roman road, called Watling Street, had been traced in Grimsargh and Elston.

Grimsargh on the Map

The Gough Map of 1360 gives an early image of the Ribble Valley. This was the first brave attempt by surveyors to record the outline of the whole of northern England and North Wales. Christopher Saxton published his map of Lancashire in 1577, followed by John Speed's in 1610. The maps indicate settlements at Ribbleton, Chipping and Longridge though the hamlet of Grimsargh is excluded. Upland areas are indicated and could be scrutinised by potential developers or battle strategists. Yates's map of 1786 gives a good impression of the county as a whole, and between Longridge Fell and the ridge at Mellor the Ribble is shown. The course of the Preston to Longridge road is now shown to bisect the named village of Grimsargh. Other features give clues to the history of the area including the lane to the south of the Catholic church at Alston which then extended to Elston Lane but today ends at Wood Farm. A site visit to the field to the east of Elston Lane reveals the course of this ancient highway which linked the townships of Elston and Alston until at least 1847. Christopher Greenwood's one inch to the mile map of Preston produced in 1818, incorporated – for the first time – the detail of Grimsargh's roads, farms and ancient dwellings and proved to be a precursor to the Ordnance Survey maps of today.

This old highway linked Alston Church with Elston Lane. The original Mission can be seen on the right.
Author's collection

Inevitably the features shown on the first Grimsargh OS maps contrast greatly with those shown on the latest OS Pathfinder 679 map with a scale of 4 cm to 1 km, covering Grimsargh. The Ordnance Survey was founded in 1791 and the first maps were conceived at the beginning of the nineteenth century with emphasis on accuracy and detail. The Grimsargh area was surveyed in 1844–47 and first edition maps covering Grimsargh-with-Brockholes were published to a scale of six inches to the mile.

The Ordnance Survey Map of 1847 reveals the two new reservoirs of Preston Water Works between Longsight Lane (Preston Road) and the newly constructed Longridge branch line which is today represented by the symbol 'track of old railway'. Old maps and antiquated books yield many surprises and overall provide a wider and more detailed perspective enabling the researcher to analyse enigmas and features of the landscape. A post-medieval sandpit was formerly situated north of Red Scar House and is shown on the first edition Ordnance Survey map. Today a synthetic fibre works has been built close to the site and there is no trace of

Grimsargh

THE STORY OF A
LANCASHIRE VILLAGE

A detail from Yates's map of
1786 showing the Ribble
Valley from Grimsargh to
Dinckley.
Courtesy of Lancashire Record Office

the ancient sandpit whatsoever. Ribbleton Moor is also shown to the north of Brockholes and next to Ribbleton Hall. The extent of the moor is further clarified with a footnote: 'shown as land common to the townships of Ribbleton and the hamlet of Brockholes'.

Numerous cul-de-sacs on both sides of the river served several old halls situated between Ribchester bridge and Lower Brockholes and the numerous farms. Where these met the Ribble, it was often possible to cross by a number of ancient river crossings. The 'Elston ferry' once plied between the hamlet of Elston and Balderstone close to Gib Holme Wood, providing a peaceful river crossing for local people and clearly indicated on the first edition map. It also solves the mystery for me of why a public footpath sign at Elston points directly into the river!

The second edition six inches to the mile OS map published in 1895 indicates that Grimsargh village was expanding along

Grimsargh on the Map

Detail of the second edition six inches to the mile OS Map (1895) showing Moss Nook, the railway and Grimsargh reservoirs.
Courtesy of Lancashire Record Office

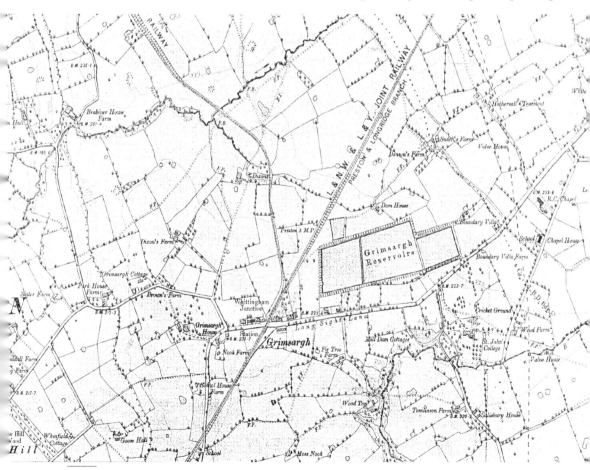

Longsight Lane. The dispersed patterns of settlements include familiar names of old farmsteads that comprised the Cross Estate. Moss Nook is shown as an isolated farmstead in meadows to the east of Grimsargh School and details of its nostalgic past are described in a later chapter. A second single track railway to Whittingham and a third Grimsargh Reservoir constructed alongside the two original reservoirs symbolise further changes to the social and economic status of the parish and the potential for commercial exploitation of the land.

The twenty-five inches to one mile Ordnance Survey Map published in 1890/93 features the woodlands of Red Scar and Nab Wood in such detail that one is left to count the trees and footpaths and scrutinise the detail of the Red Scar Mansion together with the stables and servants' quarters. William Cross planted beech and lime trees when he lived in Red Scar House. To this day the site of the former mansion is still adorned by these fine trees and his legacy gives the plateau a parkland appearance.

Archaeological evidence from Ribblesdale dates back to the first Bronze Age settlements 5,000 or more years ago and suggests that the Viking Norsemen were not the first to establish their roots in Grimsargh.

PART I

*Early Invaders and
Medieval Grimsargh*

CHAPTER ONE

Grimsargh Before the Norman Conquest

THE 'Grimsargh Story' begins with the primeval forests which covered most of Britain. The semi-natural ancient woodlands of Red Scar on their steep escarpments may be remnants of the original wild forest, which remained until man began their clearance in the late Stone Age, about 4,000 BC. Evidence of settlements was provided in 1885, during the construction of Preston's Albert Edward Dock, a few miles down river. The major archaeological legacy came from deep beneath the surface of the riverbed. A 'head count' of severed skulls comprised of thirty human skulls, over a hundred skulls of red deer, several of now-extinct wild ox, two pilot whale skulls, a Bronze spear head and two dug-out canoes. This collection has been preserved in the Harris Museum at Preston and in 2001 was the subject of further investigation and research by John Moores University, Liverpool. Research findings indicate that this material has probably accumulated since the time of the Bronze Age and the exact reason for its deposition at this point has yet to be ascertained.

Bronze Age artefacts discovered in the Grimsargh area have included a bronze flat axe found at Elston Bottoms in 1932, a flint arrowhead found less than one foot below the surface near Higher Brockholes Farm close to Horse Shoe Bend in 1930 and a damaged stone hammer head found about four feet below the surface at Stone Cross, Grimsargh, in 1950. The Lancashire Sites and Monuments Record (SMR) of Lancashire County Council's Environment Directorate at Preston contains evidence of a possible prehistoric promontory fort or other enclosure situated in Ribble Valley woodland between Red Scar Wood and the adjoining Boilton Wood.[1]

Early settlement and established agricultural land use in the area of Grimsargh is likely to have been characterised by primitive farming and the use of polished stone and flint tools and weapons. No one can be sure of the dates of the first Grimsargh settlements but they could be of the Neolithic period, from about 2500 to 1900 BC. The first human invaders of the vast tracts of primeval forests inhabited by wild beasts of the period may one day also reveal their secrets.

Following the Roman Invasion of southern England in AD 43, advancing Roman legions intent on conquering northern England, had a challenging time defeating the region's Celtic tribes known as the Brigantes. The Celts were well established in the north-west and Roman onslaughts involved armies landing by sea and using the Ribble and Lune Valleys for inland penetration. Overland advances involved the construction of roads linking the forts at Chester, Manchester, Ribchester, Lancaster and Kirkham. Just after this Conquest, a military supplies depot was set up at Walton-le-Dale. Situated alongside the Ribble and astride the road running north, and by an established ford crossing, it was strategically important and within reach of the fort at Ribchester. 'Bremetennacvm Veteranorum', the Roman name for Ribchester, was at the heart of the road network. The fort was built between AD 75 and 80 by Agricola during his campaign against the Brigantes and provided for the accommodation of a cavalry troop of at least 500 men.

Despite the initial conflict, day-to-day life involved the people working on the land, sustaining the rural economy, and experiencing a peaceful co-existence for the greater part of the occupation which lasted for over 300 years. Settlement patterns and ways of life do not appear to have been greatly affected by the Roman occupation, nor by their departure. This was in contrast to the southern counties where the effects were much greater.

The Roman Road linked Ribchester with the fort at Kirkham. Driving along the straight stretches of the urban Watling Street Road, through Fulwood, Preston, provides an opportunity to reflect on the line of the original road where Romans and their livestock hauled wooden trucks long before the modern phenomenon of road rage and thunderous juggernaut traffic.

The roads enabled soldiers and supplies to be moved quickly between trouble spots; and tracing the course of the same road through the Parish of Grimsargh may be accomplished with a trained eye, the OS Pathfinder map 679 and an indispensable guide to Roman roads.[2] From Ribchester the Roman road passes close to Ribchester Church and heads west to Hothersall and Stubbins Nook before entering the grounds of Alston Hall College.

The college was actually built on the line of the Roman road, which dispels any rumours that the Romans sought to improve their quality of life or obtain a few 'A' levels! The course of the road is shown to emerge from woods to the west of Alston Hall and cross fields to the south of Marsh House before crossing the northern extremity of Big Wood where the narrow recessed course of the road is discernible in the landscape. Between Elston Lane and the Tun Brook Woodland Nature Reserve it crosses a private driveway leading to a red bungalow, and between this driveway and Tun Brook traces of the ridge can be seen next to a ditch and the remains of isolated trees. There is little to discern in Tun Brook Wood other than signs of a curving terrace going first north and then south on the steep and inaccessible east bank. The woodland ravine is difficult to negotiate and at the point where the road cuts through the wood there is no public footpath. On the west side of Tun Brook the course of the road passes close to the aptly named Roman Road Farm and Roman Way Industrial Estate before reaching Red Scar.

An archaeological evaluation took place at Red Scar in advance

of the proposed development of the land. The Roman Road was found to be relatively well preserved, with a cambered surface composed of rounded stones and cobbles with finer gravels acting as a capping. Along both sides of the road were two drainage ditches about 9.5m apart and two outer boundary ditches about 26m apart. Roman pottery and a glass paste melon bead were amongst the archaeological remains found on the site and confirm the existence of the road during the third century. It is likely that the road would have been used by Roman regiments and cavalry, wheeled vehicles for supplies and also by local communities. The exposed excavation at the Roman Way Industrial site gives a good impression of the road and is well worth a visit.

Several items of Roman material have been found along the banks of the Ribble near to Grimsargh including a bronze coin found at Boilton Wood of a specific type issued by Emperor Antonin. In addition, three other Roman coins have been found in Red Scar Wood.

After the departure of the Romans from British shores, the Celtic influence prevailed and some of the native population

Grimsargh

THE STORY OF A
LANCASHIRE VILLAGE

OPPOSITE
A map showing important archaeological sites in and around Grimsargh, each marked with a star and number.
Courtesy of Lancashire County Council Sites and Monuments Record

LEFT AND BELOW
The Roman Way excavation, showing the original Watling Street.
Author's collection

stayed on in spite of Roman and Saxon infiltration. Large numbers of Anglo Saxons colonised the lowlands during the fifth and sixth centuries. King Ethelfrith (AD 593–613) took over the land to the north of the Ribble where Grimsargh is situated; and what is now central Lancashire was then a part of the kingdom of Northumbria based in Yorkshire. The Danes and Viking Norsemen crossed the North Sea to raid most of north and western Europe from the eighth to the eleventh centuries. In the years before the Norman Conquest there must have been considerable cultural differences and political unrest. Indeed, since the time of the Roman occupation, Preston and its rural environs have been at the heart of political upheaval and several significant battles.

Danish and German Anglo-Saxons established many Lancashire villages with names ending in 'ham' and 'tun'. Thus we have Kirkham, Heysham, Whittingham, Bolton, and Preston. The origin of the name 'Preston' and the town (attaining city status in 2002) that grew up with it have been associated with an Anglo Saxon Bishop, Saint Wilfrid, who was granted land near the Ribble, about AD 670. It has long been believed that monks from his abbey at Ripon founded a church and that embryonic Preston grew up round it, so giving the town its name 'Priest [tune] town'. The Sacrificial Lamb was Saint Wilfrid's crest and the letters PP (Prince of Peace) became the town's coat of arms. The original parish church was dedicated to Saint Wilfrid up to the time of the Reformation, when it became St John's. The present St John the Divine Church was built on this same ancient site of Christian worship in 1855.

During the early years of the tenth century boatloads of Norsemen from Scandinavia settled in north-western England. This immigration was distinct from that which had introduced a Danish population into eastern England before the end of the ninth century. The north-west invaders were Norwegians, not Danes, and there is little evidence to suggest that there were any military operations or conquests such as preceded the Danish settlements in eastern England. The surprisingly sophisticated immigrants came with well-developed agricultural skills and cultures, seeking lands to cultivate. In all probability the Irish Norse invaders would have sailed from northern Ireland and the Isle of Man before infiltrating Northern England in an atmosphere of relative calm, albeit with initial skirmishes and no doubt violence being met with violence.

Grimsargh

THE STORY OF A
LANCASHIRE VILLAGE

Proud of the local
Scandinavian heritage –
Vikings have been hewn in
stone close to the M6
intersection at Red Scar.
Author's collection

The Hundred of Amounderness, north of the Ribble, attracted many Norse settlers and many small villages owe their origins to the Norse colonies. The Vikings' influence can be seen in the derivation of modern place names including words ending in 'by' such as Nateby. Scandinavian name formations indicate the origins of both Grimsargh and the nearby village of Goosnargh.[3] Grim‚sargh‚with‚Brockholes was the name of a composite township bearing a Scandinavian and an English name. The predominance of the Scandinavian name does not in itself imply that the English were dispossessed of their lands and the flight of a few individuals cannot be read as the mass displacement of a population. The combination suggests that the Norse and Saxons of the two hamlets of Grimsargh and Brockholes may have co‚existed side by side.[4]

Grimsargh was a Norse settlement and the name 'argh' or 'aerg' was probably an equivalent for a summer farm, or a cluster of wooden huts used for the shelter of cattle in summer. This term has been connected with the Latin 'arvum', a ploughed field; with the Old Norse 'herfi' and the Danish 'harv', a harrow; or even with the Anglo Saxon, 'erigan' to plough and 'ergend', ploughing. Another view is that names like Grimsargh indicate former sites of pagan altars, derived from the old Norse word 'horgr', a heathen place of worship.[5] The name Grim is derived from Grimr which is a well‚known old Norse name.[6] It is therefore likely that the land of the Norse township would have been in pasture and this was the argh or pasture belonging to a person named Grimr.

The Scandinavians gained skills in handicrafts, accrued consider‚able financial assets, and were eventually converted to Christianity. Local evidence of the Scandinavian invaders became apparent in May 1840, when a great archaeological find was discovered at Cuerdale, close to the old Grimsargh‚with‚Brockholes parish boundary on the banks of the Ribble. The famous 'Cuerdale Hoard' of buried treasure contained the largest collection of Viking silver ever discovered in Europe and comprised of silver bullion, coins, ingots and ornaments packed into a leaden chest. There were approximately 7,500 coins of mostly Danish origin, which had been minted at York. The coins suggest that the treasure was collected around AD 905 and theories abound as to how it came to be there. One explanation is that the cache was abandoned by a Danish army, travelling one of the cross‚Pennine routes they had established in the ninth century. The treasure may have been hidden by the Danish Army in its flight before Edward the Elder in 911.

References

1. For archaeological and historic site information I am grateful for the help and co-operation of Peter Iles of the Lancashire County Council Environment Director-ate's Sites and Monuments Records. The sites mentioned here and elsewhere are, of course, only a few of the known archaeological sites. Information on finds and sites should be sent to the County Sites and Monuments Records in Preston – telephone 01772 264468. Treasure Trove laws have been repealed by the Treasure Act, 1996, and all metal detector finds should be reported to the Antiquities Officer at the National Museum and Galleries on Merseyside, telephone 0151 207 0001.

2. The route of Watling Street and Roman occupation in north-west England is described in a book, *Walking Roman Roads in the Fylde and Ribble Valley* compiled by Philip Graystone for the Centre for North-West Regional Studies, Lancaster University.

3. *Transactions of the Lancashire and Cheshire Antiquarian Society* (TLCAS), vol. 58, pp. 71–84.

4. TLCAS, vol. 60, p. 8.

5. TLCAS, vol. 8, pp. 89, 93.

6. Ekwall, *The Place Names of Lancashire* (1922), p. 145.

Grimsargh

THE STORY OF A
LANCASHIRE VILLAGE

CHAPTER TWO

Medieval Grimsargh

OLLOWING THE DEATH of King Harold a triumphant Duke William of Normandy rode from the battlefield near Hastings to seize the throne. If the English had been obsessed with Viking invasion then they had cause for concern following the Battle of Hastings in 1066. William was crowned king and most of the land of the English nobility was soon granted to his followers. William's need for money to prepare for a feared Danish invasion in 1085 inspired him to undertake the enormous Domesday Book survey of his kingdom.

At the time of the Conquest the royal estate was divided into 'wapentakes' (meaning weapon take) or 'hundreds'. Salford, West Derby, Leyland and Blackburn wapentakes were between the Mersey and the Ribble, and Amounderness and Lonsdale were north of the Ribble. In the centre of the county were Amounderness, Leyland and Blackburn hundreds. People lived in scattered farmsteads or groups of cottages and the social strata of the day included thanes, freemen, drengs and villeins, and bordars and serfs who were lower down the social scale. A significant proportion of the land was described as 'waste'.

The population of Preston at this time extended to only a few hundred inhabitants. During the period Preston had gained some importance as the Chief Manor of Amounderness and sixty-one local settlements were contained in this area. Amounderness was loosely based on the Fylde, extending between the rivers Cocker and Ribble and the Forest of Bowland in the east. In the reign of William the Conqueror parts of England were already divided into shires. At that time Lancashire did not exist as a shire and was a borderland including segments of both Yorkshire and Cheshire. North of the Ribble was nominally covered by Yorkshire and south thereof by Cheshire.

The Domesday Book is the first inventory of the assets of the people of England. To extract the maximum taxation from his people William needed to know their wealth. One respondent complained that the questioning of William's investigators was so rigorous that it was like the last judgement on Doomsday, hence the name by which the bureaucratic snooping came to be known. Compilation of the Domesday information recorded all the land held by the King and his tenants and the Manors belonging to particular estates. The names of landholders or tenants in chief and their tenants and under-tenants were fully documented. In the Domesday Survey of 1086, there were eighteen carucates of land under cultivation within the entire Parish of Preston. Prestune (Preston) had six carucates to geld and close by two carucates were assigned to Grimsargh, spelt Grimesarge in the Domesday Book. The hamlets of Elston or Brockholes are not specifically mentioned.[1]

When a tax was imposed a rate was announced, usually two shillings a carucate. Every landowner could then calculate his tax by multiplying the number of his carucates by the rate announced. For years after the Norman Conquest, land was being measured in Norse carucates (or ploughlands) and bovates (or oxgangs). A carucate geldable under the Domesday Book was around 100 acres and a unit in the tax system named after the word caruca, the Latin word for plough. Originally a bovate was the area of land that one ox could manage to plough each year, but by 1086 all these measures seem to have become tax assessment figures. After the Battle of Hastings, William the Conqueror bestowed the Honour of Lancaster upon Roger de Poictou, third son of Roger de Montgomery, who gave certain privileges to the Burgesses of Preston. As he joined in the rebellion against the Norman king at the Battle of Rochester, his estates were forfeited, and was later expelled from England after taking part in a rebellion against Henry I in 1102. During the reign of Henry II Preston's earliest charter was granted in 1179 and trade guilds became established. Roads and expanding rural settlements began to emanate around the ancient Borough of Preston.

Grimsargh has been given at least twelve spellings during its history and the following variations are represented in documented sources: Grimesarge, (Domesday Book); Grimesherham, (1189); Grimisharg, (1242); Grimsarche, Grimsharg, (1244); Grimesherg, (1253); de Grimesargh, Gremeshargh, Grymesharth, Grymesharuth, (1292); Grymesargh, (1293); Greymesargh (1301) and finally in 1400, Grymsar, the easiest pronunciation and sounding like the present day, 'Grimsargh'.[2]

The Domesday Survey shows woodland and wasteland exceeding

arable land in eleventh-century Lancashire. The medieval forests of Lancashire were of moderate extent, covering about 47,000 acres. The lands included 'within the metes of the forest' (boundaries) included the whole of Amounderness. The formation of the forest was still in process for a hundred years after the Conquest. John, Count of Montain, made a grant of £500 to the knights and freeholders to reduce to cultivation their underwoods and to alienate them by gift or sale. This was accompanied by a grant of liberty to keep harriers, foxhounds and dogs for hunting all manner of beasts except hare, wild boar and sow, and roe deer and hind throughout the forest outside the demesne enclosures or parks. On 16 February 1225 justices were assigned on behalf of the King to carry out a programme of deforestation and three years later the forest area was reduced to the localities of Quernmore, Bleasdale, Toxteth, Upper Wyresdale, and Fulwood. Fulwood consisted of 2,117 acres lying in the valley of the Savick and extending from Cowford bridge in the west to Grimsargh in the east, almost wholly on the north side of the Roman Road. The development of the regions lying adjacent to the forests began as landholders began to clear the scrub and woodland. The villeins and serfs dug out the trees and bushes and the following year crops were planted in the clearings, thus propagating the medieval strips of land worked by men with scythes and sickles.

In medieval Grimsargh the area was still extensively wooded and contained much 'waste'. Increasingly, land cultivation brought more consolidated holdings. Enclosure schemes gradually superseded the structure of open fields as the land owned by the Lord of the Manor was leased to tenants and the medieval strips disappeared under the grass. The Hoghton deeds provide evidence as to the nature of farming in the Grimsargh area during the late thirteenth century:

> Indenture dated 24th November 1284: Thomas de Grimishere for 25 marks, 7s leases for 12 years to Master Richard de Hocheton his manor with gardens, building, lands in Grimishere, namely 29 acres arable and meadow. To hold except to Sir Ad. De Hocheton and his son and the heir of William de Echeliston with all liberties, enclosures, waste, moss, herbages of wood, pannages, rents and escheats of dower. If the lessor wishes to sell the lands the lessee shall have the first option. (LRO, DDHO/640)

> Indenture dated 2nd May 1329: William son of Robert de Etheliston grants to Sir Richard de Hoghton Kt. and his heir that he may

enclose all the moors, woods, marshes, mosses in Grymesargh for his own use and retain them so that the grantor his heir and tenants may for a term of years in Etheliston and Grymesargh have sufficient common of pasture for their tenants. For this, Sir Richard grants to William the right of enclosing moors and woods in Etheliston so that his heir and tenants may have sufficient common of pasture for their tenants. (LRO, DDHO/642)

East of Marsh House Farm the old township boundary separating Elston from Alston is traceable by trees, hedgerows and earthworks. An attempt at historic land characterisation by Lancashire County Council Archaeological Services suggests that the area between Brockholes and Alston is predominantly 'ancient enclosure' – probably of AD 1400–1500 origin.

The variable field patterns of Grimsargh and Elston are a record in their own right and are best read from aerial photographs and maps. One aerial photograph shows rectangular ancient earthworks near to Marsh House Farm at Elston, thought to be restricted to a single meadow close to the Ribchester to Preston Roman Road. The exact period of the earthwork site is subject to conjecture

but could be of medieval origin. It was first recorded here in October 1991, and represents a moated site. According to the occupiers of Marsh House the complex of ditches and platforms frequently attracts people with metal detectors. On the west side of Elston Lane close to Chapel House Farm and approximately 1,000 feet from the earthworks was once the site of an ancient cross. This raises the exciting prospect that the earthworks may represent an earlier phase of settlement at Grimsargh, long before the village was developed on its present site.

The first nineteenth-century Ordnance Survey maps record the existence of four medieval crosses on the six miles of road leading out of Preston in a north-easterly direction through Grimsargh to Longridge. It is believed that the crosses were erected some time between AD 1100 and 1400. In the historical literature Grim-sargh Cross is described as: 'A pedestal of a stone cross, three and three quarter miles north-east from Preston Market Place, on the south side of the road, and one eighth of a mile south of Grimsargh Church. The words 'Three Mile Cross' appear on the map close to the pedestal'. It is possible that some of the numerous crosses shown on the map of Blackburn hundred, between Long-ridge and Whalley, were placed there for the guidance of travellers over those wild moors, so forming a complete series from Preston to Whalley Abbey. If this route between Preston and Whalley were taken, a distance of about fifteen miles, there would be almost a continuous range of crosses including those at Ribbleton Lane, Ribbleton Moor and Three Mile Cross at Grimsargh.

Prior to the Reformation there were about 500 wayside crosses in Lancashire. Thereafter only a few remained and the heads and arms in most cases were missing – hence the term 'headless crosses' – other theories abound as to their various uses. Some crosses were believed to have marked the stages at which funeral processions used to rest on their way to distant burial places; some marked spots where villagers gathered to hear sermons from travelling friars or to hear proclamations by the Lord of the Manor or to discuss other matters of public interest, and others had marked the boundaries of estates or church land.[3]

In addition to acting as one of a series on a waymarked route it is quite feasible that Three Mile Cross at Grimsargh could have fulfilled any of these functions. The base of the wayside Three Mile Cross, has been preserved as part of the war memorial, situated on Preston Road. The old shaft had long since disappeared,

OPPOSITE
The land adjacent to Ribblesdale Drive and Fir Tree and Wood Top Farms incorporates a mosaic of field patterns enhanced by marl pits and ancient and overgrown hedgerows with profusions of holly, hawthorn, buckthorn and other diverse trees and shrubs. These features further characterise the ancient landscape between the village hall and Tun Brook and provide a haven for wildlife. A development of some two hundred new houses will shortly cover this landscape.
Author's collection

but a new Latin cross of Longridge stone was erected in the socket of the ancient base in 1920 to honour the dead of the Great War and is today a Grade II listed structure and familiar Grimsargh landmark.

Grimsargh was originally assessed as two plough-lands and was a member of the Earl of Tostig's Preston Lordship with only a few inhabitants. After the Conquest the manor was divided – Grimsargh, as half a plough-land was held in thegnage (a thegn was an Anglo Saxon who held land from the King or Noble in return for certain services); Brockholes, also half a plough-land, was given to the Baron of Manchester while Elston, the remaining plough-land, was given to the Baron of Penwortham. Roger, son of Augustin de Heaton of Heaton in Lonsdale, had a confirmation of his half plough-land in Grimsargh in 1189, from John, Count of Mortain. Roger died in 1204 leaving a son of the same name. Roger de Heaton held Grimsargh in 1262, and his heir was his son William, who confirmed the title of William de Grimsargh.

In 1297 William de Grimsargh held the village by the service of 3s. a year. The rent had remained unchanged and was payable to the Earl of Lancaster. About this time the Hoghton family of Hoghton acquired land in the township. The time of purchase does not appear, but in 1301 Richard de Hoghton seems to have had a fair estate in Grimsargh. The two families continued for some time as part-owners of the land and in 1334 they sought arbitration on matters in dispute, submitting their differences to 'two neighbours and a man of the law'.

There has been no operational water mill in Grimsargh for many years. Documented sources indicate the site of one close to The Hermitage on Elston Lane, which existed in the late nineteenth century. Scrutinising wills and deeds yields many sur-prises, including the use and former ownership of the water mill. John Frederick Chadwick died in 1857 and resided at The Hermi-tage. Mr Chadwick bequeathed the whole of his property and estate, which included The Hermitage, mill and the land belonging to both and the cottages adjoining the mill to his wife Alice, and after her death to the second son, Robert. The new owners of the old mill seem to have allowed it to crumble into oblivion, although it is possible there are still faint traces on the inaccessible banks of Tun Brook. The corn mill, corn drying kiln and large mill pond are all shown on the 1847 Ordnance Survey Map as being on the north bank of Tun Brook a few metres downstream

The Stone Cross at Grimsargh, raised on the base of an ancient cross, and restored as a War Memorial in 1920. Close by is a stone which formed part of the old stocks.

Author's collection

from Elston Lane. The corn mill had disappeared by the end of the century though in 1922 Mill Dam Cottage was occupied by Elizabeth Allen, shopkeeper. However, by the time of the Preston Rural District Council Overcrowding Survey of 1936, the cottage had been condemned.

It is possible that watermills used for grinding corn had been in use in Grimsargh since the Roman occupation. By the time of the Domesday survey in 1086 there were over 5,500 watermills in England and they would have been commonplace throughout the country in the Middle Ages. Indeed water and wind power were almost the only means of grinding corn until around the time of production of those first Ordnance Survey Maps in 1847. It is probable that the medieval references contained in the De Hoghton papers at the LRO relate to this particular site at Elston Lane, where the large wooden machinery consisting of cogged wheels and horizontal shafts would have been driven by the fast-running waters of Tun Brook.

In 1265 William de Grymesargh grants to William de Etheliston, liberty to grind at his mill of Grymesargh without multure and they will be hoprefre for ever; also common pasture in Grymesargh and

Elston Lane, viewed from Preston Road. A housing development incorporating Tun Brook Avenue and Elston Green now occupies the site of the old mill pond.
Author's collection

liberty of pasture and mill in Etheliston for their cattle and tenants in Etheliston. Witness – Benedict Gernet, Sir Hen. Du Lee. Hen. De Haydok. (LRO, DDHO/ 631)

It sounds as though William de Etheliston from the neighbouring township of Etheliston (Elston) would have been on good terms with William de Grymesargh and able to share the resources of the mill and pasture, provided of course that it was left tidy and hopfree – the miller would have to clear the mill hopper of any remnants of corn before grinding the corn and without taking some of the flour produced (multure) for his own use.

Around the beginning of the fourteenth century the Hoghtons appear to have acquired lands in the township, though the date of purchase is not known. In 1362 William de Grimsargh granted to Sir Adam de Hoghton all his messuages, lands, rents and services in Grimsargh. The deed of 1362 was the completion of a sale which had taken place long before. Upon final completion of the sale to the Hoghtons, the Grimsargh family faded into obscurity. The Hoghton family held the full manorial rights for over 400 years.

There are references to Grimsargh Hall and its occupiers contained in the Hoghton deeds and papers. A documented lease of 1282 by Thomas Grimesherk to Master Richard Hocton (Hoghton) stimulates analytical thought. The archived land transactions of William de Grimsargh in 1265 even mention a derivative of the modern Grimsargh road name of Waingate (originally meaning a cart road).

Thomas Grimesherk for 14 marks leases for 10 years to Master Richard de Hocton his manor of Grimesherk with hall, chamber, kitchen and barn and the land pertaining in Grimesherk and all his right in woods, mills, waters, waste and their profits. To hold except to religious men, Sir Adam de Hocton and William de Echeliston with all liberties, enclosures, herbages, pannages, rents, escheates and free common rights. The grantee shall leave the premises in a state as good as or better than he received them. If he shall act contrary to this agreement or wish to let the lands to those excepted in this deed, the grantor shall re-enter; or if he shall wish to give or sell them he shall pay to a grantor 100s silver. Witnessed – Sir Benedict Gernet, Sir William de Hetun , Sir William de Bartun Kts., Adam de Brocholis, John de Bartun, John de Grimesherk, Gilbertt of the same, John de Wytingham. (LRO, DDHO/638)

William de Grymesargh for 3 marks grants to William son of William de Etheliston a part of his land in Grymesargh namely 9 acres within these bounds – Beginning at liolf's clearing, following the sike of raschagh nortwards to the completion of the nine acre square looking eastwards, then to Wayngate on the east and southwards to liolf's clearing. To hold with common pasture and easements. (LRO, DDH/632)

Inevitably there are many gaps in the precise medieval history of a small parish like Grimsargh including how it was affected by the plague. The Black Death reached Lancashire from the Orient in 1349. It is estimated that one third of England's population died and over 1,000 villages were depopulated. In the ten parishes of Amounderness it was claimed 13,180 people died between September 1349 and January 1350. In the parish of Preston (which included Grimsargh-with-Brockholes) 3,000 people died, with Preston alone losing at least one third of its entire population. Close to Grimsargh in the neighbouring parish of Ribchester at least 400 people died and it is quite probable that hamlets such as Grimsargh would have suffered heavy mortality and been left desolate. Successive generations suffered recurring outbreaks of the plague in 1390 and well into the Stuart period; in 1631, 1,100 people died within the town and parish of Preston. After the pestilence there were said to be only 887 people alive in the town:

> The great sickness of the plague of pestilence wherein the number of 1100 persons and upwards dyed within this towne and parish of Preston begunn about the tenth day November in anno 1630 and continued the space of one whole year next after.[4]

The irony is that nowadays the ship-borne carrier of bubonic plague, the black rat, is almost extinct in Britain except for restricted distribution on two offshore islands, where it poses no threat to anyone and even enjoys protected status.

The Township of Elston

The name Elston has roots in its ancient Saxon and medieval history. It was known as Etheliston (1212), de Etheleston with derivatives Etheliston, Ethelaston, Etherston (1246) and Elleston (1446).[5]

In 1863 a medieval ampulla (a small lead flask for holy water) was discovered in the bed of a stream, to the east of Preston. The find spot was originally described by Henry Ecroyd Smith in 1869: 'The streamlet scarcely exceeds half a mile in length and debouches into the Ribble, after running through a portion of the Elston district, about half way between Preston and Ribchester'. Archaeologist Ben Edwards has now narrowed the find spot down to a square kilometre of the stream flowing through Alston Wood/Gib Holme Wood, Elston. The ampulla was in good condition and had probably been lost by a pilgrim en route to a holy shrine, during the mid-medieval period.[6] This benign activity was in stark contrast to those of the opposing factions that once prevailed in the Saxon township of Elston.

Dobson refers to the township's history in his antiquarian book *Rambles by the Ribble.* In times past it was owned by a family that took its name from the township, Elston or Ethelston. Dobson[7] and Hardwick[8] both make reference to an ancient deed, which describes Saxon turmoil that occurred close to the banks of the Ribble at Elston. 'It was told me by Alexander Elston, who was uncle to my father and sonne to Ralph Elston, my great grand-father, that the said Ralph Elston had a deede, or a copee of a deede, in the Saxon tongue, wherein it did appear that King Ethelston, lynge in camp in this county, upon occasion of warrs, gave the land of Ethelstone unto one to whom he was Belsyre' (the word belsyre meaning godfather). In the Subsidy Roll of 1332 nine persons were rated for the township which was then described as Ethelston.[9]

Several families, possibly younger branches, assumed Elston as a surname. One of these families had long associations with the neighbouring township of Brockholes. Early lordship seems to have descended to one John de Elston, living in the time of Edward III. About a century later, it passed to the heir-general, Sir Thomas Harrington; 'that one Harrington was lord thereof, who had nine daughters, and left to every one of them lands worth 25 marks per annum and she that had Elston married Mr Hylton, of Farneworth'.

The Hamlet of Brockholes

The name of Brockhole is derived from the badger 'brocc' and 'hol' (holes or setts), which was spelled Brochole, (1212); de Brocholes (1244); Brochol, Brokhol (1246); Brocholes (1290); and Brokholes (1319).[10] The Parish of Grimsargh included Brockholes which was a member of the fee of Manchester. It was granted to the Lathom family and held by a tenant, one Award de Brockholes whose

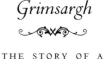

son Roger held the land in 1246. Roger's son, Adam de Brockholes, held the Manor of Brockholes of Sir Robert de Lathom by the eighth part of a knight's fee. (This was a feudal obligation by which the tenant was required to pay for his land through the performing of military service.) The Brockholes family also acquired land in Byrewath, Paythorne, Gisburn and Garstang. In 1338 Roger de Brockholes first purchased land at Claughton and to this day the family seat of Fitzherbert-Brockholes has long been established at Claughton-on-Brock.

In the feudal legal and social system of medieval England, people were given land by the lord, in return for which they worked and fought for him. Tenants also had to look after the bailiff – 'And when the bailiff or lord's sergeant of the baron, came to ride about, and overlook his demesne, and collect the rents, the tenants had to provide him, "bread, ale and victuals, and other things necessary according to the season, and for his boy and four bailiffs, such food as they provide in the household and provender for his horse".' [11]

Brockholes passed to another Adam de Brockholes in 1341, who had several children including Nicholas, his heir, and Roger. An ancient legal document dated 4 June 1372, written in Latin and on parchment, has provided further insight into medieval Brockholes, when the Manor of Brockholes and all other lands and tenements with their appurtenances passed to Nicholas de Brockholes. Nicholas had at least two sons but the Manor descended to two daughters or granddaughters, one of whom, Margaret, married Roger Elston in the reign of Richard II; and the other, who married Thomas Singleton. The Elstons, who became seated at Brockholes, were originally of the adjoining township of Ethelston. During the thirteenth century there was only one house recognised as the demesne house of the Manor of Brockholes. The Manorial rights were long vested in the Manor of Brockholes and a capital messuage named Brockehall Hall, together with the fishery of Brockhole.

The following deposition taken at Preston in Tudor times makes clear reference to the ancient seat of Brockehole Hall which preceded the Stuart period buildings of Lower and Higher Brockholes described in the next chapter. 'Edmond Felippe of Balderstone, labourer, aged 28 years, knows the mansion house called the Hall of Brockhole, three gardens, one orchard, and certain closes of arable ground, meadow and pasture, called the grene, the heys, the tentor bankes, the great wood hey and the chuchfeld, parcel of the demesnes of Brocehole, of which William Singleton was seized'.[12]

An ancient ford crossing linked Elston with Samlesbury Lower Hall to the east of Red Scar. The ruined remains of Lower Hall may still be seen on the riverbank, bearing testimony to an earlier building on the site destroyed by Robert the Bruce in 1322. Eight years after his triumph at Bannockburn, the Scottish king was determined to assert Scottish independence. The Scots looted Preston and set fire to some of its wooden buildings before rampaging throughout the pastoral landscape of Grimsargh-with-Brockholes with its timeless river and field mosaics. 'The Ribble ford was used by Robert the Bruce in midsummer 1322 when he burnt Lower Hall and robbed Samlesbury Church of valuables'.[13] After four weeks of absolute mayhem they went home to Scotland leaving the distressed inhabitants of Amounderness in a state of poverty and shock, and with not a counsellor in sight! A second building was built on the same site known as Lower Samlesbury Hall and its ruins may still be seen on the river bank. Interestingly, the staircase was salvaged from the ruins of Lower Hall and has since been reincarnated in Old Hall at Cow Hill, Grimsargh. This staircase was originally found in an outbuilding by Mr H. Mallott of Grimsargh House who incorporated it into the Horrockses offices in Stanley Street, Preston, where he was the managing director. When the offices of the old mill were demolished, the staircase was purchased and installed in Old Hall where it remains in situ to this day.

Grimsargh

THE STORY OF A LANCASHIRE VILLAGE

References

1. *History from Sources – The Domesday Book* – edited by John Morris (1978).
2. Farrer and Brownbill, *Victoria County History*, vol. 7 p. 90.
3. References to Grimsargh Cross: TLCAS, vol. 10, p. 172; and vol. 58, p. 84.
4. Philip Ziegler, *The Black Death*; and R. Sharpe France, *History of the Plague in Lancashire*, TLCAS.
5. Ekwall, *The Place Names of Lancashire*.
6. *Transactions of the Historic Society of Lancashire and Cheshire* (THSLC), vol. 9, pp. 165–80, and *Antiquaries Journal*, 51 (1971) pp. 316–18.
7. William Dobson, 'Rambles by the Ribble' (1877).
8. C. Hardwick, *History of the Borough of Preston* (1857), pp. 533, 534.
9. H. Fishwick, *The History of the Parish of Preston* (1900), p. 82.
10. Ekwall, *The Place Names of Lancashire*.
11. Dobson, 'Rambles by the Ribble', p. 66.
12. Fishwick, *The History of the Parish of Preston*, p. 292.
13. R. Eaton, *History of Samlesbury*, p. 167.

PART II

The Early Modern Period,
1350–1750

CHAPTER THREE

Grimsargh After the Middle Ages

*E*LSTON WAS A TOWNSHIP in the parish of Preston covering about 962 acres, situated between the townships of Alston and Grimsargh-with-Brockholes. Portions of the estate passed by descent from Harrington through different families to Thomas Walmsley of Preston in 1610. His nephew of the same name succeeded to it and in 1717 two or three papists also registered small estates in the area.[1] The landscape of Elston has seen little

The hamlet of Elston, showing Elston Old Hall Farm on the left; in the centre is Elston Cottage; and on the right Charity Farm. Only Elston Old Hall survives as a working farm.
Author's collection

The pristine landscape of an Elston winter, with Pendle Hill in the background.
Author's collection

change and the idyllic hamlet nestles below steep escarpments, close to the River Ribble, as it has for centuries.

A pleasant walk may be enjoyed from Elston along the Ribble Way to Brockholes, though green fields have been replaced by extensive gravel workings and the rural tranquillity has been completely transformed by the M6 Motorway.

Three miles downstream of the Elston ferry an alternative river crossing linked the hamlet of Brockholes with Samlesbury Church and operated from Ferry Boat House, on the south bank. *A History of Samlesbury* (Eaton, 1936), mentions ways of crossing the Ribble by a medieval ford and ferry and a nineteenth-century bridge. On the river just above Samlesbury Church a ferry was established linking Samlesbury with Brockhall and Preston. It was served by two ferrymen in 1379 who lived nearby on the Samlesbury side. There were incentives to 'ferry across the Ribble', for the boathouse was also a beer shop. In 1824 the ferrymen were made redundant when the river was crossed by a wooden bridge and each foot passenger was charged one halfpenny. In 1861 a modern stone bridge was built and the wooden one removed. The former toll bridge is still known locally as halfpenny or Brockhall's bridge.

The earliest maps, including Yates' of 1786, reveal ancient routes linking the farms, bordered by hedgerows and many other interesting features. Before construction of the turnpike road from Preston to Blackburn in 1824, there was no proper route between the two towns and Lower Brockholes was reached by a roadway known as Brockhall Lane. Leading from this roadway was a high parallel row of hawthorn hedges, enclosing a path linking Lower Brockholes Farm with Higher Brockholes Farm, Red Scar and Grimsargh and which today forms part of the Ribble Way long distance footpath. Samlesbury Church could be reached via Brockhall Lane and the ferry crossing, and occasionally even coffins had to be carried along Brockhall Lane and accommodated in the small rowing boat. The seventeenth-century Lower Brockholes Farm still nestles at the foot of ancient woodlands and seems an anachronistic survivor almost belying the existence of the old Higher Brockholes seat of the Elstons, now obliterated from the landscape of the riverine Horse Shoe Bend.

Eleven generations of Elstons sustained their position as lesser gentry at Higher Brockholes and the Elston moiety descended to Robert Elston who with his bride, Ann, first came to Higher Brockholes in 1643. They proudly recorded the event for posterity with a plaque above the front door bearing REA 1643 – the initials of Robert and Ann Elston. On opening the door they would have entered a spacious hall with a fine fireplace typical of the period, and a magnificent staircase which led to the upper floor. The structure was built partially of handmade bricks with the exception of the west wall of the east wing, which was of stone. Black and white work on a stone base and a unique outbuilding to the south gave it the dignity of an old manor house rather than of being the homestead of a farmer and it would have been well worthy of preservation.

Robert Elston died in 1662 and his daughters sold the estate in the same year to a Frenchman, Paul Moreau of Knowsley, who settled at Higher Brockholes Hall. In dispute at the time was the ownership of the medieval water mill at Grimsargh and trouble was brewing between Robert's son William de Elston and Richard de Hoghton.

William son of Robert de Elston claimed the sixth part of a water mill in Grimsargh against Richard de Hoghton. The plaintiff stated that his father had purchased the mill from Thomas de Grimshagh, but Agnes widow of Thomas had a third part in dower, which she had granted to plaintiff till he had received the cost of repairing the mill.[2]

Grimsargh

THE STORY OF A LANCASHIRE VILLAGE

A 1756 plan of the Ribble between Red Scar and Preston at Brockholes. Note the fishing nets across the river and the position of Lower and Higher Brockholes. A ford is indicated just above Lower Brockholes, but the only bridge across the Ribble carried the road from Preston to Walton.

Courtesy of L. Redmayne

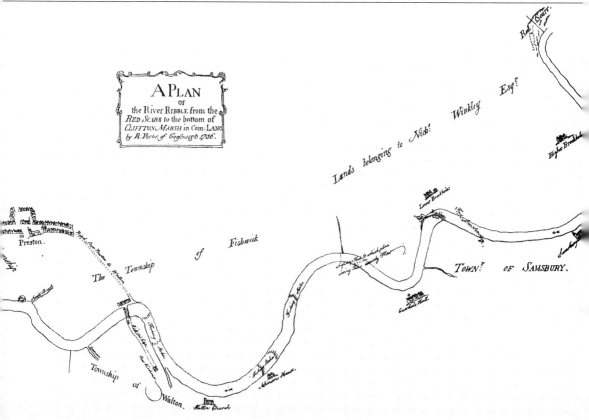

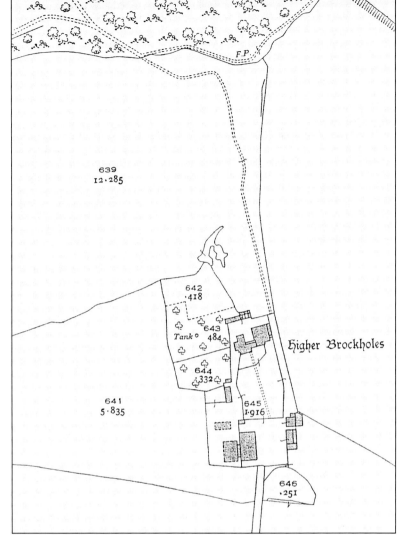

642
·418

Tank° 643
484

Higher Brockholes

644
332

641
5·835

645
1·916

646
·251

A nineteenth-century map
showing the main features of
Higher Brockholes. These
historic buildings have now
been demolished.
Courtesy of L. Redmayne

And one is left to wonder if they ever did repair Grimsargh
water mill.

The Moreaus remained at Brockholes for about thirty years.
The registers of Preston Parish Church tell of marriages, christen-
ings, and burials of members of his family there. Paul Moreau,
grandson of the purchaser of Brockholes, eventually sold the whole
estate to Mr Thomas Winckley of Preston. Four families sustained
the inheritance of Higher Brockholes for five hundred years.
They were the Brockholeses, the Elstons, the Moreaus, and the
Winckleys.

Lower Brockholes remained in the hands of the Singletons
until 1564, when John Singleton sold the capital messuage called
Brockhall Hall to Sir John Southworth of Samlesbury, son and
heir of Sir John Southworth who added the large wing to

Samlesbury Hall. Sir John Southworth died in 1597 and early in the seventeenth century Lower Brockholes was conveyed to Edmund Breres of Preston, gentleman, who in 1621 mortgaged it to Sir Robert Bindloss, Knight, of Borwick Hall. It descended to a grandson, Francis Bindloss, who built the existing Lower Brockholes Hall (now a farm) in 1634. Over the front door a stone dated 1634 was emblazoned by the arms and initials of Francis Bindloss.

In August 1648, local man Hugh Welchman/Walshman, yeoman, fought for the King at the Battle of Preston, when Oliver Cromwell led his forces to victory at Ribbleton Moor. The Royalists were defeated and Welchman was fined £3 10s. in 1649 for adhering to the forces against Parliament. In March 1654 Hugh Welchman, first took up a nine-year lease of the Lower Brockhall Estate for £60 a year, plus £40 a year for the fishery and water corn mill.

Lower Brockholes with the present occupier, Leonard Redmayne, below the coat of arms with three badgers and the date 1634.
Author's collection

On 4 August 1662 he renewed the lease from Francis Bindloss and was shown to be paying tax on five hearths in 1663. Hugh and his son John Welchman prospered despite Cromwell, and in 1662 they were both admitted to be burgesses at the Preston Guild of 1662.[3]

On the death of Francis Bindloss the estate was sold in 1668 to Paul Moreau, owner of Higher Brockholes, and John Welchman. The estate was divided and Welchman took the Hall and demesne and Moreau took portions of the land near to Higher Brockholes. Lower Brockhall was mortgaged to John Welchman, Yeoman, the lessee, for and on behalf of Hugh Welchman, his father, for £1,000.

John Welchman died soon after the death of his father and was buried at Preston in 1693. The brief mention of 'have hook and netts' in the probate inventory gives little indication of the value of John Welchman's commercial fishing rights on the Ribble at the old weir, which passed over to his successor Thomas Winckley.[4]

The Welchhman and Moreau shares were sold to Thomas Winckley in 1696 and 1698 respectively, who reunited the two moieties. Edward Winckley had settled in Preston at the beginning of the seventeenth century but the Winckley line died out following the death of Thomas Winckley. Frances, daughter of Thomas Winckley, married John Shelley Bart in 1807. Following the death of Lady Shelley in 1873, Brockholes was sold to Edward Petre in 1875.[5]

The entire estate belonged to Lady Shelley of Preston for most of the nineteenth century and it was during her time that the owners of Brockholes had a small mill near the river and close by a weir, which caused one of the most prolonged litigations ever to occupy an English Court. The lawsuits fought were in respect of the Ribble fisheries who contested the rights of the owners to dam the river, their bone of contention being that the salmon were unable to ascend the weir and swim upstream to reach the spawning grounds. The Brockholes fishery case occupied the courts and Lady Shelley figured in three lawsuits. During one of the trials the judge and jury sat for twenty-four hours consecutively. Fortunately the proceedings were brightened with a little humour during cross-examination of an elderly female by a legal luminary appropriately named Cockle. The old lady was browbeaten and asked by Cockle, 'I suppose, mistress, you like salmon?'

'Yes sir,' came the unexpected retort, 'I like salmon, but I don't like Cockle sauce to it.'[6]

It was around 1562 that John Farrington, a lessee of Sir John Southworth, built a new obstruction above the tidal reach of the Ribble at Brockhall and in 1580 we get the first mention of Bessowe Caul, afterwards known as Brockholes weir. During the same year objections were raised by special commissioners assembled at Preston. 'There is one caul weir or gorse made about 18 years ago upon the water of Ryble called Bessowe Caul. The same caul is so high and close that salmon and salmon fry canot have their full passage or course'. Thomas Weld of Stonyhurst took effective action against the owner of Brockhall Weir in 1804, the thrust of his objection being that the salmon had not secured a one-way ticket upstream to his fishery at Stonyhurst. Judgement was granted in favour of the plaintiff and in 1811 the Brockholes weir was finally demolished.[7]

The Manor of Grimsargh passed from the Hoghtons to the Cross family who built Red Scar at the beginning of the 19th Century. The Hoghton family first acquired land in Grimsargh during Medieval times but little is known of their Grimsargh Hall residence which is mentioned in Fishwick's *The History of the Parish of Preston* (p. 360).

During the sixteenth century a junior branch of the Hoghtons of Hoghton Tower settled in Grimsargh, the first of whom was Arthur Hoghton. In the Guild Roll of 1582 his residence is not given but in his will, proved at Richmond and dated 20 July 1611, he is described as 'of Grimsargh, gent.' Arthur had four sons one of whom was Richard. The will of Richard Hoghton, dated 22 June 1614, gives a few clues as to who might have been residing at Grimsargh Hall during the Stuart period. Richard Hoghton left £40 each to his natural sons Leonard and Thomas and his supposed daughter, Katherine Hoghton. He bequeathed £50 to Anne Shuttleworth, daughter of his late wife; 40s. each to Sir Richard Hoghton, Knight, and Sir Gilbert Hoghton, Knight to buy a ring with. He named his cousins Thomas Hoghton of Grimsargh and Thomas Hoghton of Haighton.

It is not certain who lived at Grimsargh Hall, but William Hoghton was living there in 1642, prior to his death in 1650. William, the eldest son of William Hoghton, was described as a delinquent and his estates were sequestrated. The capital messuage and its appurtenances called Grimsargh Hall, together with 80

Grimsargh Hall farm was
built in 1773 and today is a
private house, retaining many
original features.
Author's collection

acres of land, was put up for sale for a term of seven years on
13 April 1653. William secured the lease at a rent of £10 15s. but
was soon crying poverty!

The Hearth Tax Return of 1663 shows William to have tax
liability on four hearths. Those pleading poverty in 1668, only
two years after the Great Fire of London, were not all Londoners
nor were they paupers. 'William Hoghton appealed to the Magistrates to compel his father to assist him in time of "great poverties".
He thought his father could afford to do so as he had an estate
of a hundred pounds per annum at least.' (LRO, QSP 318/19)

The Hoghton deeds help to clarify matters in 1675:

> Sir Richard Hoghton leases for 99 years after the death of William
> Hoghton of Grimsargh to Benjamin Hoghton his second son,
> Grimsargh Hall with demesne and a smaller messuage of the ancient
> demesne of Grimsargh, all the tenants [named] of which pay their rent
> to William Hoghton, and the tithes thereof; also the water corn mill,
> called Grimsargh Mill, with houses, buildings, orchard, lands, pastures
> and all mines, quarries and delphs of lead, coal, slate and stone on
> the premises. Signature – Richard Hoghton. (LRO, DDHO 656)

On the Guild Roll of 1702 appears the name of Matthew, the
son of William Hoghton of Grimsargh, which is the last entry
referring to this branch of the family. The existing farmhouse

called Grimsargh Hall was built in 1773 at the time of the great stone reconstruction of farms and houses. There are no traces to be seen of any preceding structures, though the Grimsargh Hall of Norman times may have occupied the same site. It was not unprecedented for farms to be rebuilt on the same site or immediately adjacent to the manorial buildings they replaced. Dobson (1873) implies continued site occupancy of Grimsargh Hall with the following quotation: '… the old manorial residence having given place to one more suitable as the residence of a farmer'.

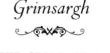
Dobson often enjoyed a walk through Grimsargh-with-Brockholes, past the sites of long-vanished farmsteads and admiring the pristine landscape of Queen Victoria's reign which would not have changed a great deal since Stuart times. 'We walked through the fields to Lower Brockholes, past Lower Boilton, a farmhouse snugly seated at the base of a hill, midway in the amphitheatre between Higher Brockholes and Lower Brockholes, which belongs to Mr Cross of Red Scar. We must here notice the mossy character of some of the fields, telling of ancient forests and subsequent ravages of water.'

Ribbleton Moor was the site of the Battle of Preston in 1648. It was mentioned by Riley in 1914 as a site of some biological importance. 'Until 1860 it appears that Ribbleton Moor was a swampy and desolate tract of land, to the east of Preston, extending north from the fringe of Brockholes to Ribbleton. The beautiful Marsh Gentian is recorded as having been abundant here and the Bogbeam scarcely less so'.[8] In 1860 Ribbleton Moor was enclosed and cultivated under the provisions of the General Enclosure Act. Relics of the engagement including cannon balls and musket shot were found during drainage and ploughing operations. The moor was initially cultivated as a source of food for the vast industrial complex expanding on its doorstep and today – approximately 200 years after the peace of the valley was shattered by Cromwell – is the site of the Moor Nook housing estates.

Amidst the turmoil of battle, no one would have been too concerned about the botanical aspects of rural Preston. The Kuerden Map of Preston showing the road out to Longridge, Goosnargh and Grimsargh would have been a more useful resource for opposing factions than the local flora. Higher Brockholes was built when the unfortunate Charles I reigned, though he had lost the authority of kingship and had been held captive by Parliament since just after the first Civil War of 1642–46. Five years after Robert and Ann Elston built their Higher Brockholes home in 1643, a second Civil War extended its ravages close to their home. The scene of the bloody conflict was Ribbleton Moor with its landmark windmill adjoining Grimsargh·with·Brockholes and Preston. As Oliver Cromwell's army advanced on Ribbleton Moor the Roundheads rounded up the Cavaliers and in so doing they eventually sealed the fate of Charles I.

References

1. *Victoria County History*, vol. 7 p. 115.
2. *Victoria County History*, vol. 7, p. 109.
3. Fishwick, *The History of the Parish of Preston*, Fishwick (Hearth Tax ref.) Eaton, *A History of Samlesbury*, and notes of Reg. Postlethwaite, of Haslingden.
4. The inventory of his goods and chattels is reproduced in the appendix..
5. *Victoria County History*, vol. 7, p. 111.
6. Riley, *The Ribble from Source to Sea* (1914), p. 171.
7. Houghton, *Ribble Salmon Fisheries* (1952), p. 42.
8. *The Ribble from Source to Sea*, p. 169.

CHAPTER FOUR

A Round-up in the Valley: The Civil Wars, 1642–51

Duntil the Middle Ages and after, warring factions and
explorers negotiated the relatively gentle contours of
Wharfedale and the Ribble Valley landscape as an east to west
route. The trans-Pennine crossing from the Vale of York to the
Ribble estuary is traceable by a chain of Norman castles including
those at Skipton and Clitheroe. Both the Romans and Cromwell
were quick to exploit its strategic value. The Battle of Preston,
fought on 17 August 1648, was probably the most crucial of the
conflicts of the Civil Wars which occurred throughout the British
Isles from 1642 to 1651.

Preston and Amounderness were well known as strongholds for
the King's cause but there were strong divisions in the town. The
Royalists supporting King Charles were dubbed Cavaliers whilst
Oliver Cromwell's Parliamentarians were known as Roundheads.
This was testament to the apprentices' close-cropped puritan
haircuts which stood for what they saw as true godliness and their
desire to do away with church ritual. Cromwell's New Model
Army was a dedicated professional force raised by and taking its
orders from Parliament. The New Model Army was prepared to
go anywhere in the country to call for 'Charles Stuart, that man
of blood, to account for that blood he had shed and mischief he
had done'. The Scots supported Charles on the understanding
that Presbyterianism should be the official religion in England
and aimed to release Charles from imprisonment and restore him
to the throne.

During the summer of 1648 the the Duke of Hamilton was
assigned to lead a Scottish army south to invade England and
capture Parliamentary strongholds. In Lancashire they were joined
by an army of English Royalists led by Sir Marmaduke Langdale
and Sir George Munro with a detachment of Scottish and Irish
forces. Opposing them for Parliament was the New Model Army
and Lancashire Militia led by Lieutenant General Cromwell and

A Civil War pikeman. In the
small fields and narrow lanes
that constituted the Preston
battlefield these fearsome
weapons, often up to 18 feet
in length, would have
accounted for many of the
casualties, particularly on the
Royalist side.
Courtesy of Dr S. Bull

A Round-up in the Valley: The Civil Wars

General Sir John Lambert. The combined Scots and Royalist forces totalled 20,000, easily outnumbering Cromwell's army of 9,000 men. Unfortunately for Preston and its rural environs the town and river had become the focus of his battle strategy and opposing factions clashed over a wide area commencing with skirmishes at Longridge.

Cromwell's army endured the long tiring walk from engagements in South Wales into Lancashire's picturesque Hodder Valley. Following a Council of War with Cromwell and his officers on 16 August 1648, it was decided to reach the Ribble's north bank and commence battling with the enemy to the east of Preston. According to tradition Cromwell marched over the picturesque packhorse 'Cromwell's Bridge' spanning the Hodder at Hurst Green before spending the pre-battle night at Stonyhurst. The

Perhaps the most famous portrait of Oliver Cromwell. The all-too-brief passage through Grimsargh by one of England's greatest generals provides a rare occasion in the village's history when it truly can be said to have taken centre stage.

Reproduced by permission of the National Portrait Gallery

Army Quarterly[1] debates this issue but the truth is that no one really knows for sure. The bridge was built in 1561 and has probably been stripped of much of its masonry over the years. About seven feet wide, it was too narrow for an army of almost 10,000 infantry and cavalry, armoured with pikes, muskets and cannons and dangerous for anyone on horseback. As is usual the officers probably enjoyed the luxury of staying dry whilst the rest of Cromwell's rain-soaked army would probably have waded the river. Having walked 500 miles, the weary troops slept in a field whilst Cromwell is reputed to have slept on a table in the Great Hall at Stonyhurst college

Cromwell was up early on 17 August and soon sent forward an advanced guard, known as a forlorn, of 200 horse and 400 foot. Their route was to take them over Thornley Fell to view any opposing forces from high ground and through Longridge and Grimsargh to the decisive battle. According to legend the origin of the name Longridge was derived after Cromwell enunciated, 'What a long ridge this is!' The name Longridge is actually on record before the Tudor and Stuarts were on the throne of England and the fanciful tale ought now to be consigned to the romantic story bin. A more likely quote is that contained in Hewitson's *History of Preston* when Cromwell expressed his views about the Vale of Chipping and said, 'I have seen no part of the country so beautiful as this.' En route to battle he apparently had time to savour the view from the uplands of Thornley and Longridge Fell, and who can blame him?

The eastern flank of the Royalists was guarded by Sir Marmaduke Langdale who may have spent the pre-battle night somewhere near Grimsargh. Langdale first engaged with the the enemy at Longridge Chapel, where he was in possession of the road and had his men firmly posted to stop the further progress of the Parliamentary troops. Cromwell's officers commanded their men to halt and decided to keep the ground until reinforced with sufficient strength to cope with the enemy's advanced guard. General Cromwell was informed of the presence of the enemy, and he rode forward to the front to ascertain the correct situation and remonstrated with his officers in command for not making an immediate charge. The General himself then ordered his men to march and the first blows in the battle of Preston were struck.

Cromwell's army was successful in driving Langdale and his men from their positions and they advanced the six miles towards

A musketeer. Most of the muskets used during the mid-seventeenth century were of the relatively primitive matchlock type, where the musketeer required considerable skill to keep his match cord alight during wet weather.
Courtesy of Dr S. Bull

A Round-up in the Valley: The Civil Wars

Ribbleton Moor, along the course of a muddy sunken lane linking Grimsargh with Preston and Longridge (now the B6243). The primitive Kuerden Map of the period indicates Preston Market Place, Grimsargh's Three Mile Cross, Ribbleton windmill, and the road through Grimsargh to be bordered by embankments with shrubs and small trees.[2] Here, in dry weather, farm workers would have endeavoured to dodge the clouds of dust churned up by the passage of more affluent yeoman on horseback, but on 17 August 1648 the peace of the township was shattered by the presence of Cromwell's army, who would have found any ongoing minor clashes with the Royalists difficult due to the incessant rain and the boggy terrain.

Langdale had 4,000 men covering the eastern approach and messages were sent to the Duke of Hamilton that Cromwell was closing in on them from the north. When the whole of the Parliamentary forces arrived upon the moor Cromwell engaged the enemy by deploying the New Model and Northern Association to the fore flanked by cavalry on either side of the army and towards the centre. The Lancashire Militia was held in reserve. Following the initial skirmishes at Longridge, the opposing forces

The scene of part of the battle of Preston. This photograph, which was taken from the old railway line, shows Brookfield (right), Eaves Brook (centre), and Hamilton Road (left).
Courtesy of Dr S. Bull

of Cromwell and Langdale engaged in battle for about four hours, across a broad front in the Eave's brook valley either side of Slack Brow, Ribbleton and where Grange, Brookfield and Hamilton Road housing estates are now situated.[3] As the battle reached its peak the closest of Hamilton's Scottish army were strewn over an extensive area about a mile away. Langdale's small force was taking on Cromwell's army despite the close proximity of the Royalists' larger forces and at this crucial stage of the battle Hamilton dispatched only part of his cavalry and 700 of the 10,000 strong army to Ribbleton Moor.

Langdale's forces fought back towards Preston to attempt to join up with the Scots, but failed to prevent the enemy's approach to the vital river crossing at Walton-le-Dale. Colonel Assheton's Parliamentarian contingent advanced along a lane which led into Fishwick Bottoms and thwarted the Scottish forces which had now been divided into two. Cromwell reached Preston where he met the Duke of Hamilton's bodyguard. The Duke and part of his command were now trapped north of the river and therefore had

A map of the Battle of Preston, 17 August 1648, showing the situation when the two armies first clashed at Ribbleton windmill, on the road from Grimsargh to Preston.

Courtesy of Dr Stephen Bull, Curator of Military History and Archaeology, Museum of Lancashire

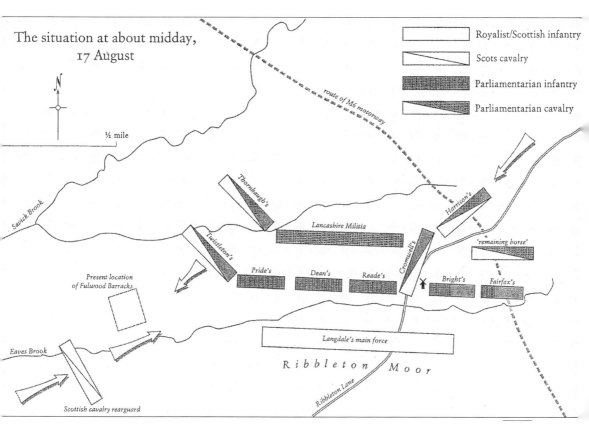

The situation at about midday, 17 August

N
½ mile

Royalist/Scottish infantry
Scots cavalry
Parliamentarian infantry
Parliamentarian cavalry

route of M6 motorway

Sawick Brook

Thornhaugh's

Harrison's

Lancashire Militia

'remaining horse'

Twistleton's

Present location of Fulwood Barracks

Pride's   Dean's   Reade's   Cromwell's   Bright's   Fairfax's

Langdale's main force

Eaves Brook

R i b b l e t o n   M o o r

Ribbleton Lane

Scottish cavalry rearguard

to swim the swollen river to join the rest of his army in Walton-le-Dale.

The battle moved to the old bridge over the Ribble at Walton-le-Dale which had been captured by Cromwell's Lancashire Militia. The fighting was particularly severe at this crucial crossing of the Ribble, but Cromwell divided the enemy and the Royalists were beaten back to the south side of the river and on to Wigan. Although outnumbered, Cromwell defeated Hamilton's Army and lost 500 of his men. About 1,000 supporters of the King were killed and 4,000 taken prisoner, before both sides ceased fighting and held counsels of war. Preston, one of the King's strongest Lancashire towns, had now been captured. Two days later most of the Scottish army surrendered at Warrington. The Duke of Hamilton was subsequently executed and Charles I suffered the same fate on 30 January 1649. An English Republic was established shortly thereafter and Cromwell became Lord Protector in 1653.

Exercise of power by absolute monarchs ceased and the Civil Wars helped to foster an increasing political stability in England, eventually leading to the development of our constitutional monarchy. It could be argued that paradoxically Cromwell's greatest legacy was courageous leadership on and off the battlefield contributing to the execution of Charles I and yielding embryonic free speech, freedom and democracy. The Battle of Preston therefore significantly affected the historical and political development of the country. When Charles II was restored to the throne in 1660 there was great rejoicing in Preston, and the bells of the parish church rang for three days. Today several roads in Grimsargh and Ribbleton are named after the officers from both armies. Where Cromwell's army advanced across the fields of Grimsargh-with-Brockholes en route to Ribbleton Moor there is now a rapidly expanding industrial park symbolically named Cromwell Park.

References

1. *The Army Quarterly*, 'Cromwell in Lancashire', vol. 27, p. 75, Captain R.A. Irivine.
2. Kuerden Map, LRO, DDX 194/28.
3. A viewing platform situated close to Longridge Road provides a facility for people to view the area of the battle and imagine the opposing forces fiercely battling for supremacy.

   I am grateful for the consultations of Dr Stephen Bull, the author of *Bloody Preston* and *The Civil War in Lancashire*. Reference was also made to a compilation of nineteenth-century newspaper reports compiled by Robert Gardner in the Harris Reference Library, Preston.

CHAPTER FIVE

Local Democracy, Crime and Poverty in the Parish of Grimsargh-with-Brockholes

The Hearth Tax and Act of Protestation

THERE IS NO OFFICIAL ESTIMATION of the population of Grimsargh until 1801. However, the first indication of population trends occurs during the Stuart period with the documented Hearth Tax returns of 1663 and the Act of Protestation returns of 1641. In Tudor times the Reformation spawned the Act of Protestation, which required all adults to sign the Protestation Oath in 1641, to maintain the established religion as opposed to Roman Catholicism. The return for 'the Higher End of the Parish of Preston' included Grimsargh-with-Brockholes and the adjacent townships for which a separate return was made for Ribbleton, Fishwick and Elston. Combined figures for Grimsargh-with-Brockholes and Elston of those who signed and abstained from signing total sixty-four men and women comprising a total of fifty mostly male persons at Grimsargh and fourteen persons at Elston. Allowing for an average of two to three children per household this suggests an approximate combined township population of between 128 and 192 which broadly corresponds with the Hearth Tax returns.[1]

Notwithstanding exemptions for the poor, the Hearth returns also yield a cautious estimate of population and accommodation in the seventeenth century and long before the days of official census. At Grimsargh-with-Brockholes there were thirty-six taxable hearths or fires levied against twenty-one occupiers. Corresponding figures at Elston were twenty-eight hearths payable by fourteen occupiers. The exact number of spouses and children is inconclusive but by multiplying a combined total of thirty-five male occupant householders with an estimated average household of between four and five an estimated population for seventeenth-century Grimsargh‑with‑Brockholes would be 140 to 175 people. Not surprisingly, farming dominated the nature of employment.

Ecclesiastical and Civil or Township Boundaries

The original parish of Preston was in the deanery of Amounderness and included eight townships in addition to the borough. These were Ashton, Broughton, Barton, Haighton, Elston, Grimsargh‑with‑Brockholes, Ribbleton and Fishwick.[2] Grimsargh‑with‑Brockholes was a township consisting of two hamlets within the parish of Preston in the Diocese of Chester, gaining its own chapelry in 1716 and ecclesiastical parish in 1875. The Grimsargh‑with‑Brockholes township embraced scattered houses, farms and hamlets within the parish boundary.

A small part of Grimsargh‑with‑Brockholes was included in the borough of Preston in 1880 and in the township of Preston in 1894. The Local Government Act of 1894 divided England and Wales into 14,000 parishes, whose boundaries generally maintained those followed by the civil parishes. In consequence of changes to the boundaries in 1894, Preston was extended to coincide with the municipal borough and Fishwick ceased to be a township. Grimsargh‑with‑Brockholes was reduced as 192 acres were trans‑ferred to Preston.[3]

The Ribble at Horse Shoe Bend represents the natural eastern boundary of the ecclesiastical/civil parish.
Author's collection

The name Brockholes finally faded into obscurity when the remaining 1,720 acres comprising the old Manor of Brockholes was absorbed by Preston in 1934. At that time the borough boundaries at Preston were extended by agreement with Lancashire County Council and Preston Rural District Council to be made available largely for industrial development by Courtaulds, and Grimsargh-with-Brockholes became plain Grimsargh.[4] Townships survived until the creation of the urban and rural district councils in 1894 and the term has now been superseded.

From 1832 the clerk of the peace kept lists, compiled annually, of those entitled to vote in local and parliamentary elections. Electoral registers came into being, with voters at parliamentary elections recorded in the poll book. The old civil parishes continued until 1894 when the newly created urban and rural district and local parish councils replaced the governing townships. Elston did not posses its own parish council and was attached to the parish of Ribbleton, with its own rural district councillor, Mr John Ainsworth. Today Elston is part of the civil parish of Grimsargh.

As a unit of local government and administration, townships were corporately administered by a Township Assembly, super-vised by the Justices of the Peace meeting at Quarter Sessions. Long before the establishment of local parish councils and the County Constabulary Act of 1845, the local community was re-sponsible for policing and governing itself with a system of unpaid volunteer officials. 'Four and twenty gentlemen' had responsibility for the parish of Preston and were known as the Select Vestry of Preston, with records commencing on 1 January 1645. They were divided into three separate groups of eight, representing a threefold division of the Parish into Preston town (or the 'middle part'), the 'upper end' and the 'lower end'. The upper end comprised the townships of the north and east, Elston, Grimsargh, Ribbleton and Fishwick. Since 1770 and before the creation of the new ecclesiastical parishes of the upper end, the renamed Select Vestry appointed the churchwardens, (of whom there were six, two for each division) the sidesmen and the vestry clerk.[5]

Civil parishes were given responsibility for the poor and the highways. The Overseer of the Poor would have had responsibility for the unfortunate poor people of Grimsargh-with-Brockholes. The prestige and responsibilities held by the churchwarden gave him regular contact with the Vicar and important landowners. A surveyor of the highways would have had responsibility for the maintenance of roads. The constable would have the onerous task of protecting life and property, the maintenance of order and enforcement of the criminal law. The business of the Manorial Court was presided over by court officials appointed at the court; and parish officers and manorial officers were two distinct, but overlapping, units of local government.

Help for the Poor

In many Lancashire villages children went to school or gained other employment without formal training. At Grimsargh many worked on the farms. Others served their masters as apprentices for seven years. On completion they became members of the trade guild and were eligible to start in business for themselves. The master taught, fed and clothed the child. Poor children were put out as apprentices by the Overseers of the Poor and masters were obliged to take them. Apprentices became subject to court orders if they were disobedient, or subjected to cruelty, lack of training or other abuse. Matters were documented in a book for entering and recording the names of such persons who were bound apprentices, together with their masters and trade. Richard Fish-wicke of Grimsargh was apprenticed to Randle Cooke of Preston, carpenter and housewright, for seven years from 1 August 1683. The boy would soon find that brick houses were becoming the norm in Preston and gradually replacing the boxed wooden-framed houses with their infilling of woven willow twigs daubed with wet clay commonly known as 'wattle and daub'.

Philanthropy was apparently not extended to Hugh Walshman's boarded-out apprentice. In 1678, the plight of an orphaned ap-prenticed child of eight years was taken up by a lady at Samlesbury, concerned about the way her neighbour, Hugh Walsh-man of Lower Brockholes, was treating the child. Jennet Heatley spoke up against him before the Court for allowing Margaret Bolton to starve. This was duly recorded by the Clerk of the Court who instructed that Walshman was to treat his boarded-out child properly. (LRO, QSP 492/2)

The borough of Preston had a number of charities including smaller benefactions for the poor. A charge of £3 15s. a year for the use of the poor of Brockholes existed as early as 1650. The townships of Elston and Ribbleton benefited equally by a charity founded in 1670 by John Farrington. He gave his tenement in

Elston to bind children apprentices or to benefit the poor in other ways. In 1737, John Charnley at Penwortham had a charge on his land, which included 20 shillings yearly for the poor of Grimsargh. At Preston Mary Cross gave £600 for the poor of the borough in 1889. The benefits of the Harris Orphanage in Fulwood were also available for children whose parents resided within eight miles of Preston Town Hall, which therefore included Grimsargh.[6]

Alternative ways of helping and controlling the poor were implemented by the legislators. The Middle Ages were charac‹ terised by oppressive measures against vagabonds. Applications made for assistance date back to the Poor Laws of Queen Elizabeth I and reflected the extreme poverty and distress to which many people had sunk.

The petition of an eighty‹year‹old Grimsargh lady, Anne Brad‹ ley, for Poor Relief shows the level of abject poverty in 1650:

> The Humble Petition of Anne Bradley of Grymsargh in the parishe of Preston, widow, Sheweth unto your good worshippes that your peticioner being aged 80‹tye yeares or thereabouts ye fallen to great povertye and want is not able to seeke releiffe, Humblye beseeches you to grant her and order to charge the Towne of the aforesaid parishe to give her your peticioner and a little chyld not 4 yeares of age which shee is grandmother too and left fatherless and motherless and borne in the aforesaid towne and parishe some monnthly pay[ment] what your worshipps thinkes fit, Otherwaies shee and the little infant wilbee lost and famished for Releiffe And shee as in duty bound will ever pray for your prosperityes etc. We certifie that the misery of this woaman is very greate and her estate is very lamentable – William Sanderson, Thos. Horne, Ric. Harrison, William Turner, Robt. Danniell, Thos. Daniell.' On the original document is inscribed the following note of the Justice's decision. 'Churchwardens and overseere to provide.[7]

No welfare state in those days, and what a way to treat one of Grimsargh's senior citizens and her three‹year‹old grandchild. The Poor Law system was established by the acts of 1598 and 1601 and was maintained with important legislative amendments in 1834 until it was finally repealed in 1946. Financial provision was made for the disabled poor by 'overseers of the poor' in each parish. At least two persons, depending on the parish, were appointed yearly with approval from the Justices, to levy a poor rate and to supervise its distribution. The petitions are contained among the invaluable quarter session records held in Preston.

Local Democracy, Crime and Poverty

The Act of Settlement 1662 empowered overseers to remove any newcomers likely to become chargeable on parish rates. It was forbidden for a stranger to settle in a parish unless he had £10 for twelve months' rent of a house or could find securities that would obviate charges on the poor rate of his parish. The principle of the legislation was that everyone should have a place of settlement, which in many cases was their parish of birth. Subsequent consolidated changes to the Poor Laws allowed people to work outside their own parish, subject to conditions. The statute also provided for the identification of paupers, who wore a letter 'P' followed by the origin of their original parish. The humiliating process was demonstrated at Grimsargh in 1698, when Thomas Greenalls of Grimsargh, a day labourer, made application.

> The humble peticion of Thomas Greenalls of Grimsargh, labourer, sheweth that your poore peticioner hath a wife and seven children two whereof is gone from your peticioner and the other five are very small and all under the age of fourteene yeres and two of the eldest of the five of your peticioners children are very infirme and lame children and can doe nothing towards their sustinance and the other three are very young and your peticioner has for this yeare last past been lame himself and at present cannot use or take any ax or spade in his right hand soe as to worke any dayes worke and has severall times offered to get imployment and worke for and towards the maintenance of his children and offered to worke for his owne meate and is very ready and willing to worke for his maintenance to the utmost and power of his strength and capacity to get and acquire a just and true livelyhood for his said wife and family but since your peticioner cannot be imployed in worke he is now reduced to great necessity that he is not able to maintain his family without the aid and assiztance of the said Townshipp of Grimsargh.

The clerk of the peace's note reads, '4s a month, wearing the Badge, January, 1698'.[8]

The 1723 Knatchbull's Act allowed parishes to unite for the purpose of maintaining a workhouse. Overseers could contract for employment of the inmates and deny relief to those refusing to enter but in practice out-relief remained the norm. The cost of providing continuous relief for families proved to be a drain on resources and the Poor Law Amendment Act, 1834, attempted to address this issue by abolishing outdoor relief and replacing the parish of administrative township responsibility with a standardised new system of union, under elected boards of guardians.

The principle of 'less eligibility' was upheld and confinement in the workhouse at Fulwood provided the alternative way of sustaining the poor. Generally, the 1834 Act was not well received in Lancashire and the workhouse at Fulwood which later became part of Sharoe Green Hospital was not built until 1869.

At Grimsargh two local men maintained responsibility as Overseers of the Poor, and attended the parish council meetings. Thomas Hothersall of The Poplars (who was also the registrar of births and deaths for the sub-district of Alston) and Thomas Patterson of Oakdene, on Longsight Lane, Grimsargh, were re-elected as Overseers at a meeting of Grimsargh Parish Council on 11 April 1922. They would not have much longer to serve in this capacity for the office of Overseer was abolished by the Rating and Valuation Act, 1925.

Constabulary Duties to be Done

The occupiers of Higher Brockholes had some rather unpleasant neighbours across the river at Samlesbury, mentioned by Eaton in his antiquarian book on the history of Samlesbury (p. 22). 'In October 1561 Sir John Southworth sent his servants over the Ribble to Higher Brockholes, when they entered the premises and broke the head of a servant then carried off twenty head of cattle, ten of which were impounded at Rigby Fold, Samlesbury and ten at Clitheroe Castle'. It does sound as though crime was rife in Tudor Grimsargh, but in the Stuart period they had greater things to think about.

The Hearth Tax was passed in the reign of Charles II 'to establish an additional revenue for the better support of the Crown and dignity of his Majesty, his heirs and successors, whereby it was enacted that on and after 20 March 1662, 'every dwelling and other house and edifice shall be chargeable with the annual payment, for every fire hearth and stove within every such house, the sum of two shillings by the year in two equal portions'. Chimney money had been around since Norman times but now the legislators sought to raise an annual tax to bolster the income of the Restoration monarchy by £1,200,000 per annum.

As with most legislation there were exemptions, which extended to those in receipt of Poor Relief and not paying the parish rate. At the time of the Act, fourteen of the thirty-six hearths of Grimsargh had been in the hands of the squires and landowners.

William Houghton had four hearths at his property, William Elston had five and Hugh Walshman was included on the return at Lower Brockholes with five hearths. At the other end of the scale was a certain Grimsargh confectioner who clearly felt ag, grieved by the imposition. In 1667 Richard Dickson appealed against the Hearth tax, which amounted to 2 shillings (10p) for every hearth.

> The Humble Petition of Richard Dickson of Grimsargh, humbly sheweth – that your said petitioner hath bine constrayed to pay for an oven house wherein there is two ovens but noe harth noe fornise [furnace] nor noe other use made of the said oven house but only backing [baking] soe that your peticioner thinkes it to be against the Intent of the acte that he should pay for the same.

On 10 October 1667, the clerk of the peace agreed and endorsed the archived document accordingly. 'It is the opinion of the court that the oven harth shall bee disburdened.'[9]

To facilitate the collecting of the tax Mr Dixon would have been required to send in a return, made to the justices at Quarter Sessions by the village constable. If the constable was not satisfied with the number of hearths and stoves shown on the return he had draconian powers to enter the house and count them. The legislation would have been a close competitor in the unpopularity stakes to late twentieth-century attempts to introduce a poll tax and with consequential non-payments the statute – like the poll tax – was repealed in 1689. The Quarter Sessions returns of those assessed in Grimsargh is no more than a list of names.[10]

Grimsargh-with-Brockholes once humiliated its miscreants in the stocks; a stone alongside the War Memorial at Three Mile Cross is all that remains of this seat of punishment. Those who went to prison may have benefited from the charity of William Edmund, son, who in 1735 left £50 to buy bread for the prisoners at both Lancaster and Preston. Long stretches of incarceration eventually led to income providing gifts for prisoners discharged from Preston Gaol. This was usually in the form of clothing or travelling expenses.[11]

In 1692 an early account of a Grimsargh shoemaker shows how some people were quite mobile and travelled to Preston to sell at the market. Richard Balshaw became a victim of crime when threatened with a sword:

> Richard Balshaw, Shoemaker of Grimsargh, while selling his goods at

a stall in Preston Market, was set upon by Richard Whitehead, lately returned from the fighting in Ireland, after the flight of James II. Whitehead helped himself to Balshaw's goods, and when asked for the money, drew his sword and threatened the shoemaker, who appealed to the magistrates for protection.[12]

No victim support in those days, and no wonder he was traumatised. The crime of robbery was not without precedent in Victorian Grimsargh, as we will see in a later chapter.

References

1. A list of non-jurors in 1715 appears in the Appendix.
2. Clemesha, *A History of Preston in Amounderness*.
3. Local Government Order (1607 – about 192 acres were transferred to Preston).
4. Local Government Act, 1929 and the Interim Report on Borough Extensions, May 1946.
5. Clemesha, *A History of Preston in Amounderness*.
6. *Victoria County History*, vol. 1, p. 90.
7. LRO, QSP 30/12.
8. LRO, QSP 822/40.
9. LRO, QSP 310/10.
10. The Hearth Tax and Protestation Oath returns for the Parish of Grimsargh and Elston are contained in the Quarter Sessions records at Lancashire Record Office, and Fishwick, *The History of the Parish of Preston* (1900), pp. 424, 429.
11. *Victoria County History*, vol. 1, p. 89.
12. LRO, QSP 718/6.

CHAPTER SIX

The Reformation and Jacobite Influences on the Church in Grimsargh

L ONG BEFORE Grimsargh-with-Brockholes gained its parish in 1875 it was part of the parish of Preston in the Diocese of Chester.[1] Walking in the footsteps of Cromwell, a little more than half a century earlier, villagers probably made at least three visits to Preston Parish Church if only to be christened, married and finally, buried. The only church in close proximity to Grimsargh was a small Roman Catholic chapel at Fernyhalgh. This was in use from 1348 as a chantry and as a chapel in 1511, during the reign of Henry VII. In Tudor times the Reformation brought about its destruction but it was rebuilt in the time of James II who tried to turn the country to Rome. After the Reformation fines for not attending the parish church were one shilling for each offence.[2]

There were undoubtedly concerns prior to the lifting of restrictions as the area was still a strongly Catholic community. With a little subterfuge Alston Lane Roman Catholic foundation, at the east side of Grimsargh, was first founded in 1761. A Jesuit priest, Sir Walter Vavasour of Hazelwood, served this district from 1700 to 1740. He celebrated Mass at Hothersall Hall and at Fairclough's Boot Farm, in Alston Lane. Having been accused of Jacobite leanings, he moved to the Mission at Preston. Other priests served this parish until the arrival of Mr Thomas Caton in 1761, who officially set up the Mission in 1765. It is not known where he lived or where he celebrated Mass. An important residence in the area was The Hermitage, the seat of the Chadwick family. Hacking Hobbs Farmhouse is a definite possibility, owned at that time by Thomas Eccles. A priest's hiding hole still exists in both houses and at that time the Penal Laws were still in force. From Hacking Hobbs, close to New Town, now Longridge, he would have been able to cover the main areas of population in the Mission which were Alston, Grimsargh, Longridge and

Hothersall. The 1767 'Register of Papists' suggests that the Catholic population of the parish at that time was about 460, many of them employed in agriculture.

In 1774, the first Catholic church in this area since the Reformation was built. It was as inconspicuous as possible, set well back from the main Preston to Longridge road. Externally the building gave the appearance of a farmstead, which belied the fact that up a set of external stone steps was a secret chapel. The unpretentious building is still situated on a public highway known as Back Lane, which in 1831 linked the village of Elston with the White Bull Hotel. Even in those days the 'local' probably provided a covert focal point for one or two clergy and not all roads led to Rome. During his twenty-three years at Alston, Mr Caton also procured a school and Presbytery on the ground floor of the Church building. Although the 'Catholic Emancipation Act' was passed in 1829, news of it, or its implications, must have taken a few years to filter through to Alston. It was not until 6 July 1837, that Alston Lane Chapel was registered for weddings and the first took place on 28 November 1837.[3]

The Vicar of Preston, Samuel Peploe, was born in Shropshire in 1668. The Vicar shared the general uneasiness regarding the popish leanings of the Stuart supporters, and was particularly worried by the activities among his flock of the priests of Fernyhalgh, who were only too willing to save people the trouble of taking their infants to Preston to be baptised. A quote from the Chetham Society ledgers (22470) of 4 April 1715, mirrored the concerns. 'Owing to the distance from their parish church and other convenient places of public worship the people were exposed to temptations and popery, there being no less than six priests in ye one parish.' The Vicar was very vigorous in combating Roman Catholicism at all costs. Many raids took place on neighbouring Catholic communities. Raids by soldiers during the late seventeenth and early eighteenth centuries on Fernyhalgh Church are believed to have taken vestments and plate and transferred the church bell to the belfry of the original Grimsargh Church.

Arising from religious division, popery and political turmoil, the peaceful haven of Grimsargh was to gain a new church. When the Reverend Samuel Peploe became Vicar of Preston in 1700, his foresight led to the building of St George's Chapel in Preston, as a chapel-of-ease for the parish church. The parish included Grimsargh-with-Brockholes, and he also applied his energy to provide for the ecclesiastical needs of this large rural area. Sir Henry Hoghton distinguished himself in the first Jacobite rebellion on the side of the government and was returned four times as Member of Parliament for Preston, from 1710 to 1735. He was very active in promoting the construction of good roads including the highway through Grimsargh that still runs close to St Michael's Church. Sir Henry and his ancestors had long held the Manorial rights for Grimsargh and he was instrumental in providing the site and building the first church, thus saving parishioners a five mile journey on horseback or shanks pony into Preston.

On 14 April 1715, learning that Sir Henry Hoghton was intending to go to Chester, Samuel Peploe seized the opportunity to ask the Lord of the Manor to take a letter from him to his predecessor, Bishop Gastrell. In it he expressed his fears, and his plans to build a church at Grimsargh. 'The site is promised by Sir Henry as well as a little money, so little that we appreciate his hope that a curate will be able to help himself.'

Letter from the Vicar of Preston to the Bishop of Chester:

My Lord,

I beg leave to acquaint your lordship that there are three townships and part of another in this parish which lie, three four and five miles from the Church, and have no other convenient place of public worship.

That by this unhappy situation they have been still exposed to temptation and popery (which is prevalent in these parts of your lordship's diocese) and are thereby an easier prey to the priests of that communion – we have no less than six of these men in this one parish.

From my first coming to this place I have wished for some hopeful remedy against this growing evil, and I hope we are now in a way for it, if your lordship please to give your approbation.

Sir Henry Hoghton, the Patron of this Church (and one who has done several good things for increasing our congregation, and is the person who does me the favour to put this paper in your hands) has promised land to build a chapel where it will be serviceable to the inhabitants above mentioned; and with his assistance I doubt not to procure a decent place for the worship of God among men.

When the intended chapel is opened, I have taken care already that there shall be ten pounds per annum at least annexed to it, besides what some of the inhabitants will subscribe, and what may be got by teaching school; it being a place where a diligent man may help himself that way. These together will be a competency for a

Samuel Peploe.
Parish records

curate in this cheap country; and I hope that if the work be perfected it will be of great use to men's souls as well as of service to our church.

I wait only for your lordship's pleasure to proceed. If I have your encouragement I will immediately set about it and hope to give you a good account of the affair in a little time.

I am your lordship's unknown but very dutiful son and obedient servant,

SAMUEL PEPLOE

I was at Chester to pay my duty to your lordship as soon after you went to London.

> Preston in Lancashire, Deanery of Richmond, 14 April 1715.[4]

Bishop Gastrell approved of Peploe's proposal and the quarries at Longridge commenced supplying the stone. As the wagons trundled down the lane, Samuel Peploe and Sir Henry Hoghton found themselves in the middle of a real crisis.

If Preston reflected some of the feelings of the country during the Civil War, there were strong elements that took opposing views at the beginning of the eighteenth century. Over 165 years

Grimsargh

THE STORY OF A
LANCASHIRE VILLAGE

A map showing Preston and the positions of the opposing forces at time of the Jacobite Rebellion of 1715.

Miss N. Carbis and parish records

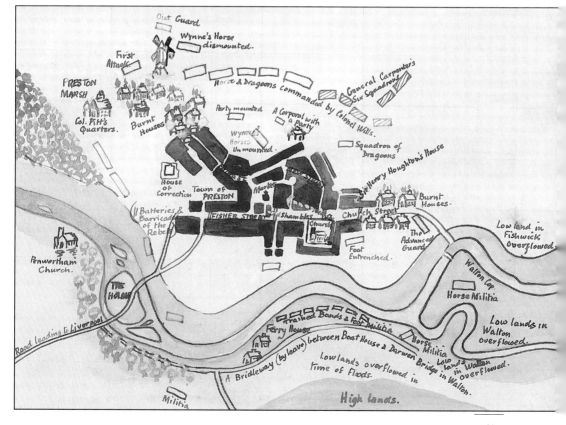

From an old painting

The original church, built in 1716.

A drawing of Old Grimsargh Church by Nellie Carbis, taken from an old painting. The founder of Grimsargh Church was the Rt Rev. Samuel Peploe, Bishop of Chester, who when vicar of Preston urged the building of the first church in Grimsargh in 1715.

N. Carbis collection

after Cromwell, another Scottish army crossed the border with the intention of reinstating a Scottish monarch. The fighting that began on Saturday, 12 November 1715 on the streets of Preston was to be the last battle to be fought on English soil.

James II had been dethroned in 1688 by William of Orange during the Glorious Revolution. Following the accession of George I, religious division began to reassert itself during the eighteenth century between the Hanoverians and the Jacobite supporters of the exiled James II.

James II had been determined to make England a Catholic country and the first Jacobite Rebellion of 1715 was an attempt to put his son James Francis Edward alias the 'Old Pretender', or James III, back on the throne. On 9 November 1715, an army of Jacobite rebels arrived in Preston from Scotland, led by Mackintosh, Foster, Derwentwater and Kenmure. There were some who welcomed the army and the Jacobites proclaimed James Edward as King in the Market Place and made Preston Parish Church their headquarters.

Captain Douglas, a member of the Pretender's army, forded the river at Elston close to Lower Hall in November, 1715, when he passed through Balderstone and on to Blackburn in quest of horses and provisions.[5]

At the same time Government armies converged on the town

and attacked the rebels. During the conflict the Vicar of Preston, Samuel Peploe was reading prayers for King George when rebel Jacobites entered the church and threatened him with death unless he ceased praying for 'the Hanoverian usurper'. Peploe retorted, 'Soldier, I am doing my duty – do yours.' Fortunately the soldier neglected his duty and Peploe lived to relate his ordeal. The Jacobites had erected barricades at the ends of the main thoroughfares and were gaining control until Sir Henry Hoghton summoned government reinforcements. By 11 a.m. the following day the town was surrounded and the Jacobites were forced to surrender. One good reason given for their defeat was that the 'ladys in this toune, Preston, are so beautiful and so richly attired, that the gentleman soldiers, minded nothing but courting and feasting during their days in Preston'.

However, there were more serious issues to contemplate. Jacobite soldiers were packed into the Parish Church and kept under guard for months. Twelve were hanged at Gallows Hill, which got its name from the hangings of the Jacobeans and is now the site of English Martyrs Church, Garstang Road, Preston. According to tradition their heads were placed outside the Town Hall. At Grimsargh they were a little more refined: public executions and 'head counts' were not the order of the day!

There is no doubt that the Reverend Peploe displayed courage by reading the prayers for the King and royal family while the rebel army was in the Parish Church. After the Jacobites had been defeated a report commending Samuel Peploe for his sturdy loyalty was conveyed to King George I. His Majesty responded with a degree of wit saying, 'Peep-low, he shall peep high – I will make him a Bishop.' Samuel Peploe became Warden of the Collegiate Church in Manchester and on the death of Bishop Gastrell in 1726, was promoted to the post of Bishop of Chester. He died in 1752 at the age of 84, and is commemorated in the Erasmus Chapel of Chester Cathedral by a white marble tablet. With the permission of the Bishop of Chester a photograph was taken of Mr Peploe's portrait which is today displayed in Grimsargh Church.

The original Episcopal chapel at Grimsargh was built by subscription and dedicated to St Michael. It was one of only five churches built in Amounderness in the eighteenth century. The modest St Michael's opened as a chapel of ease for Preston Parish Church, serving Grimsargh and adjacent townships in 1716. By deed

Pinnacles and a gargoyle from the old church, now in the Vicarage garden

A drawing of the Vicarage by Nellie Carbis. A few souvenirs were taken from the original church and placed in the vicarage garden.

N. Carbis collection

granted 22 October 1717, Sir Henry Hoghton and Miles Hale of Grimsargh, yeoman, had granted to trustees the site where the chapel stood. The inhabitants petitioned the Bishop that the chapel and yard should be 'severed from all common uses and dedicated to God by the name of St Michael's Chapel'. Within the walls of the new chapel it measured 46 feet in length and 19 feet in breadth and the site of the chapel and yard measured 50 yards by 30 yards.

Bishop Gastrell wrote in 1722: 'New chapel, lately erected anno domini 1716 in ye township of Grimsargh but not yet consecrated. Certified that nothing at all belongs to it. £200 was subscribed by Mr Peploe, Sir Henry Hoghton and others. The sum of £40 was given by a gentlewoman who desired not to be known.' An account of who first occupied the pews is shown in the Bishop's Registry. As a sign of the times distinctions were made between the esquires, yeomen and others in this original place of worship.[6]

East End – North side: William Shaw, gent; Christopher Walmsley; Miles Hale; Ann Lowe; Thomas Lomax, gent; Pulpit; The Curate's Pew.

Thomas Grimbaldeston; Henry Charnley; William Wall, gent; John Borrett, Esq.; John Killett; Roger Lund.

Font.

East End – South side: Benjamin Hoghton, Esq.; William Bushell, Esq.; Edward France; Richard Dixon; Christopher Dixon; Edward Dixon; Lawrence Charnley; John Charnley; Richard Charnock; Thomas Willasy; Thomas Cowband, gent; George Ratcliff; William France.

Entrance.

The original old tower had a four-square stone structure, with gargoyles and stone pillars at each corner. Hewitson, writing in around 1872 says: 'In the original tower were two bells, awfully ding-dong little articles; in the new tower is one and a full peal is ultimately expected.' The original bell bore the inscription 'Mater Dei, ora pro nobis. 1687 R.A.' (translated as 'Mother of God pray for us'). According to the *Preston Guardian* of 26 February 1916, the bell was taken from Fernyhalgh Church in 1689, two years after casting. The bell hung in Grimsargh Church from when it was built in 1715, and was later moved to the Vicarage garden, where it was rung by the Reverend William Harrison's housekeeper to call him from the far reaches of the garden. A larger bell, still in use, was transferred to the new tower. It is thought this bell had been brought from Preston Parish Church and is inscribed, 'Jesus be our speed, 1765'.[7] Souvenirs of the old tower including the old font, stone pillars and gargoyles were transferred to the Vicarage garden.

From 1716 the chaplaincy of St Michael's was served by curates from Preston Parish Church who walked or rode up from town to the nearby Church House Farm before ministering at St Michael's. In those days there was no vicarage and some accommodation was provided for them at the farm which today is a private dwelling. Richard Thompson was curate of St Michael's in 1726, followed by Thomas Winder in 1732, and in 1739 William Parker.

The Deed of Consecration of Grimsargh Chapel was made on 9 November 1726. The deed stated that the area around the church was to be used as a burial ground and the right of pasturage was reserved to the Vicar of Preston. The inhabitants of Grimsargh and Elston were to keep the Chapel 'repaired, roofed and decently adorned'. The signatories to the original document were: William Bushell, Rector of Heysham; Thomas Johnson, Rector of Ribchester; Thomas Clarke, Vicar of Chipping;

The Reformation and Jacobite Influences

Thomas Parkinson, Curate of Garstang; W. Birkett, Curate of Whitechapel; Samuel Peploe, LL.B.; William Johnson; Robert Willacy, Curate of St Michael's; Richard Thompson, Curate of Grimsargh; Robert Herbert, Public Notary; Edward Robert, Diocesan Public Notary; and eight others.

John Harrison held the post of the first curate of Grimsargh when he was instituted to Grimsargh in 1803 after being licensed to the village in 1799. Mr Harrison was a workaholic and much esteemed by his parishioners. He was also second master at Preston Grammar School and chaplain at the House of Correction at Preston. At the age of 56 he died suddenly of apoplexy in July 1823. Two Sundays before his death he had been walking to church with William Cross of Red Scar when a strange remark seemed to be some sort of premonition. 'Another Sunday and then I have done.' This proved true. He took the duty at Grimsargh the following Sunday for the last time.[8] The Reverend J. Harrison was buried at Preston Parish Church and is commemorated on his son's (William Harrison) tombstone in Grimsargh Churchyard.[9]

References

1. For parochial records see also T. Smith, *The Parish Church of Preston in Amounderness* (1892).
2. N. Carbis, *Grimsargh Church and Parish* (1966).
3. Consultations with Father Harry Doyle of Alston Lane Parish in 2001.
4. C. Hardwick, *A History of the Borough of Preston* (1857), p.534.
5. Eaton, *History of Samlesbury*.
6. Fishwick, *The History of the Parish of Preston* (1900), p. 150.
7. TLCAS, vol. 37, p.54; vol. 45, p. 124.
8. T. Smith, *A History of Longridge* (1888), pp. 210–14.
9. See also N. Carbis, *Grimsargh Church and Parish*, and Dobson, *Rambles by the Ribble* (1881).

OVERLEAF

Painting of Red Scar by Albert Woods

Reproduced by kind permission of Mrs E. Woods

A photograph of Red Scar Mansion (looking north) around 1890. The original medieval thatched portion at the right-hand corner incorporated the dining room and was the oldest part of the property.

N. Carbis collection and parish records

PART III

Grimsargh-with-Brockholes: The Eighteenth Century to a New Millennium

CHAPTER SEVEN

Red Scar Mansion and the Cross Family: 'The Country Squire'

G RIMSARGH‑WITH‑BROCKHOLES has always been a pastoral
and verdant rural outpost of Preston. In the southern corner
of Brockholes, the wooded landscape rises steeply from the
river. Red Scar mansion was so named after several landslides
revealed the red scars of clay, above the bend in the Ribble at
the aptly named beauty spot of Horse Shoe Bend. (One landslide
in 1950 claimed the lives of two fishermen who were swept away
and never found. Following this tragedy access to the river bank
was forbidden by warning notices.) Red Scar commanded fine
views over the river valley in a peaceful agricultural and woodland
setting. Its history is inextricably interwoven with the story of
Grimsargh‑with‑Brockholes and the manorial seat of three gener‑
ations of the Cross family.[1]

Red Scar was a real gem, built in the late Jacobean architectural
style to incorporate a long‑established thatched cottage of cruck
construction. As a very young boy I walked along the footpath
overlooking Horse Shoe Bend with my parents. Somewhere in
my mind I have the vaguest of recollections of seeing the forlorn
shell of the imposing building stripped of all its dignity and
awaiting its ultimate fate. Atmospherically it seemed to be adorned
with a shroud of mystery and antiquity as well as charm, belied
by the march of progress. What was it really like in its heyday?
An old English baronial style house, with a resident butler and
servants, which echoed to the sound of both merriment and quiet
dignity. It would only have needed a wandering minstrel at the
door and a couple of falcons outside to complete an imaginary
halt to the progress of time. The mansion's sylvan setting consisted
of impressive copper and green beech trees and long‑abandoned
formal gardens in a park‑like setting which are still part of this
scenario. Images of this eerie childhood memory are often recalled

in my mind and doubtless this has inspired me to dust away the
cobwebs, and recall the halcyon days of the country squire.

The Cross family documents discovered in a solicitor's office
in Preston in 1997 revealed that land had formerly been in the
ownership of firstly, Sir Henry Hoghton, and then of his son, Sir
Henry Philip Hoghton, each in turn Lord of the Manor of Alston.
The Manor descended in the Hoghton family and was sold to
William Cross of Red Scar on 2 May 1803, for the sum of £630.
William Cross married Ellen and brought up his family at Red
Scar. He was Lord of the Manor in 1807 and was succeeded by
William Assheton Cross, William Cross and finally Katherine
Mary Cross in 1916.

Archived material concerning Red Scar may also be found in
the Lancashire Record Office. One of the earliest pre-Cross family
references is an indenture dated 3 April, 1780, for an apprentice
poor girl from Poulton to come and work at what must have been
the original medieval house which was later incorporated into the
Cross family mansion. The indenture (LRO, PR 2027/30) sets out
the terms of reference between the churchwarden and overseers
of the poor for the township of Poulton, a certain John Kellet of
Red Scar in Grimsoy and Jane Seed, a poor girl of Poulton, the
daughter of James Seed who was not able to maintain her. As an
apprentice to John Kellet of Red Scar young Jane had to dwell
in the manner of an apprentice until attaining the age of twenty.
During this time she had to faithfully serve her master and keep

his secrets and obey his lawful commands. Further constraints were imposed on her playing cards, dice or any unlawful game, frequenting ale houses, taverns, evil company or committing fornication, adultery or marriage within the said term. Indeed she had to behave herself to her said master and all his family as becometh a faithful apprentice. One wonders what became of Jane Seed the 'poor girl' and how she fared with her long apprenticeship in 'Housewifry' and the extent of any relationship with Henry Seed, who leased 30 acres at Red Scar from 16 December 1792, though occupied by William Clarkson as under-tenant.

From 7 January, 1793, eleven acres were in possession of John Clarkson and his under-tenants – all of whom were subject 'to the same suit and service of Court as are now due and to be performed to the Lord of the Manor of Alston. All corn and grain produced on the land must be ground at the Grimsargh corn mill for which service the tenant must pay to the Lord of the Manor'. If he took his corn elsewhere he had to pay a fine to the Lord of the Manor. Henry Seed had to 'keep and provide for a dog or a cock when required by Sir Henry Hoghton and must plant every year six good young plants of oak, ash, alder or elm – maintain the buildings, hedges, ditches, gates, stiles, fences, bridges, causeways – had to grind his corn grain and malt at the mill or mills of Sir Henry Hoghton in Grimsargh or pay the penalty – must spread upon the premises and not elsewhere all the soil, dung and manure that shall yearly arise upon the premises. Must not take, kill or destroy any kind of game, fish or wild fowl nor keep any net, dog or engine for taking the same'.

Yearly rent was payable in two instalments, usually every 6 June and 11 November. 'For every acre

Grimsargh

THE STORY OF A LANCASHIRE VILLAGE

Miss Mary Cross.
Courtesy of Anthony Cross and Marian Roberts

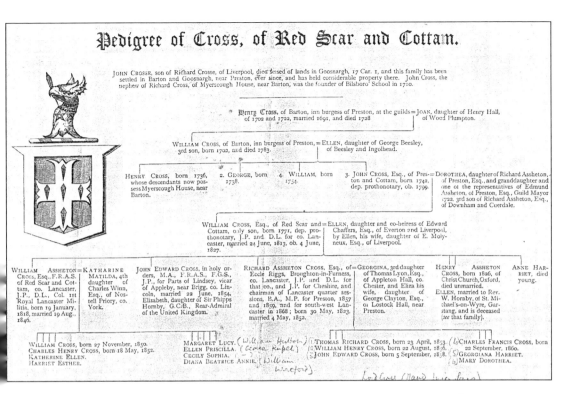

Pedigree of Cross, of Red Scar and Cottam.

JOHN CROSSE, son of Richard Crosse, of Liverpool, died seised of lands in Goosnargh, 17 Car. 1, and this family has been settled in Barton and Goosnargh, near Preston, ever since, and has held considerable property there. John Cross, the nephew of Richard Cross, of Myerscough House, near Barton, was the founder of Bilsboro' School in 1710.

HENRY CROSS, of Barton, inn burgess of Preston, at the guilds = JOAN, daughter of Henry Hall, of 1702 and 1722, married 1691, and died 1728 | of Wood Plumpton.

WILLIAM CROSS, of Barton, inn burgess of Preston, = ELLEN, daughter of George Beesley, 3rd son, born 1702, and died 1783. | of Beesley and Ingolhead.

HENRY CROSS, born 1736, whose descendants now possess Myerscough House, near Barton. | 2. GEORGE, born 1738. | 4. WILLIAM, born 1754. | 3. JOHN CROSS, Esq., of Preston and Cottam, born 1742, dep. prothonotary, ob. 1799. = DOROTHEA, daughter of Richard Assheton, of Preston, Esq., and granddaughter and one of the representatives of Edmund Assheton, of Preston, Esq., Guild Mayor 1722, 3rd son of Richard Assheton, Esq., of Downham and Cuerdale.

WILLIAM CROSS, Esq., of Red Scar and = ELLEN, daughter and co-heiress of Edward Cottam, only son, born 1771, dep. prothonotary, J.P. and D.L. for co. Lancaster, married 24 June, 1813, ob. 4 June, 1827. | Chaffers, Esq., of Everton and Liverpool, by Ellen, his wife, daughter of E. Molyneux, Esq., of Liverpool.

WILLIAM ASSHETON = KATHARINE CROSS, Esq., F.R.A.S., of Red Scar and Cottam, co. Lancaster, J.P., D.L., Col. 1st Royal Lancaster Militia, born 19 January, 1818, married 19 Aug., 1846. | MATILDA, 4th daughter of Charles Winn, Esq., of Nostell Priory, co. York. | JOHN EDWARD CROSS, in holy orders, M.A., F.R.A.S., F.G.S., J.P., for Parts of Lindsey, vicar of Appleby, near Brigg, co. Lincoln, married 22 June, 1854, Elizabeth, daughter of Sir Phipps Hornby, G.C.B., Rear-Admiral of the United Kingdom. | RICHARD ASSHETON CROSS, Esq., of = GEORGINA, 3rd daughter Eccle Riggs, Broughton-in-Furness, co. Lancaster, J.P. and D.L. for that co., and J.P. for Cheshire, and chairman of Lancaster quarter sessions, B.A., M.P. for Preston, 1857 and 1859, and for south-west Lancaster in 1868; born 30 May, 1823, married 4 May, 1852. | of Thomas Lyon, Esq., of Appleton Hall, co. Chester, and Eliza his wife, daughter of George Clayton, Esq., of Lostock Hall, near Preston. | HENRY ASSHETON CROSS, born 1826, of Christ Church, Oxford, died unmarried. | ANNE HARRIET, died young. | ELLEN, married to Rev. W. Hornby, of St. Michael's-on-Wyre, Garstang, and is deceased (see that family).

WILLIAM CROSS, born 27 November, 1850. CHARLES HENRY CROSS, born 18 May, 1852. KATHERINE ELLEN. HARRIET ESTHER. | MARGARET LUCY. (William Hulton.) ELLEN PRISCILLA. (George Rupel.) CECILY SOPHIA. (—) DIANA BEATRICE ANNIE. (William Hereford.) | (1) THOMAS RICHARD CROSS, born 23 April, 1853. (2) WILLIAM HENRY CROSS, born 22 August, 1856. (3) JOHN EDWARD CROSS, born 5 September, 1858. | (4) CHARLES FRANCIS CROSS, born 22 September, 1860. (5) GEORGIANA HARRIET. (6) MARY DOROTHEA.

Pedigree of the Cross family.
Courtesy of Anthony Cross

that shall be ploughed, broken up or grown with corn contrary to the covenant herein the further rent of £5 was incurred.'

The deeds provided clarification of what was reserved unto the Lord of the Manor: 'All the woods and timber on the estate and all manner of mines, quarries and delfs'. Also, power at all times, together with his workmen or agents, to enter the land and fell any timber and mine any mineral and cart them away; could erect any buildings or engines, sink any pits, make any drains or trenches, using any means whatsoever that might be necessary for the working of such mines etc.; had all manner of free warren (ie. the right to take game); could enter the land to take to hunt hawk, kill fish, or take away all manner of game, fish and wild fowl; could enter the land at any time to inspect the state or condition thereof – get clay for brick, sand and gravel and other materials for the making and repair of roads and carry them away 'making a reasonable satisfaction for the damage done thereby'.

Hardwick on Red Scar described the scene standing upon the plateau overlooking Red Scar.

No single picture can do justice to this beautiful and unique scrap of English scenery. The whole is not presentable on canvas from any one point of view. It contains, rather within itself, a complete portfolio

Red Scar (top left) in its
prominent setting above
Horse Shoe Bend, with a
pastoral scene on the
riverbank below. The rocky
crags (foreground) are the
result of artistic licence!

OPPOSITE TOP
The drawing room at Red
Scar.

OPPOSITE BOTTOM
The wind-braced cruck truss
in the dining room, framing
portraits of the Cross family.
The room once contained an
old hydraulic organ.
Internal pictures from *Old
and Celebrated Halls of
Lancashire and Cheshire*, vol. 4.
*Courtesy of the Harris Reference
Library, Preston.*

of sketches. It is a place to ramble about in, and not simply to stand staring at. Truly an Eden spot, fashioned by bounteous nature, to dispel the fierce burning passion and choking heart-ache engendered by rude collision with the outward world.

The Cross family, Freemen of Preston since 1700, have figured in the Guild Rolls to modern times. The family originated in Barton and Goosnargh and carried on business as tanners. There is no doubt they achieved high social status, but were nevertheless sincere and genuine in their efforts to do good to others. Their devout religion was expressed in regular church worship and successive generations of the family became closely linked with St Michael's Church, Grimsargh. Two sisters, Mary and Margaret Cross, lived at The Hollies, Barton, close to the A6. At considerable personal expense they had the steep hill on Lancaster Road, Barton, lowered, because the sight of horses pulling heavy loads to the top of the hill distressed them. Their compassion was duly recognised with an on-site memorial stone. Mary Cross also donated large sums of money to charities and founded the Royal Cross School for the Deaf which used to be situated at the top of Brockholes Brow in Preston.

John Cross, the third son of William of Barton Mill, settled in Preston and became an attorney there. He was born in 1742 and in 1770 married Dorothea Assheton. Evidently maintaining family traditions, he was generally known in Preston as 'Honest John Cross'. Dorothea died in August 1771, soon after her only son William was born. This seemed to echo her quotation that 'she

Red Scar
Mansion and the
Cross Family

was too happy to live', because her words were soon verified. Honest John died in 1799 and they are buried in St George's churchyard, Preston. Along with the Winckley family, John Cross owned much of the land around the Avenham area of Preston. Following the death of his mother, William was brought up by his aunt Mary Assheton and educated at Clitheroe Grammar School. Later he studied law at Lincoln's Inn before settling in Preston, where he lived and worked with his father. William had admired the London squares and resolved that Preston should have one. Cross Street in Preston was named after Honest John's son William, who fulfilled his ambition and created Winckley Square. On his father's death he resided in a large house he had built at the corner of Winckley Street and Winckley Square which has, until recently, has been used as an annex of Preston College. Successive generations of the Cross family seem to have been thoroughly honourable people. Indeed, the landed gentry had left their mark on Preston and William's vision of a green oasis in the centre of town has been enjoyed by Prestonians ever since.

William Cross toured extensively on horseback and made forays into the local countryside. Riding his trusty steed to the east of Preston he saw the magnificent view of the Ribble at Horse Shoe Bend and decided to buy the historic thatched cottage. Red Scar was considerably enlarged by William Cross for it had now become the residence of the Squire.

Extracts from a letter to his friend Mr Gorst from Red Scar and dated 23 February 1804 express his sentiments:

Dear John,
I am amusing myself here today with a few spademen, and after a good snack of oatcake and buttermilk I have prevailed upon myself to sit down for a few minutes, and cannot better employ them than in reminding you of the scheme once laid down for you becoming my neighbour upon the banks of this sweet river. There is now an estate which I understand might be bought ere long, if the price could be agreed upon. The edge of the bank is very beautiful and commands a noble view of the river and valley. Yours ever most faithfully, W. Cross.

After acquiring Red Scar, William extended the building and estate with the purchase of land in Elston, Grimsargh, Brockholes and Ribbleton.

The original thatched house at Red Scar was thought to have

Grimsargh

THE STORY OF A
LANCASHIRE VILLAGE

Red Scar Mansion and the Cross Family

been a Medieval place of worship, used by pilgrims on their journey to Stydd Church, Ribchester, or further afield. Red Scar was transformed into a mock timber and plaster Elizabethan style mansion. Professional advice was provided by a friend, Mr Rickman, a well-known architect and the original thatched portion of the building was retained as the dining room. The photograph of the interior of this room shows it contained one full cruck truss, i.e. with a pair of sharply carved cruck blades rising from the floor to the ridge beam, linked at the top by a short 'yoke' and with big curved windbraces to the purlin on each side. At one end was a beautifully carved altar with two wooden candlesticks. A door led to a small room behind the altar, which was very likely used as a retiring room for the preacher and close by another door opened into a tiny pitch black dungeon. A fragment of the large stained glass window that allowed the sunlight to filter into the mysterious dining room is now exhibited in the Harris Museum at Preston.

Some of the woodwork panelling for the new building was said to have come from the first St Michael's Church at Grimsargh, which was built in 1716. A library was added to the modern extension in 1840. Throughout the whole building fine oak furniture and portraits of the Cross family graced the oak-panelled dining room, music room, drawing room, library and minstrels' gallery. Outside, beautiful gardens and a cobbled courtyard enhanced the picturesque appearance of the house with its dairy, stables, and servants' quarters.

William savoured his new environment whilst spending the weekends at his 'country seat'. On Sundays he would attend morning service at Grimsargh Church. In the afternoon he walked back through Alston woods before returning to Red Scar for tea. In the evening he rowed his boat across the river to attend evensong at Samlesbury Church. William fell in love not only with Red Scar and the glorious Ribble Valley, but also with a certain Ellen Chaffers, whom he married in 1813.

Ellen and William enjoyed marital bliss amongst the cherry blossom of the woodland estate and loved the beauty and purity of the countryside. In correspondence to his friends William wrote 'that no man ever had a more happy marriage.' They improved the estate and further transformed Red Scar house into a mansion. William continued to be absorbed in his work for the various churches and in political work for the town. Sadly, at the age of

56, all he had worked for came to an abrupt end, when he caught a fatal chill. The doctor bled him, a common practice in those days, but he died on 4 June 1827. A visiting friend, Sam Staniforth of Storrs, Kendal wrote of his demise to an associate in dramatic period style on 14 June 1827:

> Oh my dear friend, how shall I tell you what we have all suffered from the moment I sent off my letter communicating the alarming illness of your valued friend, Cross, to the rapid close of his precious existence at quarter past three o'clock. All were around him to witness his peaceful end – which was only ceasing to breathe.

Canon Parkinson wrote of William Cross:

> He loved beauty of every kind, whatever was beautiful because it was beautiful, Gothic architecture, music – Handel and Mozart – were his delight – the same in scenery. The will of his God was the

William Cross was inspired to create Winckley Square in Preston, and Cross Street is named after him.
Courtesy of Anthony Cross and Marian Roberts

law of his life, in small as in great occasions. No one ever heard from his lips a calumnious censure or ill-natured remark. He was never so happy as at home, but all his domestic pleasures were mixed up with religion and hallowed by it. If a child was born to him we find an entry in his Bible with the addition, 'Laus Deo' [Praise be to God] and if he came from a long journey and all went well the words are still the same.

Unfortunately his very final journey left his widow with six children, the eldest eleven years and the youngest seven months. With the help of her three sisters and staff, Ellen carried on the work of the estate and the raising of her family. Ellen Cross outlived her two daughters and saw her four sons grow to manhood. She died in 1849. William and Ellen Cross are buried together in the chancel of St Michael's Church, Grimsargh.

One of the four sons, the Reverend John Cross, became Preben-

Ellen Cross. William married Ellen Chaffers of Everton in 1813. Together they set up home at Red Scar.
Courtesy of Anthony Cross and Marian Roberts

dary of Lincoln Cathedral. He was devoted to church architecture and almost rebuilt Grimsargh Church in memory of his parents. As a boy he had been a pupil of Archdeacon Dodgson, the father of Lewis Carroll, and played a great part in improving church music. He was given artistic inspiration by his friend the artist, Edward Lear. Like others of his family he was a keen astronomer and interested in geology and botany. The Reverend Cross was fond of sailing his own yacht and published an account of his voyage to Iceland in 1853. The keen sailor would have a tale to tell to his future father-in-law who just happened to be Admiral of the Fleet, Sir Phipps Hornby GCB.

John's brother, Richard Assheton Cross, was born at Red Scar and went on to become a politician of distinction and confidant to Queen Victoria. In 1852 he had married Georgina, third daughter of Thomas Lyon of Appleton Hall, Cheshire. Richard was a barrister but by 1857, he set his sights on a Parliamentary career, quit the bar and was returned as the Conservative MP for Preston. He represented Preston as a Conservative from 1857 to 1862 and later was returned as Member for South West Lancashire, having defeated Mr Gladstone. He held office as Home Secretary under Prime Minister Disraeli in 1873. Remarkably, Queen Victoria regarded him as a friend and he was raised to the peerage. On the death of his eldest son Thomas Richard in 1873, Queen Victoria wrote to him:

> I cannot remain for a moment silent without expressing my heartfelt, deepest sympathy in this hour of terrible affliction. You know my dear Lord Cross, that I took you on as a kind and faithful friend and that therefore I do feel most truly for you. It is inexplicable that a young and most promising, useful life should have been cut off when he could have been of such use to his sorrowing family and his country.

Lord Cross became the first Viscount Cross and between 1886 and 1892 he was Secretary of State for India.

Viscount Cross summarised his life in his family history.[2] He records that

> At the dissolution of Parliament in 1868, much to my surprise and greatly to my delight I was asked to stand for the division of south West Lancashire against Mr Gladstone, together with Mr Charles Turner, one of the former members. We had a tremendous battle and came off victorious, Mr Gladstone retiring to Greenwich. It was

Colonel William Assheton Cross in military uniform.
Courtesy of Anthony Cross

TOP

The main entrance and coach road to Red Scar – 1980.

Courtesy of Anthony Cross

RIGHT

The site of Red Scar Mansion in 2002. The large piece of concrete to the left of the photograph are the remains of Colonel Cross's observatory.

Author's collection

BOTTOM

Parkland close to the site of the mansion showing Courtaulds chimneys, 1980. Construction of the factory in 1934 sealed the fate of Red Scar mansion.

Courtesy of Anthony Cross

soon after the Election that we went to live at Eccle Riggs, which we afterwards enlarged in 1887. [It still stands today as an hotel called 'Eccle Riggs', at Broughton in Furness, Cumbria.] Since that time my sayings and doings are public property. It does not rest with myself to say anything about them. I will only place on record that altogether I have been a candidate at eight elections, six of them very hardly fought, and that I had the good fortune never to be beaten. That I have had a seat during the Cabinet during four administrations, and that I have received many favours from my Sovereign; as to my public life I will say no more. If you look back to my father's sayings, you will find a very accurate description of my own married life. I will conclude with the words which I find so constantly recorded in my father's diaries. 'Laus Deo'.

Viscount Cross died in 1912 at the age of ninety years. He wrote of Ellen Dorothea and Anne Harriet, his two sisters, 'My sisters were both delightful, both good looking, both musical, both very fair artists. I have a lovely spray of pink hawthorn painted by Ellen and a group of fruit in sepia painted by Harriet. Both wrote very fair verses.' Harriet died when only seventeen years old and is buried at Grimsargh. Shortly before her death she poignantly wrote a poem about her Bible. Another of the sons, Henry Assheton Cross, also died young and unmarried in 1851 at the age of twenty-five years. At the time of his death he was still a medical student, at St George's Hospital, London. He was buried at St Michael's, Grimsargh and left one year's income to his brothers in trust for 'such charities as they shall deem most expedient'.

The eldest son, William Assheton Cross, took up law whilst helping his mother run the Red Scar Estate, which he eventually inherited. William Assheton Cross married Katherine Matilda Winn of Nostell Priory, Wakefield, Yorkshire and they had eight children. As Colonel William Cross he served in the Crimean war, showing great courage when the ship in which his regiment was returning ran onto rocks in the bay of Argostoli. On matters more sedate at home, he was interested in music and built himself an organ. He was also a keen astronomer and had two observatories built at Red Scar where he installed some excellent scientific equipment and powerful telescopes. Day to day running of the estate saw him carrying out many improvements to the farms and implementing land drainage. He was a good and respected landlord and continued to buy farmland including Grimsargh

Hall, and visit his tenants at: Pedder House; Bank House; Rich's farm; Little Rough Hey, Sandbank; Tun Brook Head and Dixon's Farm (all of which have now gone) and the farms of Church House; School House; Cross Hill or Three Mile Cross; Roman Road; Grimsargh Hall; Wood Top; Higher Boilton; and Elston Hall.

Red Scar Mansion and the Cross Family

Alston Court Leet

And further yielding and doing suit and service at Court – beholden for the Manor of Alston upon general warning to be given in the usual manner for the holding of such Courts by the Bailiff of the Lord of the Manor.

Red Scar mansion was situated close to woodland above Horse Shoe Bend. Also shown are the areas of the former townships of Grimsargh with Brockholes, Elston and Ribbleton.
Courtesy of Lancashire Record Office

The manorial rights of Red Scar, including those of Alston, were disposed of by Sir Henry Hoghton, Bart. to William Cross.[3] Thereafter the Lordship of the Manor of Alston passed to William Assheton Cross who as landlord exercised his rights of jurisdiction over tenants in the 'Alston Court Leet'.

The business on the court agenda included the implementation of judicial rights within the manor including punishment of

offenders for those in breach of by-laws, the use of the common field and waste, the maintenance of roads, bridges and footpaths, prevention of nuisances including the containment of cattle, the related rights of lord and tenant and surrender of land. Proceedings were enforced by the lord or his steward and attended by his tenants and the constable. Court officials enforced the by-laws of the court. The names of those owing suit were read out, and – apologies for absence – duly noted. If the excuse for absence was not a good one a fine would be imposed.

The Court Leet exercised judicial rights within the manor, whilst the Court Barons were concerned with the regulation of the tenure of the tenants. Records show that the venue was often in a local public house and one wonders if absolute sobriety prevailed over the allegations of offences and whether the fine imposed was a fair one. An extract from the *Preston Chronicle* of 18 May 1850 provides further insight into this aspect of our local history.

'On Tuesday last W.A. Cross, Esq., of 'Red Scar', Lord of the Manor, held his usual court at the house of Mr John Parsons, the 'Duke William Inn', Longridge. The attendance was pretty numerous, but many retired to their homes, immediately after having performed their accustomed suit. After the general outline of business was concluded, about fifty sat down to an excellent dinner, which was got up in the worthy hostess's customary style, and reflected great credit on her catering skill. At the table was W.A. Cross, Esq.; J.B. Dickson, Esq., Steward of the Court; J. Fletcher, Esq., Alston Lodge; the Reverend W.C. Bache; Messrs. J. Nuttall, C. Parkinson and others. The officials left at an early hour but many of the farmers remained to enjoy the conviviality, till the evening was somewhat further advanced.'

A further court report showed conviviality again flowed at a change of venue, the Wheatsheaf at Longridge. 'The annual Court Leet of the Lord of the Manor of Alston, Dilworth and Grimsargh, William Assheton Cross, Esq., was held at the "Wheatsheaf", Longridge on Tuesday. Mr Dickson of Preston acted as Clerk of the Court; Mr Thomas Alston of Grimsargh being foreman of the Jury, empanelled according to ancient custom. The only business of the Jury was the change of footpath in the Township of Alston, which was subsequently arranged. Afterwards those attending the Court were entertained at dinner when a most convivial meeting was held.' I am sure that the dignity of the court was maintained, after the homage had been sworn in, and before proceedings were formally adjourned to atmospheres of subsequent merriment.

The decline of the Manorial Court was influenced by judicial responsibilities passed to township meetings and Justices of the Peace. The 'copyhold' customary tenure of land was provided by evidence of the title, which consisted of a copy of the Manorial Court Roll. The diaries of William and Joseph Briggs Dickson, partners in Buck & Dicksons, of Preston, who were solicitors for the Cross family, are quoted in the publication, *A Firm of Families* by Colonel D. Houghton. They performed the office of Steward at the Alston Manorial Court of William Assheton Cross and in 1889 Joseph Briggs Dickson, in his last year, attended the Alston Manor Court Leet.

It was not only the manorial courts that disappeared. It seems a shame that all the descendants of the Cross family parted company with Lancashire and Red Scar in particular. One of the descendants is sixty-nine-year-old Mr Anthony Cross who farms near Tiverton, Devon, and still has treasured souvenirs from Red Scar including a grandfather clock and another clock which was a wedding present to Colonel William Cross in 1846. Tony Cross tells me that no one regrets the loss of Red Scar more than himself, and during 1980 he visited the site of the ancestral mansion along with his wife Ann and Miss Nellie Carbis and took some photographs.

The Leasehold of Red Scar

In February 1887, the two remaining unmarried Cross sisters, Kitty, now aged forty, and the writer of the journal described later, and Cecily Sophia, aged thirty, left Red Scar to make their home in London. In May 1889, Kitty's brother, Charles Henry Cross married Edith Mackintosh at Plymouth. They went to Red Scar for part of their honeymoon. Kitty always regretted that the bride saw the house in a very dishevelled state and so different from the beautiful home of her childhood. The 1891 census records that only two rooms at Red Scar were then occupied. The residents were a gamekeeper, his wife and two young children. Presumably these people had looked after Charles and his bride two years earlier. How very different from the 1861 census when there were nine members of the family and fourteen servants resident at Red Scar. Admiral Charles Henry Cross died on 1 January 1915, and was buried with full naval honours at Plymouth. There is a memorial to him in Grimsargh Church.

Katherine Ellen Cross, spinster, died in hospital on the Isle of Wight on 16 March 1928.[4] William Cross inherited Red Scar on the death of his father, William Assheton in 1883. William spent most of his working life in Hexham and worked as a shipyard designer with Sir Charles Parsons to develop the first marine turbine boat, 'The Turbinia', in 1890. William Cross retired to south Devon and leased the building out to several tenants. He died on 30 August 1916. His elder daughter was Katharine May Cross of London, who is mentioned as Lady of the Manor in Kelly's *Directory of Lancashire* in 1924. Miss Cross became the last member of the family to own Red Scar and secure its fate when she sold it to Messrs Courtaulds on 9 April 1934. Miss Cross died on 27 February 1959.

On 5 May 1887 a new era had begun at Red Scar when William Cross first advertised the mansion and estate:

> Notice by William Cross of intention to lease Red Scar, together with Shooting and Sporting Rights. All that Messuage or Mansion House called Red Scar with the gardens, grounds, stables, coach houses, Vinery, Greenhouses, buildings and other appurtenances thereto belonging. Also the Messuages or Cottages situate near the said Mansion House one of which has been used as a keeper's cottage. Also the exclusive right of hunting, coursing, shooting, and sporting in over or upon the lands belonging to me Also the right of fishing in or upon the streams and brooks on the said property and in the River Ribble (so far as I can grant such right and to the extent only of my right to fish in the said river).

Of those tenancies recorded in trade directories and existing documents, the first was that of Mr Walter M. Daniel from 1898 to 1901. This was followed by a lease to Mr Caleb Margerison of White Windsor Soap, who was succeeded by his brother George when he left to live in the Isle of Man.

On 8 June 1925, the contract was renewed for the building and land to be rented to Mr Thomas Stanley Walker who was already an established tenant. In 1927 Mr Joseph Hollas and Mrs Hollas moved in and became the last to hold the tenancy of the mansion. Mr Hollas desperately wanted to purchase Red Scar, but sadly it was bought by Courtaulds in 1934 to enable the firm to build a new rayon factory for Preston. This was a crucial time for employment and by now the building had outlived its usefulness for the local gentry. Miss Carbis once told me about the time she was a guest of the Hollas' family at Red Scar in 1935, the year she arrived in Grimsargh. As a keen gardener she was naturally in her element in the gardens and there was even a hothouse with peaches, nectarines and grapes. At one time the Hollas's even kept a private zoo with some strange animals lurking in the grounds of Red Scar. Mrs Frances Potter of Grimsargh can remember the zoo when she delivered papers along the long coach road to Red Scar and was rewarded with a bar of chocolate by the kindly Mrs Hollas. According to Mrs Potter the lady of the house went shopping to Grimsargh in her red sports car and was often accompanied by an unidentified beast from the menagerie which was sprawled over the front passenger seat.

Mr and Mrs Hollas were still in residence at Red Scar when, in March 1936, Kitty Cross came to Preston and stayed at the Park Hotel. Accompanied by her solicitor she visited Red Scar, which was by now the property of Courtaulds, and selected all the furniture and pictures she wanted for her Villa Bagatelle in Bath. Later that day she wrote, 'I feel like a murderess today as if I had torn the insides out of something living. I hope to goodness the poor furniture will like the Villa Bagatelle and settle down there.'

Mrs Hollas left Red Scar and moved to Wiltshire at the beginning of 1936, taking with her the head gardener, Mr Piner and his family. They had a special train to transport their animals and agricultural implements. A few years later Mrs Hollas returned to Longridge to farm at Hothersall. Mr Hollas stayed on at Red Scar and took on a new gardener, Mr Wilfrid Simm, who came from Balderstone. He and his wife, son and two daughters lived in the gardener's cottage; one of the daughters was Miss Olive Simm who attended Grimsargh School and was taught by Miss Carbis before entering the teaching profession herself. Miss Simm today resides in Longridge. In May 2001 I spoke to her and she fondly recalled those early days at Red Scar. 'There was a large rose garden and dad provided white roses for Grimsargh Church at Easter. I can remember that Colonel Cross's red brick observatory was close to our house and was then being used as a cattle shed. Some of the fine beech trees are still there but the once abundant red squirrels are long gone.'

Mr Hollas eventually moved to Lytham in 1938. During the war years the mansion lay derelict, decaying along with its romantic history, and was finally demolished in the late 1940s. The site of the mansion has never been built on and need not have been sacrificed and today would have been worthy of listed building status. So much for so-called 'progress' and how unfortunate that there seems to have been an appalling lack of effort to come and rescue it. Courtaulds radically transformed the estate by demolishing the mansion and erecting a huge factory. The farm-land was sold off in stages. Tun Brook Head Farm was sold to Preston Corporation in 1962, and included the land that is now used by the crematorium.

The old coach road is still in situ near the crematorium and on walking along the half-mile length one can imagine the former pastures and meadows on either side ringing with the sounds of the shooting parties of the squire. Doubtless, the coveys of par-tridge that used to be common in the old copses and hedgerows graced the tables at Red Scar from time to time. On reaching the woodland site of the mansion there are still faint traces of the left fork which led to the front main entrance of Red Scar, whilst a right fork went past the rear of the mansion to the servants' quarters and gardener's cottage. The foundations of the mansion are barely discernible.[5] A huge upright piece of concrete which once formed part of Colonel Cross's observatory may be seen from the Ribble Way footpath next to the ghostly yet serene woodland site. Many trees were planted to adorn the estate and still stand as a legacy to the Cross family. Two copper beeches provide clues to the approximate location of the mansion and nearby rhododendrons are controlled, to prevent the invasive shrubbery taking over the Red Scar woodland. Woodland paths originally enjoyed for genteel walks by the Cross family and their visitors may now be sought out by those who value our local countryside and wildlife.

In May 2002, the East Preston Historical Group discovered a fragment of pre-industrial pottery dated around 1740 at the site of the mansion. The glazed pottery with piecrust edging was part of a piece of a decorative plate and is now on display in the Harris Museum at Preston, thus providing a further insight into Red Scar's forgotten history.

Grimsargh

THE STORY OF A
LANCASHIRE VILLAGE

References

1. See also *Victoria County History*, vol. 7.
2. 'Family History', by Viscount Cross.

Red Scar Mansion and the Cross Family

3. Baines, *History of the County Palatine and Duchy of Lancaster* (1893) vol. 5, p. 349.
4. Cross family papers, discovered at the Solicitors, Buck & Dicksons, Winckley Street, Preston.
5. For five excellent original black and white photographs of Red Scar Mansion see 'Old and Celebrated Halls of Lancashire and Cheshire', vol. 4, in Preston Reference Library.

CHAPTER EIGHT

A Family Manuscript: The Evocative Writings of Katherine Ellen Cross

I T WAS in the late 1980s that local historian Mrs Marian Roberts, the author of *The Story of Winckley Square*, met and became friends with Miss Carbis and Tony Cross. Mr Cross kindly allowed Marian access to the vaults of his Preston solicitors and thus the story of the Cross family at Red Scar was slowly revealed.[1] Marian has afforded me her valued time in researching this chapter and I acknowledge her help and that of Tony Cross. Indeed it is thanks to them both that 'A Family Manuscript', representing the second generation of the Cross family, has been resurrected from the archives and that I now have the privilege of being able to reproduce for posterity extracts from the evocative writings of Katherine Ellen Cross.

Katherine Ellen Cross was born in 1847 and was the eldest daughter of William Assheton Cross and his wife Katherine. It was Katherine Ellen (Kitty) who wrote a 'Family Manuscript' entirely by hand in a big leather bound ledger. From her came the most vivid memories of Red Scar as a delightful home which she described as 'the place on earth, beloved over all'. Following the death of grandmother, Ellen Cross in 1849, the family moved from Stodday Lodge, Lancaster to begin their life at Red Scar. Another daughter, Harriet Esher (Hatty) was born in 1849. Next came the longed for son William (Willy) and in 1852, Charles Henry (Charlie) destined to become a sailor and his mother's favourite. In continuing order of succession Ellen Priscilla was born in 1855. In 1856, Margaret Lucy (Maggie) was born and in 1857 Cecily Sophia (Cecy) came along. Lastly, in 1859, Diana Beatrice Annie (Di or Didy) completed the second generation of the Cross Family, and just in time for the 1861 census details.

Katherine Ellen wrote affectionately of her grandmother Ellen Cross:

A painting believed to be Katherine Ellen Cross as a child. She wrote, 'I must also mention a little watercolour picture of myself at Red Scar taken when I was about 3 years old, with fair hair and dark eyes and a striped blue sash.'

Courtesy of Anthony Cross

96

My grandmother died when I was only one year and six months old, the month before Hatty was born I always think. I remember her, but it can hardly be possible, and yet I feel I saw her in our 'day nursery' at Red Scar. Our grandmother must have been a very lovable character. My father and uncles were all devoted to her and she was very clever and wise also. She brought up her six children carefully and well, a widow with six children, none of them nearly grown up. She must have had an anxious life but was greatly helped by her sisters, the Everton aunts. My grandmother and Aunts walked the mile and a half to Grimsargh Church every Sunday and remained there all day, taking their luncheon with them, that they might teach at the Sunday school in the afternoon. Our father used to talk so much about her and in his last illness he said, 'I think I could eat one of my mother's puddings.

It would seem that Grandma Ellen Cross was more than capable of keeping an eye on her tenants.

She would say to a tenant, 'Well Martha, your house doesn't look at all nice, it's untidy and not as clean as it should be. Then she would pull open the drawers and the cupboards and say that they must be put tidy and kept so, and all in better order for the future. They seemed almost proud of being so carefully looked after and scolded. She must have had a pleasant way of doing it, as there is no doubt she was very much loved by all who recollected her there.

Of her father – William Assheton Cross, who was born 19 May 1818 and died 25 January 1883, she wrote:

In January, 1849 my grandmother died and our father and mother moved to Red Scar. In 1850 my eldest brother William was born. Willy's birthday was always kept with great éclat – we always had fireworks on the lawn and several times, a dance in the coach house for the servants etc. In those days there were large oval shaped flowerbeds on the lawn, in front of the drawing room windows, with open wire work sides and they were planted with red geraniums which were dug up in the autumn and put 'by the heels' into sand in the apple house for the winter. The fireworks were let off from these beds, which were also of use for all the Christmas greens, on Candlemas Day.

Dinner in my early days was at 6 o'clock, half past on weekdays, but still at 6 on Sundays, to give the servants more time to themselves. This early hour enabled us to have strolls after dinner in Summer, with our father and mother. I remember so well the Sunday evening walk, mamma in white muslin, my father in evening dress. We often went up the carriage road and through 'Kitty's little stiles', into the field beyond. My mother always arm in arm with my father. They always walked arm in arm like this to and from church and if she was not able to go I took her place – a fussy little creature I must have looked stepping along, the pink of propriety, a little old woman in a black silk jacket and a bonnet, at the age of, say – 10!

In 1854 came the great event of our quiet lives. The Crimean War had broken out, and my father's Militia, in which he was a Major, embodied and went to Portsmouth. We all went there too, and much enjoyed the change of air and scene after our quiet life at home. We used to walk on the ramparts and on the common. After three or four months the Regiment volunteered for foreign service and was sent to Corfu to relieve some regiments of the line sent to the front. My father came home on leave the following October, when Nellie was born.

While we were at Portsmouth we saw the whole of the Baltic fleet come into Portsmouth Harbour under sail. How well I remember my mother telling me to' look at it well, for we should never see such a sight again.

Among the officers I remember often coming to our house were Colonel Clayton, Captain Whittle, Captain Pudsay Dawson and Captain Thornhill. My father came home when peace was signed, full of admiration of the Ionian islands which of course then belonged to England. His admiration of their beauties led Uncle John to give him the two beautiful pictures of Corfu and the olive groves and Mediterranean, by Mr Lear. He also gave one almost more beautiful of the ruins of Baalbec, by the same artist.

My father's chief characteristic was his extreme modesty and humblemindedness. There was nothing small about him, he never thought of applause or cared for it. He did his best and that was enough.

He was very fond of astronomy and had two observatories, where he looked out many nights through his telescopes. He polished his own speculums and it was a sad day indeed when one cracked or otherwise came to grief during the polishing. He forgot time and lunch when engaged on one; and I remember often being sent out as a very little girl to tell him his luncheon was waiting for him. Not that it would have taken much harm, as it generally consisted of brown bread and butter and beer, with a glass of sherry to end with. He seldom ate meat, fish and eggs he liked, and had a boiled egg for breakfast every day of his life.

In the evenings he read the newspaper (*The Times*) diligently, after having glanced at the news at breakfast time and then some interesting book of history, astronomy, biography etc. He was very clever and had a knowledge of very many subjects. I think it never occurred to

Grimsargh

THE STORY OF A
LANCASHIRE VILLAGE

us that papa could not answer questions on any subject we liked to ask about. He taught himself to play the organ in a humble way, with the help of a few lessons, and almost built the beautiful organ we had in the dining room at Red Scar, with the aid of a musical carpenter. Afterwards it was improved by an organist workman from Liverpool, the blowing done by water power.

On Saturday mornings he always went to Preston in the dog-cart (driven by our coach man Hodgson) while he smoked a cigar and attended meetings of various kinds.

There is a reference to John Hodgson the coachman, in a letter to Kitty from her father William in September 1864.

Everton, Thursday.
My dear Kitty,
I write a line to say that I come home tomorrow. Tell Hodgson to meet the 2.20 train, and as I have some luggage he had better bring the carriage.

The 1861 census shows John Hodgson from Millom, Cumberland as groom and footman. A gentleman tutor was on hand for Katherine Matilda's eight children who are described as scholars. Also on the staff was a dancing mistress, a housekeeper, a butler, a nurse, two housemaids, two nursery maids, one gardener and a lady's maid, (Françoise Heiney born in Switzerland).

Kitty makes reference to her uncle Canon John Cross who was a great benefactor for St, Michael's Church, Grimsargh. The church was rebuilt and enlarged by him in memory of his parents.

A visit from him always meant a holiday and his favourite game of damming up 'Tun Brook', which he enjoyed fully as much as any of us. Then in the evenings he would sing to us in his beautiful tenor voice; 'Tom Bowling' and the 'Cork Leg' were our great favourites.

Of Uncle Richard (Viscount Cross) she records:

I remember Uncle Richard staying at Red Scar in very early days, probably before his marriage and hearing with a sort of awe that when we were all in bed – even papa and mama had gone to bed – that he was sitting in the library working and reading. He was always very fond of music and Aunt Gregory also, and like our father and Uncle John always liked to have some music in the evening. He married Georgina and I was one of the bridesmaids ... Another of my recollections concerns the 'great election' of 1868 when our Uncle Richard turned out Gladstone for south west Lancashire. We went to Liverpool for the polling day.

John Hodgson (footman).
Courtesy of Anthony Cross

Kitty records that her mother always suffered from the most terrible headaches, and could not bear noise of any kind. This had a most profound effect on the lives of the children who always had to be very quiet. The only time that they were allowed to be noisy was at Christmas, and what a delightful picture Kitty has left us of that time.

Christmas at Red Scar

Christmas Eve was a great day. The gardeners brought in ladders and evergreen wreaths which they had been busy making in the potting sheds for some days before and they were fastened up to the black oak beams in the dining room, with a big bush in the shape of a bell, and mistletoe hanging where the clapper of the bell should have been. The best pieces of holly with berries were put over each of the ancestors' pictures, and then we children 'did' the windows, sticking in choice little bits of green into the latticed panes. The church was decorated with green wreaths up all the arches, and in later years with our paintings and later still came Altar vases and flowers.

At six o'clock on Christmas Eve we all assembled in the Servants' Hall, to give away beef to all the men, coachman, gardeners, bailiff, carter and labourers. They had a good piece of beef of 10 or 12lbs. each, with a piece of holly stuck in the middle. My father stood at the head of the table, all the men round it, while we all stood round the fire in the corner. A large silver tankard of hot spiced beer stood on the table in front of my father, in which he drank their healths. We followed in succession and then each man came up received half a crown and his beef and drank our healths; the man who had been with us the longest had two half crowns.

On Christmas morning, before our parents were up, we all assembled round their door and sang, 'God bless the Master of this House, and Mistress also, And all the little child/er/en, That round the table go, With a pantry full of good mince pies, And a cellar full of beer, We wish you a Merry Christmas, And a Happy New Year.' Then we often sang 'Once in Royal David's City', after which we heard 'Come in', and in we all trooped to get our kisses and thanks for the songs and our Christmas presents.

After Church and luncheon on Christmas Day my mother used to give presents to all the servants and we were the messengers to take these round – a print dress or a warm petticoat or something else useful and often a thick cardigan knitted waistcoat for Hodgson, our Coachman. Then came the Christmas trees! First, Mama's tree, with presents to us all. Then our tree, things we had made ourselves and that had kept us busy preparing for all the year nearly. Pincushions, needlebooks, and all sorts of things that Miss Turnbull, our Governess (generally known as Tubby) had helped us to make. The third tree was in the saddle room for the gardeners and the other men's children.

After dinner on Christmas Day, the singers, the church choir, used to come into the dining room to sing Christmas hymns and carols and anthems and afterwards had supper. Another evening the servants sometimes had a dance in the kitchen, and we would open the ball with a country dance, a 'Sir Roger de Coverly'. We always enjoyed the Christmas festivities, even after we were grown up. One good result of a very quiet life was the enjoyment we had in very small things – our lives were so very quiet that any little variety was welcomed.

Life at Red Scar

Visiting was very limited; a few days at St Michael's and Appleby Vicarage now and that was about all, except to Mr Staniforth's at Storrs, Windermere, generally for the Yacht races on the lake, which my father enjoyed as much as we did, and could explain the whole mystery of it to us, and once he took Hatty and I up the Langdale Pikes, greatly to our pride and delight.

At Red Scar the garden was quite in the old-fashioned style to suit the house, with hedges, and borders under them for the old-fashioned flowers. The present flower garden was the vegetable garden, with a few flower beds in the part nearest to the observatory. This was always filled with red carnations which my father liked for a buttonhole and on Sundays the gardener always made a bouquet which was placed by my mother's plate at dinner. Cinerarias are always connected in my mind with the bouquet, at one time of the year, and in summer coloured verbenas and mignonette.

I have said very little about our lives after we were grown up. I may now say without vanity that Hatty and I were considered very good looking, and certainly Hatty was a remarkably tall, handsome girl, while I was a shrimp by her. What I think we liked best of all was the 1st Royal Lancashire Militia Review and luncheon, and often dance in Lancaster. There were also some good private balls in those days, but our Mother was very particular about where we went, and who we talked with, and we were never allowed to go anywhere alone or unchaperoned.

Kitty puts on record '… the way our mother worked at the time of the great cotton famine of Lancashire. She collected several hundred pounds all among friends and relations, and with the money bought blankets, and warm things to distribute among the poor starving people. I have copied it (the accounts) to show what an immense amount of labour my mother gave herself and what a terrible time of distress it was.'

In the autumn of 1869, whilst mother and daughters were on a visit to Thurland Castle, Mrs Katherine Matilda Cross was taken ill. She asked Kitty to 'Write and tell papa about it, but don't frighten him.' Their visit was curtailed and Mr Cross took his wife to see specialists in London. For a while she seemed much better then, whilst on Preston Station awaiting a train to take them on a visit to Smithhills, Bolton, she was again taken very ill. The family's omnibus was still outside the railway station and she underwent further medical attention. Her death on 16 April 1871 was said to be caused by cerebral paralysis.

Two Fashionable Weddings and a Funeral

On 21 January 1875 Grimsargh Church witnessed the wedding of Hatty to a Captain Pennethorne, duly recorded in her elder sister's journal. 'They were married at Grimsargh Church by Special Licence, as it was still a Chapel of Ease under Preston. Her bridesmaids were her four sisters Maggie, Nellie, Cecily, Didy and Pussy and Mary Cross, Uncle Richard's daughters.' The officiating clergyman was her uncle, the Reverend John Edward Cross, Vicar of Appleby, Lincolnshire. The local newspaper reported that 'the beautifully decorated church was crowded in every part and a covered way, laid with carpet, was formed from the churchyard gate to the porch. After the wedding breakfast at Red Scar the newly married couple left, amid a shower of old shoes and rice, for London, en route to the Isle of Wight where they spent their honeymoon.'

Another four years were to pass before the next wedding of her sister, Margaret Lucy Cross to Mr W.W.B. Hulton JP.

In May came Maggie's marriage to W.W.B. Hulton. He often told the tale of how he brought his father on a drive one Sunday, just timed to catch us coming out of Church, that his father might have a look at her (this was before he had proposed to her) and his father's crushing remark, What! Do you think a girl like that will look at you? Maggie was very good looking with auburn hair and a good figure, and he was a widower with four children. So there was perhaps some justice in his father's view. People flocked to the wedding from all parts of the surrounding district, converging on 'the perennially isolated church of Grimsargh', by train. Maggie wore a white moiré dress trimmed with orange blossom and white lilacs. She was led in by her father and attended by six bridesmaids dressed in white muslin trimmed with pearled Breton Lace, each carrying a bouquet and wearing a gold locket set with pearls – gifts of the bridegroom. Again, the church was beautifully decorated, and amongst the invited guests was the Right Honourable Richard Assheton Cross, Home Secretary, 'Uncle Richard', to the bride. This time the bride's uncle the Reverend John Cross, assisted the Bishop in conducting the wedding ceremony and as the couple left for Red Scar two of the children of the bridegroom's former marriage strewed flowers in their way. On the death of Mr Hulton's father they removed to Hulton Park, near Bolton. When in later years, her husband was knighted, Maggie became Lady Hulton.

In January, 1883, Grimsargh Church witnessed the solemn funeral of Colonel William Assheton Cross and Kitty stated in her journal, 'I cannot write more about that dreadful time.' William Assheton Cross and his wife Katherine Matilda are buried in the family vault in the graveyard of St Michael's Church, Grimsargh.

Thus ends the story of the Cross family at Red Scar. The loss of the mansion and estate has created a poorer yet surreal landscape still worthy of exploration. Driving past the entrance to the coach road or observing the lonely woodland site of the mansion, one can almost rekindle the life of the Grimsargh country squire and his caring and socially aware family. The family manuscript and writings of Kathleen Ellen have undoubtedly altered my perception of nineteenth-century *hoi polloi* and the relationships between the social classes. As the scale of urban encroachment marches relentlessly on one wonders what Mr Anthony Cross's ancestors and great landowners of yesteryear would have thought of the landscape of the next millennium – the conjectures are unrepeatable!

Reference

1. Probate, London, 20 April, to Diana Pennethorne, spinster. Effects £8,761 15s. 6d. (from LRO, Wills and Admons, 1928).

CHAPTER NINE

Churches in the Grimsargh Landscape

St Michael's Church

THE CROSS FAMILY became generous patrons of St Michael's Church, Grimsargh and in 1815 the chapel was enlarged. In 1823 Richard Grainger MA was appointed curate. Mr Grainger was therefore the first occupant of the Vicarage, which was built just a year later, in 1824. Today the Vicarage still complements the church as a part of Grimsargh's heritage and is set in an equally idyllic and tranquil haven on the other side of Preston Road. The Reverend Grainger remained at Grimsargh until his death in 1849 and is buried in Grimsargh churchyard outside the east window.

He would have witnessed the rebuilding of the ivy-covered chapel which commenced in 1840. Stone from Longridge quarries was again brought to the site and a new chancel replaced the original smaller one. In addition a north aisle built to the same height as the old nave was built. The costs were defrayed by one of the four sons of William Cross, the Reverend John Cross. In 1868 the same gentleman funded the rebuilding of a new nave and tower at a cost of £3,000. The old square tower disappeared and the familiar landmark of today began to dominate the skyline. The new nave was larger and exceeded the height of the old one. Today the apex marks of the old nave may be seen across the wall of the chancel which was built in 1840, and perhaps symbolically represent the old church and the religious devotion of past generations of the community of Grimsargh-with-Brockholes.

Dobson made reference to adding the finishing touches to the new church: 'To finish the Church it wants a spire on the small tower. There are few churches that occupy so commanding a position for such a structure; when the spire is added it will be one of the most prominent features of the landscape for many miles around.' The church acquired its stumpy red tower which

The east window of St Michael's Church.
Parish records

Grimsargh church took on its present appearance in 1868.
Parish records

An interior photograph dating from around 1920, when lighting was still by oil lamps and candles.
Parish records

became the familiar local landmark it still is. The new church was re-opened on 2 January 1869; during the rebuilding the congregation had attended services conducted in Grimsargh Parochial Church School.

John Winstanley Hull succeeded Richard Grainger and took over at the new church in 1849. A copy of the original 1726 Consecration Deed was made on 16 September 1851 and certified as a true and faithful copy by Mr William Assheton Cross of

Red Scar. The architects, Austin & Paley of Lancaster, had done a good job of building a more commodious building with pleasant features in a woodland setting. It must have been quite an atmospheric place with oil lamps and candles providing illumination before the days of electricity. One lady in the choir did not share the sentiment when she nodded off during the sermon. Suddenly her large feathered hat dipped onto a candle and she began to feel the heat. The lady survived her ordeal and was fortunately able to carry on singing after someone snatched the hat from her. The new curate, one William Pilling who served Grimsargh from 1854 until 1865, was bemused by the occurrence, and didn't know what to do next – there were no fire extinguishers in those days. We will never know if he related the anecdote in Leicestershire before he returned to Preston in 1885 to take over as vicar of the newly built church of St Mary Magdalene, Ribbleton.

Grimsargh was for centuries part of the parish of Preston in the Diocese of Chester and parochial records were compiled in parish records at Preston. Originally a chapel-of-ease for Preston,

Grimsargh church choir outside the church about 1889.
Parish records

Grimsargh first became a parish in 1875. An order assigning St Michael's Church to the district chapelry was made by the Ecclesiastical Commission on 14 May 1875 and appeared in the *London Gazette* on 19 May 1875.[1]

The Reverend William Harrison, son of John Harrison the first curate of Grimsargh, was appointed the first of nine of Grimsargh's listed vicars. Mr Harrison died in October 1885, aged 76 years. 'A large and sympathetic gathering of friends followed his remains to the grave at Grimsargh.' (*Preston Chronicle*, 31 October 1885).

Another sombre occasion was reported in the *Preston Chronicle* in January 1883 describing the funeral service of Colonel William Assheton Cross of Red Scar. 'With marked simplicity and an entire absence of ostentatious mourning, the obsequies of the late Colonel W. Assheton Cross, of Red Scar, Preston, were performed on Wednesday at Grimsargh Church. No invitations were sent out to the gentry and the attendants at the funeral beyond the relatives of the deceased comprised only of those gentlemen connected with Colonel Cross in his Magisterial work and one or two friends. Leaving Red Scar shortly after 12 o'clock the cortege proceeded slowly through the grounds and up the Longridge Road to Grimsargh Church. About twenty of the principal tenants on the estate walked in front of the hearse then, in the carriages which followed were Mr William Cross, the deceased's eldest son; his brothers, the Reverend Canon Cross and the Right Honourable Sir Richard Assheton Cross MP, and his sons in law, Captain Pennethorne and Mr W.W.B. Hulton, his brothers-in-law

The Vicarage, which was built in 1824. Before that time, clergy rode up from Preston on horseback to take services at St Michael's Church.
Parish records

Grimsargh Church in a bygone landscape, when the main road resembled a dirt track with not a single car in sight. On the left is the entrance to Church House Farm.

Painting by Albert Woods, courtesy of Mrs E. Woods

Mr Rowland Winn MP and Mr Edmund Winn and many promi‚ nent people. The coffin was received by the officiating clergyman, the Reverend Phipps Hornby, Curate of St Michael's on Wyre, who preceded the remains, reading as he went the Church of England Burial Service. A minor voluntary by Mozart was played and afterwards Mr Stothert played 'Dead March' in Saul. On the conclusion of the Service the coffin was carried to the Vault in the Churchyard, where lie the remains of Mrs Cross who died in April 1871. Friends gathered round the vault to take a farewell glance at the shell, which contained the remains of one whom they had held in the highest esteem. Upon the shield of the coffin was the inscription, William Assheton Cross – born 19th May 1818 died 25th January 1883.'

The death of the Lord of the Manor marked a milestone in the history of Red Scar and indeed Grimsargh‚with‚Brockholes. Grimsargh has had plenty of interesting characters and quite a few of them have been vicars. The Reverend Francis Drinkall Pritt, MA succeeded the first vicar, the Reverend W. Harrison in 1885. Mr Pritt introduced the wearing of the surplice, Gregorian chants, altar lights, and coloured stoles. Clear signs of the approb‚ ation of Grimsargh Church were mirrored by 'Sunday services being well attended, the collections good and the singing truly admirable.' Technological innovation at the vicarage extended to the luxury of piped water for the first time.

It was in 1889 that the distinguished-sounding Reverend Tertius Augustus Buzzard, BA was appointed. He built up the organisations of the church and laid out the beautiful gardens which are a well-known feature of the Vicarage.

Marriages within the farming community were commonplace, exemplified on 19 April 1897, when Richard Mason's daughter, Jane Mason of Dixon's Farm, Grimsargh, married local farmer William Margerison at St Michael's Church. The Reverend Buzzard officiated over their marriage and also at the marriage on 12 May, 1897, of Edward Cowell, thirty-two years, who farmed at Alston Old Hall to Annie Burrow, twenty-four years, of Elston Hall Farm. Typical weddings of the period included not just those of the indigenous farming community. Love blossomed at the manorial seat of Red Scar when two members of the household staff paid Mr Buzzard a visit and decided to tie the knot at St Michael's Church. A twenty-one year-old gamekeeper, James Cundall, married servant, Elizabeth Jane Kenyon, also twenty-one years, on 18 June 1896.

Church magazines of the late nineteenth century suggest familiar problems involving church income. Monthly collections commenced in 1890. Tithes and Easter dues supplemented the income but the Friday Harvest Service of 1894 was not too well received. 'Considering the beautiful weather the congregation was a poor one, and so was the offertory, £1 11s. 11d.' Christmas Day 1895, fared little better. 'Christmas Day was not so well attended as formerly. A jolly good dinner seems to me more thought of nowadays, than the services of Him in whose honour the feast is provided.'

The Reverend Buzzard's work was recognised in 1897 when he won a dozen silk handkerchiefs for good conduct. He must have been quite a character, serving the local community both as squire and doctor while administering home-made medicines and comforts as well as spiritual counsel. With an ornithological-sounding name like Buzzard it was perhaps appropriate that he had a collection of peacocks which roosted in the churchyard and village trees and gave lusty warnings of imminent rain and visitors! A brass plaque graces the chancel wall in his memory. It is inscribed, 'To the glory of God and in affectionate memory of the Reverend Tertius A. Buzzard MA, Vicar of this Parish, 1889–1928. Died 31st

A carving in a corner of the tower in Grimsargh Church.
Parish records

January 1928, aged 78 years. This tablet was erected by parishioners and friends.'

St Michael's Church became part of the Diocese of Blackburn in 1926. The Reverend Robert George Stanley researched the early history of the church when he was appointed vicar in 1928. The Reverend Stanley retired due to ill health to Morecambe and was succeeded by the Reverend George Oswald Rubie MA, in 1935.

The Reverend Rubie was remembered by the schoolchildren of his time for his many gifts to the school, his bonfires, and firework displays. The vicar also regularly took along his own cinematograph and Charlie Chaplin films to the Grimsargh Assembly Rooms, where he relieved the wartime anxieties of children evacuees and villagers alike. At the Vicarage he attended to the cleaning of his study because only he understood its layout.

The church in mid-winter, 2001, showing the tower and the graveyard.
Author's collection

Churches in the Grimsargh Landscape

The desk was piled with letters and papers and tobacco tins were placed strategically in handy places. Electrical 'bits and pieces' and projection equipment littered the room as befits a man with numerous hobbies. No woman was allowed to enter this beautifully untidy man's room with a duster, brush or shovel in case she told him to put this or that away or not to leave his newspapers lying about. The vicar must have been a shooting man and his two guns propped against the wall seemed to imply the desired effect – 'KEEP OUT'! His eighty-one-year-old mother resided with him and was President of the fifty-strong Mothers' Union and Mrs Margaret Mallott of Grimsargh House was secretary. Mr H. Myerscough and Mr H. Latham were Vicar's and People's Warden respectively. It was during the incumbency of the Reverend Rubie that pew rents were abolished and the choir led a congregation, which often exceeded two hundred.

In post-war Grimsargh the Reverend Philip Douglas Butterfield, MA was appointed in 1945. Grimsargh had to move with the times and the brass candlesticks were removed from the pews and choir stalls. In June 1948, he installed a carpet in the chancel to protect the engraved brass covering the tomb of William and Ellen Cross and wrote in the parish magazine, 'I am glad to

acknowledge a cheque from Miss Cross of Red Scar, the present head of the family of William Cross whose body lies with his wife's below the large brass in the Chancel floor. I saw Miss Cross recently in London, and she fully approves of our proposal to protect the brass from further damage by covering it with a suitable carpet as part of our improvement scheme.'

The Reverend John Harold Brindle took over in 1951. He introduced a robed choir, and an elaborate pine screen, paid for by parishioners, which enhanced the church interior and screened off the robing room. The churchyard was simplified and the vicar became fully committed to the cause of replacing the Victorian Parochial Church School with a brand new school. In 1966 he arranged an exhibition to celebrate the 250th anniversary of the building of the first church. A booklet, *Grimsargh Church and Parish* by Miss Carbis, was prepared for the event and the vicar's foreword recognised her dedication. He wrote, 'Like the mason of whom she has written, she has put heart and mind into the work as well as skill.' [2]

By 1977 the church required re-roofing and a joint initiative with Mrs Ruth Lister, the wife of the school headmaster, was inspired. Mrs Lister embarked on a tremendous undertaking, painting the individually numbered old roof tiles which were subsequently sold to offset the considerable cost of the new roof. The Reverend Brindle was vicar of Grimsargh for thirty-seven years and his successor was the Reverend Andrew James Haslam who came in 1988 and stayed for nine years.

During his incumbency a new extension was built incorporating a boiler room and serving as a venue for church meetings. At the same time the font was moved to its present position, near to the front of the church to afford access to the new extension and to enable holy baptism to take place during the service. In 1999 the Reverend Geoffrey Richard Loxham, from the Parish of St Barnaby, Heapey and St Paul, Withnell arrived just in time to get to know his church and parishioners as Grimsargh celebrated the new millennium.

Today's church is a Grade II building listed by the Department of National Heritage as being of special architectural or historic interest. The five-bay aisle arches of octagonal columns and bosses on which the great roof beams rest show intricate designs of lilies, acanthus leaves and trefoils, whilst moulded fine stone heads of angels, queens, bishops and monks adorn the granite capitals. A

Grimsargh

THE STORY OF A
LANCASHIRE VILLAGE

The Reverend Tertius
Buzzard.
Parish records

Churches in the Grimsargh Landscape

Mr Rubie in retirement on the Isle of Wight with the old Cunard Liner *Caronia* in the background.
Parish records

magnificent candelabrum over the chancel is at least 250 years old. Obscure in origin, it was apparently brought from Longridge to Grimsargh. The stained glass east window of the chancel was installed in 1953 and made by Shrigley & Hunt of Lancaster. The centrepiece is Christ triumphant, with his feet crushing the serpent's head. The two other panels are of St Michael, the patron saint of the church. St Michael is the warrior angel, portrayed in the Book of Revelation as waging war in Heaven against the dragon; thus with a sword in his hand. The other angel, with staff in hand, is St Raphael. In the chancel there is also a window in thanksgiving for all who worshipped in the church. It depicts the feeding of the five thousand, with Jesus giving thanks. The window above the font is of more modern design, but is worthy of detailed study. The variety and interplay of colours are aesthetically pleasing.

Mr William Pritt of Preston played the original pipe organ built by Foster & Andrews of Hull. Initial funding for this instrument amounted to £1,500, and was paid for by the Cross family. William Pritt was also a talented artist, specialising in Lancashire landscapes and exhibited one of his paintings at the Royal Academy. His oil painting of Grimsargh Church is currently displayed in the church. An electronic organ replaced the original instrument in 1950. Miss Kathleen Conroy was the church organist from 1954 until her death in 1983. Miss Conroy gave the Stewart cup in memory of her Godson, Mark Stewart who was tragically

Reverend G. Loxham in front
of the window above the font,
Christmas 2001.
Author's collection

killed in a road accident. The cup is awarded annually to a junior member of the choir. Her dedication speaks for itself in that she served the church and the community as organist for thirty-nine years. Following her death her cherished Compton organ was replaced by a new one in 1983 at a cost of £5,750.

The beauty and serenity of St Michael's Church makes a visit well worth while. There are a number of old gravestones still remaining in the churchyard with familiar names of the people of the Grimsargh of yesteryear. The large plain stone of the Cross family vault may be seen in the eastern portion of the churchyard outside the vestry door. William Assheton Cross and his wife and brother Henry are buried here.

The Lord of the Manor and his family at Red Scar had a mile and a half to walk to church, although from all accounts they enjoyed their Sunday morning constitutional. St Michael's Church commemorates this family with eleven brass plaques on the wall and floor of the chancel and a fine memorial brass over the chancel burial place of William and Ellen Cross. The memorial measures eight feet by four. William is portrayed in his lawyer's gown and Ellen in Victorian matron's dress. It has a Gothic canopy inlaid with shields and ornamented with allegorical figures. It is engraved with the words, 'A good man leaveth an inheritance to his children's children. She opened her mouth with wisdom and in her tongue was the law of kindness. Here lie the remains of William Cross, Esq. born 24th July 1771. Died 4th June 1827. Also the remains of Ellen, his wife, born in December 1783. Died 27th January 1849. Their four sons erected this monument'. The plaque honouring the memory of John Cross who rebuilt the church is inscribed, 'In memory of John Edward Cross, Prebendary of Lincoln Cathedral and Vicar of Appleby, Lincolnshire. Born April 10th 1821. Died February 28th, 1827. Buried at Appleby. I will joy in the God of my salvation.'

Another plaque honours the lives of four Grimsargh men who died in the Great War with the following inscription: 'To the Glory of God and in memory of Lieutenant James Willasey Stevenson – Royal Naval Reserve; 2nd Lieutenant John Howard Vincent Latham – Royal Air Force; Captain John James Parke – 9th Battalion Loyal North Lancashire Regiment; Lieutenant Captain William Henry Lofthouse – 11th Battalion 3rd Brigade, Australian Imperial Forces.

Who gave their lives for their country's honour in the Great War 1914–1918'.

The three-stage tower with pyramidal roof and three light belfry louvres dominates the Grimsargh skyline. The more observant will have noticed the fine water heads at the top of the lead drain pipes bearing the 1868 date of rebuilding of the church and the two bizarre stone beasts – doubtless a species new to science!

The distinctive Grimsargh Church and grounds are very well cared for by the verger, Mr Brian Woodburn The listed status of Grimsargh St Michael's Church should help to ensure its long-term survival. Of greater importance than the architecture, however, is the concept of a living vibrant church fulfilling the purpose for which it was consecrated.

The Roman Catholic Church at Alston

St Michael's Church, Grimsargh, and Alston Lane Church have been prominent in the local landscape for an almost equal length of time. The Roman Catholic Church of Our Lady and St Michael and its primary school are situated a few hundred metres east of Boundary Cottage at Alston. For at least two centuries many people from Grimsargh have both walked to school and worshipped here. The parish boundary of Alston Lane Church extends through Grimsargh to the Preston side of the Rough Hey Trading Estate and eastwards along the River Ribble towards Knowle Green. The church is within the Diocese of Lancaster. Alston Church has seen the holy ritual presided over by some interesting characters. This applies equally to Father Harry Doyle, the present parish priest and to whom I am extremely grateful for his assistance in compiling this chapter.

The first entry in the baptismal register by the Reverend Henry Sharples is dated 28 May 1848. Father Sharples was born in Liverpool, where his father was a timber merchant and shipbroker. He was ordained at Ushaw College, Durham in 1835 and had wide experience before coming to Alston Church. The superlatives make him sound like a modern-day Friar Tuck: 'He preaches short sermons and kills nobody with his impassioned eloquence.

Grimsargh

THE STORY OF A
LANCASHIRE VILLAGE

Drawing of the first Roman Catholic Church at Alston by N. Carbis. The building now comprises several dwellings.

ALSTON LANE CHAPEL
MISSION FOUNDED 1765
CHAPEL BUILT 1774.

Churches in the
Grimsargh
Landscape

We hope his fine portly shadow may never grow less'. 'A sunshining clerical King Cole, doing his duties regularly and on general terms with all about him'. 'A good and genial pre-eminently fat priest with a mind made up of contentment and a face with as much radiance in it as an ocean sunset!'

On 27 December 1855 Father Sharples saw the need to have the original church building registered as a place of worship for Roman Catholics. The early effects of the Emancipation Act, meant he had a lot more paperwork and a growing congregation. In 1856 the first proper registers for baptisms, confirmations, marriages and deaths appear at Alston, making the historian's work easier.

With the advent of the power loom and the railway the Grimsargh area was beginning to expand and local quarries were reported to be employing over 400 men. Congregations of around 200 had discovered that the disguised Church was no longer to be regarded as a covert institution but it was too small for the Catholic population of the neighbourhood. Clearly there was a need for a new chapel which was completed in September 1857.

The old chapel and school (extreme right) and the nineteenth-century Roman Catholic church of Our Lady and St Michael, together with the presbytery, in the winter landscape of Alston.

Author's collection

Building work began and the cornerstone was laid and blessed by Bishop Goss of Liverpool on the 1 September 1856. The architects employed were J. and C. Hansom. This was Joseph of 'Hansom Cab' fame, who also designed the impressive St Walburge's Church in Preston with its impressive second-highest church spire in Britain standing at 300 feet. Nevertheless, Alston Church was not so impressive and Goodhart Randel disparagingly pontificated, 'I am afraid that any parallel design of 1857 by an Anglican would have been much better proportioned.'

In 1872, the local historian, Atticus, wrote about the features of the new Catholic church.[3] 'In 1857 a new Catholic chapel was erected by subscription in Alston, not far from the old building. It stands within a stone's throw from the high road, and has a plain yet comely appearance. The graveyard, which fronts it, is square, level, and in good order. There are about eighteen headstones in it, of various designs. In the centre of the ground there is a carved monumental stone over the vault of the Chadwick family. The internal proportions of the chapel strike the eye at once as being extensive and substantial. The roof is very high,

The Roman Catholic Church at Alston was built in 1837.
Author's collection

is pointed, and filled in with stained wood. The walls are sparingly decorated and are pierced with two light windows. On the right of the entrance within iron rails there is a massive stone font, octagonal in shape. Close by the bell rope there is an opening leading by some steps to a wide gallery above. A considerable number of country lads and lasses sit in the gallery, and they scamper up the steps in a quick and most original fashion. The chancel is faced with a fine arch, neatly painted, and filled with sacred mottoes. Within and on each side of it there is a deep recess. All the walls hereabouts are tastefully decorated. The chancel window is a four-light one, of good proportions. In the gallery there is an organ – a moderately well built instrument but not too particular in its harmony. The congregation consists principally of farmers and working people, whose specialities are strong shoes, roseate features and mental quietude. The chapel will hold 400 people but the average attendance is about 300.' The cost of the new 'simple and unpretending country church with a wide nave and shallow sanctuary' was £2,000.

When the new church opened the opportunity was taken to extend the school to the first floor of the old 1774 building, by transforming the former church into a classroom. Private accommo-dation was provided on the ground floor for the caretaker. In 1927 a new school was built and in the early 1930s worship and rote learning eventually gave way to changes of use for the old church and school building. The external steps were removed and a conversion now incorporates three separate dwellings.

Father Henry Sharples must have been proud of his new church and shared the same rosy complexion of some of his farmers in the congregation. His legacy of the building of a new church, after the penal restrictions had been lifted, has earned him a place in the history of the diocese. His last entry is the baptismal register is shown as 16 March 1873. Following a 'good innings' he died aged eighty-seven years in February 1874 and is buried in the parish cemetery. Father Walton took over in 1874, and com-plemented the church with the presbytery which was built along side it.

Between 1897 and 1913 families endured the long sermons of Father Thomas Bridges – good or bad they lasted anything up to an hour! 'Wake that man up, he is asleep,' shouted the Father from the pulpit. On one occasion he dismissed the entire choir during a service and told the altar servers in no uncertain voice,

'Sing up, and if you can't sing, shout.' Overall he must have been pleased with their efforts because at Christmas he always gave the altar servers a threepenny piece. Ecumenical relations with the vicar of Grimsargh must have been on a 'sound footing' for he had the vicar as a partner in the three-legged race on Grimsargh playing field on the occasion of the Coronation of King George V. There were discussions with the water authorities concerning a number of issues including the installation of central heating in the church. Father Bridges eventually opted for a well-earned retirement and was succeeded by Father Ignatius Harris, who was at Alston from 1914 to 1927.

His sermons were not quite so long as his predecessor's but took on a different style and captivated his congregation. He had the great gift of being able to separate people from their hard-earned cash and do so with a smile. Consequently his charity sermons or monetary appeals were in great demand. His achieve-ments at Alston Lane were significantly the building of the Lourdes Grotto in 1921 and the building of the new school. In 1926 the same trowel that was used in laying the cornerstone of the church just over one hundred years earlier was again used for the official stone-laying ceremony of the new school. On 1 February 1927, the new school was opened for business and the old schoolroom had outlived its use.

Father Pat O'Sullivan took over after Father Fred Gillett in 1933. Father Gillett was given the following tribute by a local newspaper: 'He was very human and approachable to everyone he met. His walks around the parish were prompted by halts for a chat at various farms he was passing, and he was ready to talk to anyone at all from children to adults, and from farmer to landowner.' By contrast his successor, Father O'Sullivan, was a big, tough Kerryman, who never lost his accent, or as they say round these parts, 'he never scraped his tongue'. He was also strong and resolute in character where principles were concerned. Pat was capable of standing his ground, quite literally, over territorial matters. A dispute occurred with his neighbour, who happened to be another strong-minded Kerryman, Father Henry Marshall of St Wilfrid's, Longridge, within the Diocese of Salford. At the end of 'round one' it was decided that they could not amicably solve their problem concerning parish boundaries and a very high-level decision needed to be made from Rome. Father Marshall left Longridge before the decision came from above.

Miss Mary Bamber, former
Headmistress of Alston Lan
R.C. School, later became a
nun. Here she is on a visit t
Grimsargh in the School
Garden.
Parish records

Father Harry Doyle is the urrent parish priest at Alston Church.
Photograph R. Woollam

Father Marshall was promoted to become Bishop of Salford and Father O'Sullivan was able to maintain the same boundaries – it would seem there were no losers in this dispute!

In 1936 the Tithe Redemption Act was passed and in June 1938, Father O'Sullivan bought out the tithes that existed on the property for £33 12s. 0d. In October 1944, a letter from a Dick Barnes proclaimed that 'I have deposited £150 in the Trustees Savings. I agree with you that a new set of 'Stations of the Cross' would be a fitting memorial to my aunts, Ellen and Mary Hother-sall.' They were in place for the beginning of Lent, 1945. Father O'Sullivan never managed to start Mass on time. He spent many hours with his head under the bonnet of his old Ford Anglia car which would not always start. The old car made it with a one-way ticket to Lancaster in 1959, when he informed the Bishop of his intention to retire from the ministry. The nun who was the Bishop's housekeeper asked him if he would like a drink, but did not perceive what he had in mind. The Father enlightened the Bishop's Secretary, who asked him, 'Have they attended to you?' 'Yes.' he replied. 'She asked me did I want a drink and she brought me a b – coffee!' Wee dram or otherwise he died in Dublin during March 1976, aged ninety years.

Father Joseph Walmsley was a Prestonian who attended Stony-hurst College, before commencing work at Leyland Motors. At twenty-three he began his studies for the priesthood and attended Beda College in Rome. On returning to his hometown of Preston as priest at English Martyrs, he opted for the rural way of life at Alston Church in 1951. It seems he had a good ear for music and considered that the organ was 'not too particular in its harmony'. In 1952, he somehow discovered that there was an organ for sale in a disused chapel in Oldham. This instrument stretched the finances at Alston when it was purchased for £1,050. On Sunday 8 February 1953 the official 'christening' of the instrument was performed by no less than Reginald Dixon. The recital was actually played by the organist from Lancaster Cathedral and not his famous namesake, AWOL from Blackpool Tower Ballroom!

When Father Horricks arrived in September 1954, he realised that the centenary of the church was just round the corner. With some willing helpers and no doubt a few conscripts, fundraising events were set in motion to cover the cost of a new pulpit, new communion rails, a new floor in the sanctuary and redecoration of the church. At a cost of approximately £1,000 the refurbishment work was completed in time for Bishop Pearson, who consecrated the church. A copy of his homily in the Parish archives shows that he reminisced about the church as it used to be and of his boyhood days in Grimsargh. Father Horricks's memories included the Cumberland coast and his hometown of Millom. In September 1971 he decided to call it a day and returned to Millom, where he enjoyed thirteen years of retirement.

Father Edwards also hailed from Cumbria and after leaving Ulverston adopted a nomadic lifestyle before taking up the priesthood at Alston in 1971. Scarcely were his cases unpacked when the headteacher was after him wanting more structural alterations to the school. The Diocese put the money up front for new classrooms and improvements but it had to be repaid with interest. Three years later there was a problem down at the cemetery as burial space was running out, and an extension was provided. In 1975 the head was wielding her might once more and a new school hall and kitchen had to be provided. In 1976 someone decided that the septic tanks were a bit smelly and going out of fashion and, at a cost of £1,000, modernisation of the plant took place. Despite being a sick man, Father Edwards continued to run the parish until his retirement in 1981. In addition to offering spiritual guidance and a host of other duties he cleared all parish debt, and left his successor with £1,200 invested with the Diocese.

On 13 March 1982 the present incumbent, Father Harry Doyle, became the thirteenth priest at Alston. The parish, first founded in 1761, has prospered throughout most of its 260 years and today this is self-evident with packed congregations. Born of farming stock Father Doyle is quite at home in a pair of jeans and can be seen working with cattle and sheep and helping his friends down on the farm. There is no doubt that the kindly figure is an integral part of the local community and during a conversation, he further clarified my thoughts about the versatility of the parish priest. 'I came from English Martyrs where I spent seventeen years in a house just slightly bigger than the Alston Presbytery. It had twenty-six rooms including three in the cellar and I know this for I decorated all of them in 1971, starting in May and finishing in October. It was therefore easy for me to adjust to the size of the Alston Lane Presbytery.' Long may the traditions he has maintained continue.

Grimsargh

THE STORY OF A
LANCASHIRE VILLAGE

Grimsargh Congregational Mission and United Reformed Church

The founder of Methodism, John Wesley, made several visits to Preston between 1780 and 1790. This was at a time when non-conformity paraded itself and Primitive Methodism was making an impact among the rural communities of Lancashire. Wesleyan Methodists converted all sorts of buildings for worship before Methodism acquired the identity of a separate denomination in 1795. Usually the chapels had started life as simple buildings such as cart sheds, joiner's shops, or indeed converted houses or farm-steads. This level of frugality resulted in the spread of modest Methodist structures such as the old Grimsargh Congregational Mission, where no money was wasted on superfluous architectural display.

The Congregational Mission was used for worship before Grim-sargh United Reformed Church was built to serve a combination of Congregational and Presbyterian denominations. The site for

the new church is today occupied by two houses and is situated at the junction of Lindale Avenue with Preston Road.

A perusal of the original minute book shows that it was proposed that construction of the new church would take just over two months and for an estimated total cost of £477 10s. 0d. An extract from the book dated 31 August 1913 states, 'The contractors promising to have the building in a sufficient state of completion for service to be held within it on the first Sunday in November next. The names of persons to be approached for stone-laying to be submitted and discussed.'

The official stone-laying ceremony was accomplished on 20 September 1913 and duly minuted. 'An informal preliminary meeting proposed an agenda for the official opening of the church. It was reported that satisfactory arrangements had been made with Mr Myerscough at the post office to provide tea (6d. per head) and that the contractor, Mr Rigby would provide a suitable platform. That arrangements be made to borrow a harmonium to accompany the singing. That cards had been provided with

Grimsargh

THE STORY OF A
LANCASHIRE VILLAGE

Grimsargh United Reformed
Church was situated on
Preston Road prior to
demolition in 1979.
Photograph courtesy of Mrs N. Wille

the order of service. It was favoured that no speech making take place after tea; that friendly chats over the table would be more of the occasion.' The contractor fulfilled his obligations and the new church was opened and dedicated on 6 November, 1913.

On the big day, '… a goodly number of friends from Preston, Longridge and other places gathered together. After the ceremony about 80 of the friends sat down in the Mission Room and the collection here more than covered the cost of the tea. A good hearty Christian feeling prevailed. Cards with the order of service were distributed.' The chosen hymns were 'All people that on earth do dwell', and 'O God our help in ages past.' [5]

With a dwindling congregation of a dozen or so, the old church closed its doors for good in 1979. The original Congregational Mission wooden building later became Grimsargh's Assembly Rooms and entertainment venue.

References

1. LRO, PR 2845/23/2.
2. N. Carbis, *Grimsargh Church and Parish* (1966).
3. 'Atticus' (A. Hewitson), *Our Country Churches and Chapels* (1872), p. 88.
4. This chapter is based on consultations with Father Harry Doyle, of Alston Lane Parish. I am one of many who has valued his good humour, willing help, and co-operation.
5. Congregational Church records kindly provided by Mrs N. Willet of Grimsargh.

CHAPTER TEN

Educational Establishments in Nineteenth-century Grimsargh

The old Grimsargh Parochial Church School of St Michael's

T HIS GRANITE BUILDING is familiar to those who pass along the main road and is situated between the old railway bridge and St Michael's Church. During medieval times the church was the guardian of learning and at Grimsargh most of the population would be illiterate. The children of Grimsargh walked from remote farmsteads and often in the dark to the Dame School

A Grimsargh classroom about 1914, with the teacher Miss C. Coupe. The children in the picture are J. W. Wilkinson, Janie Gornall, Jimmie Elliott (later of music hall fame), Renee Taylor, Hilda Elliott, Lizzie Beesley, Frank Coar, Clifford Hall, Daisy Singleton Fred Rhodes, Alice Mason, Sidney Hunt, Harold Massey Florence Sanderson, Roger Foster, Annie Hoyle, Robert Rhodes, Mary Hewitson and Arthur Latham.

Photograph courtesy of Mr D. Wilkins

at School House Farm. It is easy to imagine the children seated eagerly behind their desks at the Grimsargh Parochial Church School of Saint Michael's when it opened with one classroom in 1809. In the days of pre-census reports it is not known who taught there in the early years. In 1851 the schoolmaster was Thomas Billington who had responsibility for seventy children. Both the original Dame School House and its 1809 successor survive to this day, as private dwellings of considerable charm.

My friends Don and Margaret Wright and family were the first occupants to reside at the transformed dwelling of St Michael's. Attractive flowerbeds now lie where generations of Grimsargh children had laughed, cried and played together in the yard. What were the beliefs and visions of the Cross family, who in 1809 donated the site for the school? How many teachers had been strict disciplinarians with a family of canes and had imprinted their own philosophy and personality on the village children? What happened to the countless numbers of children playing in the yard who became our forebears and together made up the soul of the school for nearly two centuries? Set against a backcloth of the changing social face of Grimsargh, many children would leave the village. Others would follow the traditions of their farming ancestors or make their home locally, with their own anecdotes to tell of the Story of Grimsargh.

The stone over the door of the oldest part of the school gives the date of construction as 1809 and states 'built by public subscription in 1809'. This was in the days when the Reverend John Harrison performed his pastoral duties for the school, and before Grimsargh became a parish in its own right. There is no record of who subscribed unless it was the farmers who took their wagons and horses to the quarries at Longridge to haul the stone to be used in construction of the school. The earliest part of the school was a single room, thirty-five feet by sixteen, with a stone floor, open fireplace, and two oil lamps suspended from the ceiling.

In 1838 the building of a new railway line almost took the trains through the middle of the classroom. Some of the land which had been donated by the Cross family for construction of the school was now subject to compulsory sale. A section of the school yard was leased to the railway authority for the princely sum of £2 a year which was still being paid up to the last 'chuff' of the Longridge trains. Passenger and goods trains started to pass through a cutting at the rear of the school. Generations of children who 'watched the trains go by', now began to realise that perhaps there was life beyond Grimsargh School playground after all.

The old school log book dates back to the year of compulsory education in 1870. A school attendance officer was appointed in 1885 to enquire into the medical condition of the children or otherwise. Throughout the summer the children worked hard on the farm and in the fields. Indeed, many boys and girls were expected to earn money to supplement the family income. The Grimsargh farming community was busy in September when only nine scholars were present out of sixty-eight children. When the weather was bad the primitive roads and footpaths were turned into mudbaths and the children would be lucky to wear a mackintosh on their long trek to school. There was often poverty at home, with no free meals or unemployment benefits to help. Nor was it easy to send for the doctor, because he presented the patient's family with a bill. Consequently many children did not

receive proper medical attention and their physical and mental well-being degenerated.

In 1882 the schoolmaster was Mr H. Bramwell followed by Mr Slater, Mr Harrison, Miss Critchley, and latterly by Miss N. Carbis. Mr Slater had sixty-eight children under his supervision in a single room. Next door to the old school the old schoolmaster's house is still occupied as a dwelling. The year '1809' above the front door and the initials of village blacksmith, John Hothersall and his wife Alice, indicate original occupancy. Deeds concerning the house show that on vacation by the Hothersall family it was given by the Cross family to the Diocese of Blackburn. It became the master's safe haven from the parochial school during the second half of the nineteenth century. Did I say safe haven? Mr Slater earned himself a 'busman's holiday', with his own ten children. In 1879 dinner money went up by 1d. a week, payable every Monday morning, and another drain on housekeeping re-sources, even for teacher. Mrs Slater taught her husband plenty of housecraft, for he invariably got a good report at the annual school inspection for needlework!

Imagine the Victorian classroom with two classes of infants and seven standard classes seated on wooden forms without backrests, having to endure the cold stone floors and draughty accommo-dation. The emphasis would have been very much on the three Rs, with children systematically chanting their times tables. Rote learning and the copying out of documents and texts to improve handwriting were, I am reliably informed, very much a part of the learning process in those days. Reminiscent of a character from Dickens, the schoolmaster single-handedly endeavoured to earn his own good report. The children used slates and pencils and if the teacher showed them how to do their drawing he could earn more money; but that meant an extra inspection, and was it really worth it?

Mr Slater's salary was dependent on a satisfactory report from the Inspector at the time of his annual visit to the Victorian classroom, but considering the difficulties, teacher's efforts some-times went down like a 'lead version of an Ofsted report'. 'The examination may be regarded as creditable'; 'Handwriting on paper is not very good'; 'The infants do not know much'; 'Numer-ation is still weak, and the younger children are wanting in attention and intelligence. Several things are wanted — that is reading books, log book, portfolio, account book and copy of regulations. The room is draughty and it has a stone floor.' A report of the Inspectorate in 1898 contributed to the luxury of a second classroom two years later: 'The room is too crowded for teaching purposes and a classroom must be provided. When this is done the offices must be removed further from the school, apex ventilation supplied and the lighting very greatly improved.' Apart from the structural improvements, Grimsargh School now boasted a second assistant lady teacher, of whom it was stated, 'was over 18 and had been vaccinated'!

In 1933 a wooden extension costing £800 was built, partly from the proceeds of fundraising by the Grimsargh Women's Union. Miss Carbis took up her duties as headmistress on 1 July 1935. As head teacher Miss Carbis was regarded as quite strict. A good standard of discipline prevailed: after all, she was an excellent shot with the chalk and sometimes the board duster! Political correctness – who had ever heard of that? I am also told that with the passage of time Miss Carbis began to mellow and

Grimsargh

THE STORY OF A
LANCASHIRE VILLAGE

'Generations of school children who watched the trains go by began to realise that perhaps there was life beyond Grimsargh Station after all.' 'At term end boarders at St John's College left for home in special carriages provided by the LNWR company.'
Photograph counrtesy of Tom Heginbotham collection

The new school, January 1982 — the children in costume for a school production. It is interesting to see just how much conditions had changed compared to the picture on page 126!

Photograph courtesy of Mrs J. Butterworth

demonstrated her love of animals (especially her new cat Jeannie) and the natural world which, of course, included children. Miss Carbis and her two assistants Miss Knowles and Mrs Baron educated the children in the three Rs and introduced themes to stimulate the interests of children. 'Our daily news' hung on the wall and the infants duly endorsed it with all sorts of 'howlers'. As they sat at their desks the children gained inspiration from the BBC nature broadcasts and other programmes for schools. Current affairs were widely discussed and newspaper cuttings and large scrapbooks were part of the interior wall decorations. On a calendar the children meticulously recorded the dates of emerg, ing snowdrops, primroses, the sighting of the first swallow in April and on hearing the first cuckoo in Spring.

On 22 January 1936 the timetable was suspended to allow the children to hear the broadcast of the Proclamation of King Edward VIII, from 9.50 a.m. to 11 a.m. and the special afternoon broadcasts to schools by the King's Librarian. Before the days of official

school meals the children brought their own dinners which were warmed in an oil stove. Miss Carbis and her staff also supervised the children brewing their own tea, cocoa or Horlicks and ensured they placed their own cloths on the tables: the cutlery was provided. Mr Rubie, the vicar, provided malt and cod liver oil from the Poor Fund for children in special need and occasionally, as a special treat for the children, brought his cinematograph. School attendance was still a problem on 16 January 1936. 'The attendance all this week has been very poor owing to sickness, colds and influenza. This morning only 62 children are present out of 93. The infants' attendance is particularly low – 11 children present out of 27.'

Eight days earlier the Inspector Mr R. Phillips had visited the school to check performance and on 20 January 1936, the Reverend G. Rubie had endorsed the school log book – 'checked registers and found them correct'. Such was the practice at a church school, where the vicar kept a close eye on the teaching and the scholars regularly attended church services as a school group. The course of events in the late 1930s were now set to change the village school dramatically as routine inspections ceased to be prioritised, with the implications of the outbreak of war.[1] Towards the end

Miss Carbis with another class of children, about 1940.
Parish records

of the war an area of rough pasture was leased by Mrs Mallot of Grimsargh House as the school garden. The rent payable was one shilling a year and the garden was directly opposite the home of Miss Carbis. Following the cessation of hostilities the land was transformed into a delightful haven and educational resource by Miss Carbis and the school children.

There were herbaceous borders, a circular pond and planted with purple iris, bird nesting boxes, vegetables growing beneath cloches, miniature trees and rows of fruit bushes intersected with walkways. From the time the snow receded to reveal the fresh white and green of the first snowdrops. The garden was a blaze of colour until the last chrysanthemums were gathered and the Autumn leaves swept away. The garden still contains many of the original 140 species of exotic and ornamental trees and plants. The planned phases of colour included contrasting copper beeches and shades of green conifers, which became both prominent and beautiful features of the village.

Documented and superb photographic records were kept by Miss Carbis relating to the origin and history of each species. She gave me many personal tours around the garden and rattled off the tongue-twisting names of her joint creation. 'This is the snowy mespilus, and here we have some cotoneaster berries for the birds, or how about this cupressus nootkaensis' – quite! A later acquisition was the giant sequoia which is making a very fine tree at around fifty feet. Yet it is still a mere baby for a sequoia.

Miss Carbis decided to call it a day in 1964 and her retirement party was attended by the Vicar of Grimsargh, the Reverend J. Brindle and Mrs Brindle, officials, friends and staff and of course, the children who presented her with a transistor radio and two bouquets. After twenty-nine years at the school she recalled there were many children whose parents she used to teach and also mentioned the four waves of additional evacuee children, taught during the war years. Mrs Mallot from Grimsargh House insisted that she carried on looking after the garden. Today Nellie's garden legacy is remembered as a permanent tribute to a quite remarkable lady. A modern Primary Church School has replaced the Grim-sargh Parochial Church School which opened in 1809.

The Hermitage – A Victorian College and Latter-day Restaurant

The true origins of The Hermitage, set in natural woodland on the banks of Tun Brook close to Elston Lane, are obscure. It has certainly had a varied history and is now the home of Jonathan and Jane Heaton and family. The Hermitage was occupied as a dwelling house by the Chadwick family in the nineteenth century, but parts of the building are believed to be of earlier construction. The Chadwick family are recorded as having acquired The Hermitage 'with other hereditaments' in 1780 and subsequently sold it in 1873 to the Reverend Thomas Abbot Peters, who had started a school in Longridge. A copy of the census for 1851 shows John Frederick Chadwick living there with his wife Alice Francis, their sons Frank, aged ten years and Robert Newton, aged eight years and their mother, Margaret. The staff included a nurse, a nursery maid, a cook, a dairymaid, a butler and a coachman.

The west wing was commissioned by John Chadwick in 1842 and today this ornate Victorian portion exhibits the year of construction of 1842, carved in the front decorative eaves. The middle part of the building has extensive beamed ceilings and has been dated around 1680. The eastern end of the building has undergone many changes over the years and there is some evidence that the east wing was once destroyed in a fire.

The gardens appear to have been laid out at or about the time that the west wing was built for Mr Chadwick. There appears to have been considerable thought in the design of the inner circle of trees surrounding the rear lawn in that the varieties are almost alphabetically located in a clockwise direction, from a cracked ash round to an evergreen yew.

William Dobson in his book *Rambles by the Ribble*, discovered The Hermitage for himself in 1883. He describes his walk into Grimsargh and how he came up Elston Lane from the river. He found himself at a hall, which had been bought by the Reverend T. Abbott Peters, who had enlarged the house and extended the grounds. This was St John's College, described as one of the few high-class schools in the district.

The Reverend Peters was born of humble parents at Preston and was a self-made man. At the age of nineteen he started night school classes at Alston and in 1854 opened his first college at

Alston between College Villas and Spout Farm. The short-lived venture proved a great success entirely through his untiring energy and perseverance. In 1873 he purchased The Hermitage and re-named it St John's College when Alston College was demolished to make way for the present reservoirs. St John's College was described by Smith, 1888:

> The school is fitted up with the most modern improvements, including airy and pleasant class-rooms, a large swimming bath and gymnasium, besides cricket and football fields of nine acres in extent. There is also a beautiful Chapel attached to the school which is licensed by the Bishop. We do not suppose that in any school in England better provision is made for the bodily comforts of the boys than at St John's College. A matter, though of such vital importance to growing youths, which are often neglected. 'Mens sana in corpore sano' is evidently the motto of the Reverend T.A. Peters MA, the respected Principal and Mrs Peters. The successes attained by the pupils at the various Universities, the Army and Civil Service, prove conclusively that every attention is paid by the masters of this school to developing the mental faculties of the students. A striking proof of the fame which the college has attained is afforded by the number of pupils, which is now upwards of a hundred. We may add that the sanitary condition of the school is excellent. The greatest possible praise is due to Mr Peters, who has been ably seconded by his wife. Both of them are beloved by their pupils, and are also highly respected by all their neighbours.[2]

St John's College was one of the first buildings in the country to have a system of gas lighting installed. An early trade catalogue of the period extolled the virtues of gas lighting with a Muller's Alphas Gas 40 light machine and denounced the other modern invention known as the electric light. The college featured in a trade catalogue of the period with a full page illustration and citations, which belied the true innovative potential of gas and electric installations. 'The Hermitage, Grimsargh, Near Preston. A select preparatory school lighted with Muller's Gas 40 light machine, supplied February, 1879.'

> Much public attention has of late years been given to the best mode of artificial lighting. Patent after patent has been taken out for this purpose — most of them without practical satisfactory result, having to be abandoned after a very short existence — including the electric light, which for all practical purposes, as yet is not applicable for the lighting of private buildings, or the requirements of premises isolated

from coal gas centres, as a steam engine must be kept at work if only one single light is in use.

The Reverend Peters gave it a 'good report'. 'I like your Alpha Gas making apparatus very much, and am recommending it to my friend's notice.'[3]

The Reverend T.A. Peters wanted the college to be an integral part of the village community. There was a chapel in the grounds, which was consecrated in 1882 and cost £1,000 to construct. Local people were invited to attend the services there and in addition to boarders many local lads studied at the college. A full-page prospectus of the school was advertised in the Preston Guild programme for 1902, while the following is an extract from the St John's College Year Book at the close of midsummer term, 1891.

The morning was bright as a mid-summer morning should be. Seldom if ever, have the beautiful grounds round and about the college been seen to greater advantage. They have been heartily admired by the mid-summer prize day visitors. In the fields not far away, the sweep of the scythe could be heard, in the waving grass and on the breezes came the grateful odours of new made hay. But the college grounds have their own attractions. There are the well-kept gardens, rockeries, the shrubberies, cool grottoes, ornamental waters, and level lawns. The visitors enjoyed the peacefulness and repose of the surroundings. They enjoyed also, in a more tangible and substantial way, the hospitality of their host, the Reverend T. Abbot Peters, M.A., the popular principal of the college.

What may be termed the more public part of the day's proceedings was commenced by a short service in the college chapel. About noon there was a move made towards the college, in the large hall of which the pleasing ceremonial was to take place. The students headed the procession; they were followed by the robed choir; then came the resident staff, also robed; after them the Mayor of Preston and the Reverend Principal walked together; and they in turn were followed by the numerous visitors, the whole forming quite an imposing spectacle. All being in readiness, his Worship the Mayor of Preston (Alderman Galloway) took the chair and was supported on the platform by Lieut-Colonel Feilden (of Witton House Blackburn), the Reverend Principal and masters, the Reverend C.F. Wood, Mr W. Hill (an old boy), and one or two more. The Reverend Principal then said the first duty was to read the list of students who had recently distinguished themselves at University and other examinations. The prizes were distributed by the Mayor of Preston and the speeches were made by Reverend Principal, Colonel Feilden and the Mayor of Preston.

Mr W. Hill said he felt great pleasure in moving a vote of thanks and encouragement to the Principal – (hear, hear). It was not necessary for him to enlarge on the education given at St John's, as the list just read to them was sufficient to show that the college turned out as good men now as it had formerly done – (hear, hear). The position of St John's College among the schools of the country was too well known to need comment from him. The National Anthem was sung, at the end of which the boys called for three cheers for the ladies, which were heartily given. The visitors afterwards gave three cheers for Mr and Mrs Peters, and the proceedings closed with three cheers for the Mayor.

The medical report of E. Eccles, visiting surgeon from Longridge was dated 7 July 1891, and further extolled the virtues of the college.

Having had the privilege, a few day ago, of inspecting the students of St John's College, Grimsargh, upwards of 100 in number, I have much pleasure to be able to say that I found them all in the enjoyment of robust health. Their physical development was all that could be

Educational Establishments in Nineteenth-century Grimsargh

Engraving of St John's College showing grounds and Chapel.
N. Carbis collection

St. John's College, Grimsargh
(The Hermitage).

desired, and was fully borne out by the part they took in the various sports on the 24th ult., and indicated that no means had been spared to conduce to their comfort and health. This excellent educational establishment still maintains its long-earned reputation of enjoying a marked immunity from sickness, as during many half years, it has entirely escaped from disease of any kind. This may be justly attributed to the sound sanitary arrangements of the College, and not least to a wholesome and liberal dietary.

At the conclusion of the closing service the boys packed their bags.

On the following morning the students, numbering upwards of 100, left the Grimsargh station of the London and North Western Railway, shortly after 8 o'clock. Special carriages were provided by the Railway Company, and in due time the students all arrived safely at their various homes in England, Ireland, and Scotland.

The new boys had an inventory of articles to be brought by each pupil to the Victorian college:

Clothes as at home; three dinner napkins; six small hand towels; three shirts – woollen preferred; travelling rug; one bag for soiled linen; two pairs of sheets; one knife, fork and spoon to be marked with

Hermitage Lodge Grimsargh. 12

A postcard of The Hermitage Lodge, situated on Preston Road at the junction with Elston Lane. The two scholars on bicycles from St John's College date the photograph as late Victorian.

Parish records

The picture opposite shows The Hermitage at the beginning of the twentieth century. Throughout its chequered history The Hermitage has been a school, a restaurant and is now a private dwelling. The Hermitage was bought by the Rev. T. Peters as a boarding school known as St John's College. The boys' dormitories were still on the top floor when it became The Hermitage Restaurant.

Parish records

initials; Bible and church service; one pair of leather slippers; three pairs of boots; clothes, nail, hair, and tooth brushes; one box of tooth powder; one pocket comb; one college cap and Scotch cap.

NB all linen, clothes, and other articles to be marked with name in full.

The lengthy college yearbook recounts an important chapter in the story of Grimsargh. There is no doubt that the college had a good reputation and old residents have described the excitement in the village at the beginning and end of term when the local 'fly' was in great demand conveying boys and their trunks to and from Grimsargh Railway Station. The trains on the branch line featured in their lives and provided a link with the outside world and home. Tragically, two college boys engaged in a 'paper chase' drowned in the River Ribble and this may have led to the school's decline.[4] With the death of the Reverend Peters in 1909, the college closed. The Reverend Principal's grave may be seen in St Michael's Churchyard, Grimsargh.

About 1910 The Hermitage entered another chapter in its history when it was purchased by Patrick Joseph Moore for use as a family home again. The family remained there until 1926, when they emigrated to Canada. The Hermitage was re-occupied as a dwelling and rather ignominiously became a duck farm. The valley and stream to the west of the property were excavated and concrete pens were built in which ducks were bred. The concrete pens remain to this day although the ducks have long since migrated to that duck reed marsh in the sky. If they had lingered they would no doubt have provided a heavenly meal, when in later years, The Hermitage became a restaurant. During the Second World War, 'Donald' made way for the families of private evacuees and the old dormitories were once again in use.

In the 1960s after a succession of owners including the Hartleys – who made lovely jam – it was converted into a very pleasant restaurant known as The Hermitage and later Rembrandts. During the 1980s we enjoyed the ambience of the restaurant on a number of occasions. The most enjoyable aspect for me was the setting and heritage of the place, while Dorothy enjoyed the meal! Together we looked out from the coffee lounge at a handsome copper beech providing a natural frame for Mr Chadwick's vision of a beautiful landscaped woodland garden. Alas, this dining out experience was not to be savoured for much longer. Trading at the restaurant was generally unsuccessful and in 1989 Thwaites closed it for good. The building lay unoccupied for four years until the Heaton family realised the enormous potential for re-occupancy as a dwelling. Following extensive renovation of the building the family moved in on 17 December 1993.

Another view of The Hermitage and grounds, which can be compared to the picture on page 138. There was also a chapel in the grounds of the former boys' college and neighbours were invited to attend services there.
Parish records

The restoration process yielded one or two secrets. Whilst the overgrown garden was being renovated a stone walkway between large boulders was discovered alongside the present driveway. At the end of this walkway nearest the house is a hidden area in which there is located a small shrine. There is plenty of opportunity for retreat in any of the building's forty-two rooms including what appears to have been a priest-hole ledge concealed in the kitchen chimney. In 1761 Thomas Caton was the first Catholic Rector at Alston and before the mission was established other priests served the local area, who on occasions may have used the chimney facility.

As to ghosts, Mr Heaton states, 'In the house there are none, indeed the house always has a restful and tranquil feeling about it without any form of disturbance from the past.' It would therefore be imprudent to recount local stories concerning a so-called white lady and the apparition that walks across the field outside The Hermitage or a mysterious visitor to nearby Wood Top farm who specialises in unheralded visits to the lounge and then departs through the wall without even bidding the occupiers good night – at The Hermitage, things that go bump in the night can always be attributed to the resident pair of wild badgers on their nocturnal perambulations – er ... yes, of course! [5]

References

1. The account of Grimsargh School is based on discussions with Miss Carbis and several of her former pupils including John and Philip Cowell, Gladys Hundziack, Tom Heginbotham, Mrs Anna Fisher, Miss Eileen Parker, Miss Olive Sim and the late Mr Peter Wild. I am grateful to them all and for the help of Mrs Janet Butterworth for allowing access to the school's historical documents.
2. Tom C. Smith, *A History of Longridge* (1888).
3. Report in *The Times* 'Saturday Review – Antiques', 2 February 1974.
4. *Nellie Carbis's Grimsargh* (1989) p. 12.
5. I acknowledge the help given by Jonathan Heaton at The Hermitage in compiling this account of his home.

CHAPTER ELEVEN

Employment and Population Trends

THE ANCIENT WOODLANDS have provided man with limited timber resources for commercial exploitation, though the steep escarpments have not been cleared on a vast scale owing to the nature of the terrain. Cherry was used to make charcoal for copper smelting as it gave a hot burn, and alder was also used for charcoal and for clog making. At the top of the west bank of Tun Brook Wood, near Grimsargh Hall, a stand of poplar was planted on the flat area for matches, but was never used as imported poplar became cheaper. Much of the larger timber was removed from Red Scar woods during the First World War and horses were used to drag it out. This would explain why virtually the only big trees are at the edge of the wood, where they were left for their appearance. During the Second World War the west end of Boilton wood (next to the M6) was clear felled, but the stumps left. This ties in with a relatively poor ground flora in this area.

During the eighteenth century large quantities of timber and brushwood from Osbaldeston, Alston, and Elston were used for work undertaken on the Ribble's salt marshes to the west of Preston. In 1731/32 rafts of timber felled in Tun Brook were floated downriver to Penwortham and Hutton where it was retrieved for the upkeep of marsh defences and marsh reclamation schemes. This unrecorded use of the River Ribble for the commercial exploitation of timber provided employment for the men who recovered the wood from the river and to a John Comeleach who was paid for seven-and-a-half days' rafting.[1]

The first national census began in 1801, when the statistics were entirely numerical. It was not until 1841 that a reasonably accurate picture of the population can be made when the returns gave the house and details of occupants including name, sex, age, occupation, and their relationship to the head of the household. Information is used privately by the Government and detailed

Employment and Population Trends

information concerning individuals is not released into the public domain until after 100 years. Local historians can gain useful information from the released census returns about populations and accommodation density and the size of families. This information may then be supplemented by probate returns, deeds, newspaper reports, and the personal reminiscences of Grimsargh's citizens. The census returns are provided every ten years and the last census was completed in 2001.

Examination of Grimsargh's Enumerator's census return of 1851 reveal that the majority of the population was born in Grimsargh or local villages like Chipping, Dilworth, Goosnargh and Whittingham. Children under the age of fifteen years are shown as scholars although one ten-year-old boy in 1861 (before the Education Act of 1870) is recorded as being an errand boy.

Village expansion is commensurate with the social and economic needs of small communities and in Grimsargh the local tradesmen and shopkeepers helped to fulfil the needs of the established farming community. Associated with the farming industry of mid-nineteenth-century Grimsargh were the blacksmith and farriers, wheelwrights and joiners and other artisan occupations. The Preston Parish Directory of 1851 records that George Bleasdale was station master and coal agent; Thomas Billington, schoolmaster; Robert Hothersall, blacksmith; Edward Hothersall, joiner; Christopher Parkinson, tailor; Alice Dawson, miller; Reverend Winstanley Hull, incumbent and James Blanchard was the 'gent' at Grimsargh House. At Elston only nine dispersed dwellings/farms and no business premises are shown in the small township.

It is likely that Grimsargh, like the rest of the Ribble valley, had a large amount of domestic industrial production long before the Industrial Revolution. Textile production began in the countryside as a home industry and gave rise to the Industrial Revolution. By the 1830s the system where whole families worked together in their farms and villages was rapidly coming to an end and employment was sought elsewhere.[2] The farming economy was transformed by the proximity of large urban populations from the mid eighteenth century onwards and to maintain a workforce farmers were obliged to increase wages and alter the nature of the labour contract. During the nineteenth century the local communities of both Grimsargh and Elston saw both depopulation and repopulation. Localised movements of the inhabitants of

Grimsargh and Elston from 1801 to 1921 are illustrated by the following graph.[3]

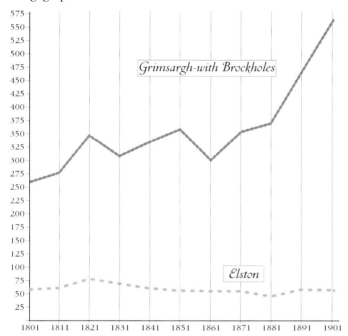

It is possible that a sudden increase in population at Elston from 58 in 1801 to 76 in 1821 and at Grimsargh-with-Brockholes from 262 to 343, within the same period mirrors the swelling of the labour force into the farms and cottages of Grimsargh, at a time when there were seasonal demands for gangs of men, women and children to work on the land to produce more arable. The Education Act of 1870, with compulsory primary education, effectively removed a percentage of the child labour. The population of both townships took a dip in 1831 at a time when there were greater opportunities and prosperity in Blackburn and Preston and other cotton mill towns of Lancashire. Steam looms in the cotton mills gradually replaced the handloom weaving industry and led to the erosion of the workforce from rural areas at the beginning of the 1830s. It was the coming of the railway in 1840 that facilitated the growth of Grimsargh as a linear village and offered a wider choice of employment. For the first time the 'iron horse' provided a real alternative to the equine variety before the 'horse power' engendered by the age of the motor car.

As Preston expanded during the Industrial Revolution some villagers went to live in the town. One such family to move into Preston were the Hothersalls who at first occupied the dwelling which became the schoolhouse and is still situated on the north side of Preston Road between St Michael's Church and the old school. Above the door is a stone plaque bearing the legend: HJA 1809. This is a reference to the first occupants, John and Alice Hothersall. In 1835 John died and in 1840, Alice bequeathed her property, one third each to sons John and Robert Hothersall and the interest on the final third to daughter, Ellen.

John Hothersall (senior) was the village blacksmith working in premises at what is now Ivy Cottage, situated on Preston Road opposite Schoolhouse Farm. This had been the site of the village pinfold for the containment of stray cattle until John Hothersall petitioned the Lord of the Manor, William Cross, to build a new cottage and village smithy in 1807:

Grimsargh September 7*th* 1807
J. Hothersall
Older petitions the Lord of the Manor (William Cross) These are to certify all whom it may concern that J. Hothersall, Elder, Blacksmith, Hath solicited the favour of the Chief Lord and freeholder within the Hamlet of Grimsargh, to inclose a certain place of waste land called Pinfold Nook to build a smithy upon. Granted by us: …

'School House' was first occupied by the Hothersall family.
Author's collection

John Clarkson, Richard Dixon, Edward Hothersall, Robert Sumner, his Thos X Claton, mark, John Charnley.'

William Cross gave conditional acceptance in the following terms.

> As Lord of the Manor of Alston I have no objection to the above plan upon the arrangement proposed of giving an Equivalence in land adjoining to the School But this is upon Condition that the plan is approved by Mr Heatley and his Lessee to whose Land the Waste adjoins.

In the first half of the nineteenth century members of the Hothersall family served the Grimsargh community as tradesmen before taking up employment in Preston. At Smithy Cottage John's sons John and Robert Hothersall sweated over the furnace and the anvil in the terraced property which also housed other tradesmen and their families. One of Robert's nephews, Edward Hothersall, became a joiner and wheelwright and occupied a house and workshop near to the Plough Inn, with garden and two fields, comprising over five acres. By the time of the 1851 census Robert Hothersall was still shown as the Blacksmith at Smithy Cottage. In September 1852, Robert Hothersall sold the smithy, cottages, and land to the Lord of the Manor (William Assheton Cross), in accordance with the following indenture:

> This Indenture made 11th September 1852 between Robert Hothersall of Grimsargh, Blacksmith of the one part and William A. Cross of the other part. Robert Hothersall sells to William A. Cross the hereditaments for £110. All that piece or parcel of land on garden ground situated in Grimsargh called or known by the name of the Pinfold.
>   Together with the cottage or dwellinghouse and Smithy with the outbuildings thereunto belonging standing upon part of the said land … now in the occupation of the said Robert Hothersall.
>   John B. Dickson, Solicitor, Preston. Witnessed the signature of Robert Hothersall.

John and Robert moved to Preston where John became landlord of the Vulcan's Arms and Robert is recorded as residing with his brother. On 9 May 1853, Edward Hothersall similarly conveyed the messuage, joiner's shop, garden and hereditaments on the east side of the highway leading from Preston in Grimsargh, to William Assheton Cross. Edward also became an innkeeper in Preston. In moves that were not without precedent in the mid nineteenth century the Hothersall family were moving out of Grimsargh and seeking employment in Preston. Incomers from the same village often congregated in the same part of town to maintain contact with each other and with the places they had left. Many would not settle in one house, however, and with overcrowding and the stench from the privy who can blame them? Edward Hothersall, married twice and came back to Grimsargh for his last resting place and is buried in the family grave outside the east window of Grimsargh Church.[4]

Preston's population in 1851 was 70,000, mainly due to the effects of migration. The social implications for countryside workers moving to Preston would have included a wider choice of job opportunities in the cotton industry with better wages for shopping and perhaps even a night out at the music hall. Two bedrooms were the norm in Preston's houses and inside conditions were very cramped, frequently damp and with poor hygiene standards. It was a time of economic instability, however, and after the longest cotton mill strike of thirty-nine weeks in 1854 there was the great cotton famine of 1861. The rural population at Grimsargh started to rise again where the population was 301 in 1861, 357 in 1871 and 369 in 1881.

Rows of Victorian terraced houses were built to meet the demands of an expanding population. The Poplars, Primrose Villas, Sunny Bank, Myrtle Bank, and Longsight Terrace began to skirt Preston Road, supplementing older dwellings including the original Pinfold Cottages (1807), Kitchen Terrace (1875) and the established eighteenth-century farmsteads. The Police Station was situated at No. 2, Sunny Bank, Grimsargh, and was one of eight consecutively numbered dwellings making up the same terrace. At various times Sunny Bank terrace has been occupied by local coalmen Robert and James Wilkinson and their families, the local doctor, undertaker and stationmaster, Howard Latham. At the time of their construction the main road through Grimsargh was called Longsight Lane which successively became Longridge Road and Preston Road.

In 1861, Jacob Bilsborough, twenty-eight years, a blacksmith, born in Thornley, his wife and two daughters, together with Thomas Bibby, a twenty-eight-year-old lodger blacksmith, born at Hothersall, were tenant blacksmiths at Smithy House. As repopulation increased the origins of people moving into the village became less parochial by the time of the 1871 census. The occupiers of 20 Grimsargh Road at the time of the 1881 census were twenty-one-year-old Francis Bennett, police constable, who originated from Ulverston, his wife Caroline from Wallasey and daughter Maud, aged two weeks, born in Grimsargh. Next door on the same terrace resided John Fitzsimmons, a gardener from Ireland, his wife Mary from Richmond, Yorkshire and their five children. The Irish influx was at its height during the 1840s Irish famine resulting in mass immigration of Irish people into Liverpool and the north-west. Some Irish farmers provided seasonal agricultural labour and were boarded in Lancashire farms. At Grimsargh thirty-two year old Margaret Hill had crossed from the Emerald Isle and was residing at Ivy cottage with her two sons and employed as a laundress (possibly at Whittingham) in 1891.

By 1881 John Walmsley, twenty-eight years, born in Chipping, was working in the blacksmith's shop, next door to the Plough Inn and Thomas Rhodes the joiner and wheelwright worked in close association with him. Joseph Walmsley took over from his cousin John Walmsley in 1919. In the 1930s Ralph Ireland became the last blacksmith and farrier to occupy premises next to the Plough Hotel which latterly became the village garage. School

Grimsargh

THE STORY OF A
LANCASHIRE VILLAGE

Ivy Cottage, Preston Road, Grimsargh. Built as a terrace of three houses and a blacksmith's workshop in 1807, the Pinfold cottages included Smithy Cottage (Ivy Cottage). The cottages were later converted into four and are today well below the level of the main road.

Photograph courtesy of Ms K. Cunningham

House was subsequently occupied in 1881 by schoolmaster, Harry Bramwell, a twenty-eight-year-old teacher from Preston and his family, long before Kathleen May Cross conveyed it to the trustees of Grimsargh School in 1933. The school caretaker, John Beesley, lived there in 1950, before it was later sold by the Blackburn Diocese for use as a private dwelling.

John Salthouse, thirty-six years, and his wife Isabella, were farming at Church House Farm in 1871, together with five family members. It was the practice to take in lodgers and farm labourers in those days. Census returns show that a young couple, James and Elizabeth Maylor, both twenty-two years, shared the accommodation as lodgers. Jim was employed as a bricklayer at a crucial time in the history of Grimsargh, when several linear dwellings would be under construction.

An overall total of twenty-three people were in residence at Red Scar between 1851 and 1861. The staff hierarchy was complex but those who erred were answerable to the butler or to the housekeeper. The footman, John Hodgson, was a native of Millom, Cumberland and so was servant Hannah Bowman, known affectionately by members of the Cross family as 'old Nanna Bowman'. In the overall scheme of things, John Hodgson came somewhere between old Nanna Bowman, and the prestigious position of Cross

By the late nineteenth century Red Scar was a grand mansion which employed large numbers of domestic and other staff, many drawn from Grimsargh and further afield.

Courtesy of Anthony Cross

family butler and was still a faithful member of staff in 1881. It was not unusual for people from Cumbria to come to the industrial towns of Lancashire seeking employment and coincidentally my old nanna Bowman, crossed the Cumberland border when she moved from Millom to Preston in 1918. As a fourteen-year-old Winifred (Tina) Bowman had to leave her home in Millom in 1914 to become a housemaid at a large house in the Lake District before venturing forth to Preston in 1920. Like her namesake Hannah, at Red Scar, she mirrored the social trend of those days and in her twilight years Tina settled at Grimsargh, where she died in 1992, aged ninety-two years, the epitome of a wonderful old gran.

Late nineteenth-century returns for the townships of Grimsargh-with-Brockholes show a fifty per cent increase between 1861 and 1901. Separated from the agricultural workers and tradesmen was the Lord of the Manor at Red Scar and the wealthy occupiers of The Hermitage, Grimsargh House, and Grimsargh Manor. Originally the occupiers of Grimsargh House and Manor and other middle-class dwellings introduced a new economic dimension and to some extent changed the physical landscape of Grimsargh.

Grimsargh

THE STORY OF A
LANCASHIRE VILLAGE

Kitchen Terrace, opposite the Plough, still bears the date of construction as 1875.
Parish records

Employment and Population Trends

Professional and business people could now travel by train to work in Preston. Grimsargh was beginning the long transformation from agricultural hamlet to dormitory for people who chose to live in the village yet carried out their employment in Preston and elsewhere.

Thomas Nathaniel Thornton of Thornton & France, wine merchants of Preston, had occupied Grimsargh House by the time of the 1881 census. The Thorntons employed three servants, one of whom was thirty-seven-year-old Fanny Bond from Dublin, to help to look after their home and six children. Wilfrid Trubshaw became a high-ranking Chief Constable of Lancashire in 1927 and came to reside at Grimsargh House. Mr Trubshaw was appointed Deputy Chief Constable of the Lancashire Constabulary in 1914 and Chief Constable in 1927. The exercise of firm leadership through the Great War and impoverished 1930s culminated in a challenging career and he had earned his retirement by 1935.[5] Doubtless he found time for a little relaxation and was able to conceive a few policies along the leafy lanes of Grimsargh or the

Another shot of Victorian Grimsargh showing Lynwood villas built in 1901 overlooking what is now the village green. Courtesy of Mr T. Heginbotham and parish records

WHITTINGHAM LANE, GRIMSARGH.   No 17

gardens of Grimsargh House. The Chief Constable employed the local policeman gardener, William Cadwelleder, from Moss Nook who had to 'get fell in' for the boss during periods off duty.

Herbert and Margaret Mallott followed the Chief Constable into Grimsargh House in the 1920s. Mr Mallott was the Managing Director of the Preston Cotton industry of Messrs. Horrocks, Crewdson. Mrs Mallot was the daughter of James Allsup of Whittingham Hall, who bred a famous herd of large white pigs. Her grandfather built the covered market at Preston and his boatyard on the Ribble turned out many fine coasting vessels.

Grimsargh Manor was first known as Grimsargh Cottage and in 1851 was occupied by Edward Sidgreaves, his wife and three children who are recorded as being scholars at home. Thirty years later the same residence was occupied by solicitor Mr William Blackhurst. At the beginning of the twentieth century two divisions of the Thornton family, who were Preston wine merchants

Grimsargh

THE STORY OF A
LANCASHIRE VILLAGE

Longsight Lane later became Preston Road. The view here is looking towards Preston.
Courtesy of Mr T. Heginbotham and parish records

occupied both Grimsargh House and Grimsargh Manor. The Thorntons had joined a succession of Preston businessmen and professional people, who were now moving out to the countryside and settling in villages such as Grimsargh.

At the beginning of the twentieth century the local registrar would have had his fair share of work. The population of Grimsargh had risen from 262 in 1801, to 561 in 1901. Thomas and Jane Hothersall, who became the Registrar of Births, Marriages and Deaths for the sub-district of Alston, lived at The Poplars on Longsight Lane. Grimsargh had originated from an agricultural manor and was still basically agricultural but with a less permanent industrial population working in Longridge, Ribbleton, or Preston. Local employment and commerce began to prosper with the establishment of the Preston textile industry, three cotton mills in Longridge, the Whittingham Mental Asylum and Courtaulds Factory. Barrett's guide for 1901 shows an increased diversity of locally based employment including more shopkeepers, a water-works manager, a coal merchant, a druggist (at Preston), a plumber and painter, a fireman, assurance agent and dressmaker and a total of thirty farms at Grimsargh-with-Brockholes and nine at

Elston. Victorian developments impacted on rural areas like Grimsargh as it absorbed the expanding population and the village took on its familiar appearance either side of the main road and on Whittingham Lane.

During the twentieth century many of Grimsargh's inhabitants were employed at the County Mental Hospital at Whittingham, and at Courtaulds Factory. Radical development commenced in the 1930s when Courtaulds acquired part of the Red Scar Estate and needlessly demolished the former Cross family seat at Red Scar Mansion. A huge factory on the boundary with Preston at Ribbleton was built. Commensurate with an expanding population in Grimsargh was the construction of linear 1930s semidetached houses by local builder William Houghton who built The Towers, Woodlands Grove, Nook Glade, Nook Crescent and the semidetached houses on Preston Road east of the railway bridge. Tom Heginbotham and his parents moved into their new house in Nook Glade, in 1931. He still resides there with his wife and is the only original resident of the Close.

For over forty years Courtaulds Preston Factory was one of the largest viscose works in Britain. In 1980 market forces brought

When the station was demolished the stone was used to build attractive bungalows for the elderly which now form Old Station Close. (The author's parents, Joan and Norman Hindle, standing in the doorway, resided at No. 1).
Author's collection

about its closure and nearly 3,000 people were made redundant.
In 1982 Central Lancashire Development Corporation bought the
150-acre site to turn it into the revitalised Red Scar Industrial
Estate. The closure of Courtaulds Factory signalled the end of
the two giant 'Courtaulds Chimneys' and what was left of the
former Preston to Longridge railway. I had been brought up
within the shadow of the twin 'biros', which at 385 feet were the
tallest chimneys in Lancashire and was there to watch the last
smoke emissions before they came crashing down to the ground.
Preston's crematorium was built in the same woodland as the old
mansion and opened its doors on 25 January 1962.

Grimsargh's population had risen to 835 in 1961 and was to more
than double by the time of the Millennium. Car ownership has
increased rapidly and transformed urban and rural relations, re-
versing the trend of rural depopulation. With more houses built
towards the end of the decade the population had risen to 1,325
in 1971. At the time of the 1991 census the population had reached
1,676 and although the 2001 Census figures are not yet available,

Grimsargh's population is now estimated to be in excess of 2,000 people. The urbanisation of the local countryside and repopulation of Grimsargh have transformed it into something of a commuter village to the city of Preston or Manchester with consequential loss of traditional village character. In contrast to home textile production, blacksmiths, wheelrights and farming industries of yesteryear John Turner and Sons Ltd, are now the most prominent employer within the existing parish of Grimsargh, employing 300 people in a variety of traditional building trades. Operating discreetly from premises for which they have won design and environmental awards, Turners is one of the major building companies of north-west England. They have balanced their commercial success with investment both in the community through training and in the Grimsargh countryside through planting woodland, meadowland and hedges.

Notwithstanding their environmental contribution, it could nevertheless be argued that the generic sociological profile and lifestyle of the rural community is rapidly heading towards extinction. Distinctions between villages and towns and urban and

Grimsargh

THE STORY OF A
LANCASHIRE VILLAGE

Grimsargh Village centre an level crossing. The undated postcard was sent by a lady called Mary to her friend ir Manchester to say she 'was having a lovely holiday here in Grimsargh'.

Courtesy of Mr T. Heginbotham

GRIMSARGH.　　　　No 16

Labels within image: Alston Hall · Squire Andertons · FROM · The Church · GREETINGS · GRIMSARGH. · The Hermitage · St. Michael's Ch. School.

'Greetings from Grimsargh'.
A postcard featuring aspects
of Victorian Grimsargh and
district.
Originally provided by Mrs E. Latham

rural have become increasingly distorted and reflect what is happening in many other parts of England.

References

1. Centre for North West Regional Studies, *Bulletin* 14 by Dr Alan Crosby. I acknowledge helpful discussions with Dr Janet Edmunds concerning the Red Scar woodlands.
2. Michael Anderson, *Family Structure of Nineteenth-century Lancashire.*
3. Fishwick, *History of the Parish of Preston,* p. 74.
4. I acknowledge the help of Mr George Hothersall of Sussex.
5. Bob Dobson, *Policing in Lancashire* (1989).

CHAPTER TWELVE

'Grimsargh Junction: Change Here For Whittingham'

ONE OF THE MOST SIGNIFICANT developments for Grimsargh took place on 1 May 1840 with the opening of the Preston and Longridge railway line, which bisected the fields of the township on an embankment, the remains of which may be seen from the reservoir causeway. The railway was built to the annoyance of some local farmers who threw stones at the first trains. The daily goods train to Longridge and the unique Whittingham passenger trains soon became a feature of the Grimsargh landscape and epitomised those wonderful days of steam.

Grimsargh has a particularly interesting railway heritage and was once a junction served by two stations on separate lines. The first railways in the Preston area were opened in 1838 and 1840. The privately-managed Grimsargh to Whittingham line was constructed during 1887 to connect the huge Whittingham Mental Hospital with the nearest railway at Grimsargh. The diminutive

An aerial view of the Bowling Green, at the rear of the Plough Inn, which was reshaped by the railway.
Courtesy of Miss E. Parker

station was a few yards from the main LMS station and the site is now occupied by Langden Fold. The Longridge line closed to passengers in 1930 and to freight in 1967, whilst the Whittingham line survived until 1957. The two rural branch lines once made an important contribution to the social and economic infrastructure of Grimsargh.

The Preston to Longridge railway was conceived as a means of conveying large blocks of stone quarried from Tootle Heights, Longridge. The first meeting was convened at Preston Town Hall on 9 September 1836. The chairman, Thomas Batty Addison, met with twelve shareholders who became Directors of the railway and included James Blanchard of Grimsargh House.[1] Stone from Longridge quarries was used in the construction of Preston's Harris Museum and Art Gallery and many other important buildings in the north-west including Liverpool Docks. The original Preston terminus of the seven-mile Longridge branch was a station at Deepdale, situated near to the former coal sidings on Fletcher Road.

Mr H.W. Bushell was the engineer and a prospectus stated that there was to be capital of £30,000, in 600 shares of £50 each. 'We hope that the spirited proprietors will form themselves into a trading company for the conveyance of stone, limestone from the kilns and quarries near Longridge; and the transit of corn and other commodities from Preston to Clitheroe and other parts. But to ensure success cheapness must be the order of the day.' Two conveyances for passengers ran between Preston and Longridge on Sundays, Wednesdays and Saturdays. The fare from Preston to the Plough Inn at Grimsargh was 4d. and to Longridge it was 6d. A description of the route through Grimsargh towards Preston was described in a local trade directory:

At Tootle Heights, Longridge the railway is cut out of solid rock. There is a fine view of the Chipping Hills and the diversified scenery, which adorns the landscape below. Further west it proceeds towards the Plough Inn, in Grimsargh, which it passes within 10 yards and then it is carried in a straight line to the eastern part of the 'Parsonage House' in Grimsargh, and to the south is the antique residence of Mrs Cross, called The Red Scar House. In this direction another bridge occurs, of wood [the site of the old bridge on the B6243 on Preston Road near Grimsargh School], under which the line is constructed. It then passes the garden of the School House, and thence, without any material angle or curve, proceeds under another bridge [Gamull Lane] near to Ribbleton Brow; thence it proceeds in a regular direction to the terminus near to Barton Terrace [near Deepdale Road].[2]

The railway company reshaped the historic bowling green at Grimsargh's Plough Inn when track-laying necessitated 'all change' from a round to an oval green. Originally the locomotion was provided by horsepower with horses supplied by Mr Hayes of Riche's Farm, Grimsargh. On 1 May 1840 villagers along the line cheered the inaugural passenger train drawn by a horse decorated with ribbons. The first excursions at holiday time provided new delights of travel for passengers from Preston, Grimsargh and Longridge. The *Preston Chronicle* of 5 June 1841 reported that 'three hundred and fifty seven passengers were conveyed on the newly opened Preston to Longridge Railway, with four trains despatched each way to explore the fells and quarries of Longridge, and the good folk had a chance to witness the festivities of Preston on Whit Monday.' Occasionally the horses jibbed on the gradient between Grimsargh and Longridge, and male passengers were requested to push. After being unyoked from their carriage at Longridge the horses earned a sugar lump and boarded their own special carriage to hitch a lift back to Grimsargh. The incline was such that the trucks freewheeled under their own gravity and the shires gained a well-earned complimentary ticket.

The Board of Directors of the new Fleetwood, Preston, and West Riding Junction Railway had grandiose plans for the Longridge line. A one-mile extension to the detached line at Deepdale to link it with a junction at Preston was proposed. The associated railway companies also planned in 1846 to run a connecting line from a point near to Grimsargh to reach the east Lancashire coalfields and onto the railway network in Yorkshire. Through the determined opposition of Lancashire landowners the bill put forward was thrown out in the House of Lords. There was a panic among the shareholders, and the ambitious proposal to establish a railway extension from Longridge to link up with the rail network in Yorkshire was abandoned. At Hurst Green a railway cutting of over 200 metres survives in the landscape as a monument to this ill-fated Victorian enterprise. In 2001 a local farmer directed me to the site and over 150 years after construction, the shallow cutting of double track width was easily discernible. Either side of the cutting, it is obvious that steep wooded valleys

Grimsargh

THE STORY OF A
LANCASHIRE VILLAGE

would have necessitated the building of high viaducts, which never came to fruition.

The abandoned railway was described by Dobson (1877):

> This was a huge unfinished embankment. Climbing it we saw for some distance an excavation, with level bottom and sloping sides, continuing to the next dingle where there was again the beginning of an embankment, as if to cross over the valley through which runs Clough Brook. I soon saw that this was a detached and uncompleted portion of that once ambitious project, the Fleetwood, Preston, and West Riding Junction Railway. It was to go up the Preston and Longridge line at Deepdale, leave that line below Grimsargh, and pass by Hothersall, Dutton, Hurst Green, Mitton to Whalley and into Yorkshire. Beyond improving the Longridge line and making the Preston tunnel, they did nothing but excavate this one field in Dutton. Had the line gone on, it would have traversed some lovely scenery and have disclosed to the traveller many a pretty look of Ribblesdale which few now take the trouble to go and see.[3]

Celebrations were held at Deepdale to mark the departure of the first steam locomotive to Longridge on Whit Monday, 1848. Officials of the railway company, along with some 200 invited guests and a band of the 89th Regiment and a large party of officers from Fulwood Barracks were hauled by the engine, 'Addison' to the Longridge terminus. Celebrations included processions through the town to Tootle Heights, whilst in the grounds of the railway company the band struck up for the dance. Various young ladies with their delighted partners tripped it lightly to the astonishment of villagers. Country dances and polkas followed and a carnival atmosphere seems to have been enjoyed by all. All of this was too much for the horses who succumbed to the marvels of modern technology when steam took over, and hopefully the beasts of burden enjoyed a well earned retirement in the fields of their home station at Grimsargh.

The new one mile extension was opened at Preston in 1850 to link the line with the town's developing railway network. The west side of Grimsargh's Plough Hotel was originally used as a booking office for the branch line. Some passengers may even have treated a certain George Bleasdale to a pint, for he was stationmaster at Grimsargh in 1851.[4] The Plough stables were used by people who rode into Grimsargh to continue their journey by train and who could now reach Preston or Longridge on the 'iron horse'. Alternatively they could reach Longridge and even Bowland if they had seen the advert in the *Preston Guardian* dated Saturday, 7 June 1851: 'Whitsuntide holidays, cheap excursions from Preston, by train to Longridge, Whitewell and Chipping. By rail, to the Townley Arms, Longridge, where conveyances can be had for Whitewell and Chipping. 1s. 6d. first class, 1s. second class, and 6d. third class.'

In 1856 the Preston to Longridge Railway was purchased by the newly re-formed Fleetwood, Preston and West Riding Junction Railway Company. The line served Grimsargh and Longridge and there were intermediate stations at Maudland, Deepdale Road, and Fulwood (Gamull Lane). In 1867 this company lost its identity to the Lancashire and Yorkshire (L and Y) and London and North Western Railway (LNWR). The two companies owned the railways around Preston and operated the Longridge branch as a joint line.

Their enterprise included the building of a new station at Grimsargh in 1870, replacing the Plough Inn halt, which now had more space for serious drinkers. Grimsargh Station was of single-storey granite construction situated adjacent to the level crossing of Longsight Lane and on the south side of the single-track line. The coalyard and railway sidings at Grimsargh were immediately behind the railway station with its single platform and semaphore

Grimsargh

THE STORY OF A
LANCASHIRE VILLAGE

The Langden Fold development was built on the site of the Longridge branch line and the Grimsargh station of the Whittingham railway. The site of the original booking office at Grimsargh Station is shown at the west side of the Plough Inn.

Author's collection

signals situated either side of the white wooden level crossing gates.

A dark cloud hung over the next station down the line from Grimsargh when disaster struck at about 9 p.m. on 10 August 1867. A serious accident occurred at Fulwood (Ribbleton) Station when an excursion train from Longridge collided with the rear of the scheduled train, which had stopped at the station platform alongside Gamull Lane bridge. Signal error and a further breach of regulations was established as it became evident that the tail light on the 8.25 p.m. stationary train had not been displayed. There was no loss of life but at least sixty passengers returning from the Guild Festivities at Longridge sustained injuries, some of which were serious. The joint ownership got off to a bad start and two employees – a guard and a signalman – were subsequently dismissed from the service.[5]

Three years later another accident occurred. A newspaper account detailed the events of 1 October 1870.

> An alarming railway accident occurred though unattended with harm to life or limb, but yet which caused considerable alarm to the passengers on the 5.40 p.m. train from Longridge on Tuesday. The train was originally started from Preston as a luggage train but as it was found very convenient for contract and ticket holders, it has for some time run a passenger train as well as a luggage train. The train passed up all right but on its return journey, it was not so fortunate. About 500 yards from the station and arriving at a place known as Waring's siding, the engine and tender, two carriages and the brake-van all left the rails, tearing up the metals and proceeding over sleepers, chains etc. for about 30 yards. It was brought to a stand and the passengers lost no time in alighting. From what we can gather the cause of the accident may be attributed to the mischievous meddling of a pair of points by a number of children, who constantly congregate near the place where there is a siding for the purpose of loading stone from the Chapel Hill delph of Messrs. Waring Bros, and also the weighing machine at which waggons are weighed by the company. The engine and the tender were much strained and the latter was broken in several parts. Men were engaged during the whole of the night in getting the engine upon the rails again, in which they succeeded, so that the first morning train at half past seven might pass.

Despite these accidents a second railway station was built at Grimsargh in 1887 on the north side of the level crossing gates

'Grimsargh Junction: Change Here For Whittingham'

and thus Grimsargh became a railway junction. The newly constructed Whittingham Railway was privately owned and had connecting facilities with the 'main line' to Preston, thus providing a boost to the economic sustainability of both railways. At the joint line station the porter now greeted his trains with 'Grimsargh, change here for Whittingham'. The extra freight and passenger traffic increased returns on the Longridge line, which enjoyed its heyday up to the time of the Great War.

In 1917 a second proposal was made to extend the Longridge line into Yorkshire. Plans for an alternative route to the north of Longridge Fell 'ran out of steam' during the following year. The route would have seen stations built to serve the villages of Chipping, Whitewell, Dunsop Bridge, Newton, Slaidburn and Tosside before linking up with the Midland Railway at Hellifield. With alternative rail links to the Midland line it would have been uneconomic and left a permanent scar on some of Lancashire's prettiest villages and countryside. In 1923 the line to Longridge was under the management of the London, Midland and Scottish Railway Company and was then destined to become a quiet backwater of a passenger and freight line.

Nevertheless there was the daily excitement in Grimsargh of the level crossing gates being opened several times and the sight of stationmaster Latham emerging from his office to welcome

Grimsargh Station in 1909 is remarkably busy with intending passengers. The sig on the gable end states: 'Onl passengers allowed on the platform', and there are separate waiting rooms for gentlemen and ladies. There has been some speculation a to the nature of the group waiting for a train: some hav suggested a Conservative Ladies' trip; others a local Temperance Movement outing – the absence of crat of brown ale could be taken as further evidence of eithe of these! In fact the passengers were actually a party of Oddfellows on an excursion. This postcard wa posted in July 1909 by Mis Jane Heyes (housekeeper t Tertius Buzzard), to her sist Eleanor in Liverpool.
Courtesy of Mr T. Heginbotham

Grimsargh Station before closure in 1930. Gas lamps and station name of Grimsargh are still in situ.
Courtesy of Mr T. Heginbotham

passengers. Freight trains were shunted into the yard where the milk, cattle, coal and other merchandise were handled with calm professionalism. Anyone running for the train was usually accommodated by the guard, who always checked the main road in both directions before signalling to the driver to open the regulator of the veteran engine at the head of the train. However, you cannot please all of the people all of the time:

Little Margaret Finch was barely ten years old when she was sent with some clogs to the cobbler's shop adjacent to the Plough Inn. What transpired had such a profound effect on her that she ran home to Longsight to report the choice language used by an errant Grimsargh farmer. As the level crossing gates made their customary clank across Longsight Lane to afford the morning passenger the 'road to Longridge', a herdsman was driving his cows home and was stopped in his tracks. The farmer did not mince his words: 'You shitten-arsed bugger' – clearly a very articulate man – was directed at the humble porter for allowing the train to proceed. One could write that he 'remonstrated' with the porter, but in charting the social history of Grimsargh is it not better to use the actual colourful language of this down-to-earth local? I am reliably informed that it could have been much worse and the abuse was by normal standards, a term of endearment!

Undaunted by her earth-shattering experience in the 1920s Margaret paid a penny for a bar of Nestlé's chocolate from the machine on Grimsargh Station before catching the train to Preston to see a music hall performance at the old Empire Theatre. It made a change from the 'Physic Revellers' and amateur plays and pantomime on offer at the old 'tin tabernacle', more politely known as the Grimsargh Assembly Rooms.

From his rear garden at Blackrock Farm, Grimsargh, young Nicholas Swarbrick watched the trains struggling up the steep gradients of 1 in 94 steepening to 1 in 59 on the approaches to Longridge. The slipping of the engine's wheels was exacerbated by wet and frosty weather and on occasions, freight trains had to uncouple half their train and then return for it from Longridge yard. At Blackrock Farm the fascinating rasping call of the corncrake from deep within the hay meadows served as an alarm clock for the young schoolboy, Nicholas Swarbrick, to get up and catch the 8 a.m. train to Preston. Today the once-abundant corncrake is almost extinct on mainland Britain and, like the official 'knocker-upper' of urban areas, is but a memory. Over seventy years after he last used the service, Grimsargh's centenarian resident, Mr Swarbrick, told me of his recollections of the line with nostalgia and a degree of sentiment. 'We did not need to go out of the house until the train was in the station. When the train coasted down the gradient from Longridge and the crossing gates closed that was the signal for me to walk onto the platform.' Before the Roaring Twenties he used the same service as neighbour Esther Rigby and Margaret Mallott from Grimsargh House. The train stopped at Ribbleton before Margaret Mallot alighted at Deepdale Station to attend the Park School whilst young Nick and Esther Rigby went on to Preston Station for the Catholic Grammar Schools.

Tom Heginbotham of Grimsargh can recall at least one instance of trains coming down the incline from Longridge with wheels grinding and sparks flying and as the runaway freight train came down the line she most certainly blew, usually just before taking the level crossing gates at Grimsargh. Stops at Grimsargh – scheduled or otherwise – were out of the question and but for the steep escape route siding at Courtaulds factory it is likely that Preston Stations days would have been numbered! Not surprisingly in the aftermath of the tornado-like spectacle with its columns of hissing steam, young Tom gave up trainspotting to steady his nerves, and together with his companions greeted the infrequent motor cars passing along Longsight Lane by proclaiming, 'Here comes a car!' Now, of course, it is the cars that tend to debilitate one's constitution.

They say all good things come to an end and this was to include the Longridge branch line passenger service. In the late 1920s the first omnibuses operated by the Pilot, Majestic and Claremont Bus Companies from Clitheroe and Preston were on track to eclipse the local railway's passenger service. The line was scheduled to close on Monday, 2 June 1930, but in the absence of a Sunday service the last train from Longridge was at 10 p.m. on Saturday, 31 May 1930. The last stationmaster at Grimsargh, Howard Latham, bade farewell to his passengers for the last time. Mr Latham continued to serve the community as churchwarden and organist at St Michael's Church, about half a mile down the permanent way. There was more than a tinge of sadness at the time of closure and a column in the local newspaper on the Monday after closure evoked those feelings:[6]

> The last journey on the Longridge line sharply contrasted the aloof austerity of Preston and the warm feeling which the villagers showed as the train passed them for the last time. It was as well that someone should have remembered for there was nothing at Preston to indicate that engine 10646 was to make the last passenger journey on the 90-years-old line. No notice was taken of the short train drawn up at the end of one of the departure platforms; for what significance and status had it amongst the 'monarchs of the permanent way', that clank their corridor coaches into Preston. But at the village stations it was different, for it was their train and they were seeing it for the last time. Driver Billington aptly summed up his last journey. 'Use is second nature and people get to know each other, that is why they are sorry.' When the train steamed out seven minutes late it suffered the indignity of having to pull up within a few hundred yards of the platform to give way to main line trains. Perhaps after all there was recognition of the mournful last trip, because the carriages were unlit as they ran through gloomy yards and into dark tunnels.
>
> After leaving the town the 9.22 p.m. came into its own at Longridge. Its arrival was heralded by three short reports caused by fog detonators placed on the line. The cobble stone platform was crowded and the booking clerk was issuing the last tickets. 'No, I won't book return', said someone. Unusual interest was taken in the coupling of the engine for the last time. An optimist with a pocket camera tried to immortalise the event and a Clergyman, to give it a Benediction, as it were, shook hands with the driver and fireman. A porter gave the all clear by whistling with his fingers and on the stroke of ten the

'Grimsargh Junction: Change Here For Whittingham'

Longridge to Preston train started for the last time. Passengers leaned out to wave to those left on the station, the engine whistled a prolonged goodbye to the village and the bridges and embankments were lined with people anxious to see the last train. Then came a stretch of line studded with fog signals. Report after report rang out and as the train approached each station the steam whistle sounded and more fog signals exploded. There were groups of officials at each of the stations and passengers and onlookers insisted on shaking hands with the driver.

There were at least 40 detonations before the train emerged from Deepdale tunnels. At Maudland there was an enforced delay and the train stopped over the shadowed canal. What the railways did to canal transport was now happening to locomotion on the line. Other methods had superseded them and they were no longer wanted. Reaching Preston Station, exactly an hour after leaving for the outward journey, the driver and fireman and a few passengers inspected a wreath, which had been tied onto the engine on the return journey. A few minutes afterwards the train ran into the sheds and so ended

Engine 10646 on its last stop at Grimsargh Station. Driver Billington of Lostock Hall Shed bids farewell to Stationmaster Lathom on 31 May 1930.
Courtesy of Phillip Cowell

the 10.30 p.m. on Saturday, 31 May 1930. The service which was begun with the hope of linking Lancashire with Yorkshire on 1 May 1840, never got beyond the seven miles to Longridge and now even that distance is seven miles too long.

'Grimsargh Junction: Change Here For Whittingham'

Freight and parcel traffic continued to operate from Grimsargh Station and during the Second World War the Longridge branch line was pressed into extra service with at least two freight trains a day. The local Home Guard walked onto the station platform to commandeer station master Howard Latham's office and agonised over their strategy to keep the Führer firmly on the German rail network. A Ministry of Defence war supplies building was constructed next to the coal sidings and the logistics of clandestine operations within the building were partly met by the railway. Following closure of the passenger service there were several unusual workings and a handful of special passenger excursions, mainly operated for rail enthusiasts.

On arriving in Grimsargh in 1935, Miss Nellie Carbis witnessed the extraordinary sight of the Bradley family of Preesall moving their entire farm stock aboard a specially reserved train to Grimsargh Station. The cattle were rounded up in the pens at the end of the platform before proceeding in an easterly direction through Grimsargh to Boot Farm at Alston, where they gained pastures new. In January 1936, it was reported that a Noah's Ark of a train left Longridge destined for Wiltshire. This was a special train ordered by Mrs Kate Hollas who was the last lessee of Red Scar. Together with all her animals and farming equip-ment she was now migrating south, as this interesting account can reveal.

Resembling a 'Noah's Ark', a train left Longridge this afternoon for Highworth, near Swindon, a distance of two hundred miles. It comprised eleven trucks of livestock and thirteen of farm implements and sectional cabins and practically the whole of the farm stock from Holworth and Hacking Hobbs Farms at Longridge, the property of Mrs Kate Hollas of Red Scar, Grimsargh. Mrs Hollas has taken up Parsonage Farm, Highworth, following the sale of Red Scar, to Messrs Courtaulds. There were on the train six shires, a hunter and two foals, a Shetland pony, forty-five sheep, a bull, fifteen cows, twenty-seven stirks, eighteen yearlings and four calves. The farm implements included carts, traps, plough, harrow, turnip-cutter, harness and feeding utensils. The cows were milked before leaving and will be at Parsonage Farm in time for the early morning milking. By 9 a.m. tomorrow it is expected that the whole of the livestock will have been safely transported and will be grazing in the fields of Wiltshire.

After all that the journey was done in reverse in about 1939 when Mrs Hollas came back north to farm at Hothersall, near Longridge.[7]

Miss Olive Simm of Longridge lived in one of the cottages at Red Scar and her father was employed by Mr Hollas as the gardener. At that time Miss Simm was a schoolgirl at Grimsargh and in 2000 she told me of a school train excursion she went on from the by-now disused Grimsargh Station on 22 May 1936. On searching the old Grimsargh School log I found the appropriate entry duly recorded for posterity. 'The School was closed today to allow fourteen children and two teachers to visit Worcester and Stratford on Avon on an excursion organised by the L.M.S. Railway Company'.

The building of the Courtaulds factory in the 1930s provided a lifeline for freight services on the Longridge branch. Courtaulds' own industrial steam engines now hauled coal wagons from the factory to newly constructed sidings adjacent to the Longridge line. The building of large housing estates at Ribbleton saw the LMS railway playing a crucial part in the installation of electricity supplies. British Railways gave permission for the electricity auth-ority to lay their cables beside the line and I witnessed this unusual operation on a bitterly cold Sunday in January 1955. The normal method of one engine in steam over the single track to Grimsargh and Longridge was suspended on a day when the line saw no traffic. The special train had a couple of vintage 0–8–0 locomotives numbered 49150 and 49382 at either end. These engines were regulars on the line and I had already underlined them in my well-thumbed trainspotting book. In between the grimy engines were several cable wagons and a huge steam breakdown crane which was depositing the cable drums at the side of the track. From the bridge at Cromwell Road I saw that the engine at the head of the train was shunting empty wagons into the sidings outside the Ministry of Food cold storage depot.

I grew up with this freight railway and its engines and was sad when the last goods train trundled to Grimsargh and Longridge on an uneventful day in November 1967. Following closure Grim-sargh Station's granite setts were utilised in the building of the old people's bungalows and the station building was immortalised

Grimsargh

THE STORY OF A
LANCASHIRE VILLAGE

by the street name, Old Station Close. It was the demolition of Courtaulds chimneys that sounded the death knell for the last remaining section of the Preston to Longridge railway line. The line from Preston to Courtaulds continued to see trains operating until the factory closed in 1980. Today only a small stretch of long-abandoned track exists from Maudland to Skeffington Road, marking the final chapter of the Longridge line.

Love blossomed for quite a few Grimsargh couples within the precincts of Grimsargh's railway environment and a parallel line could be drawn with the famous film 'Brief Encounter', in which Trevor Howard met Celia Johnson at Carnforth Railway Station. Here, against a background of plumes of white steam, mugs of tea, and Rachmaninov's Second Piano Concerto the encounter seemed to be doing quite well, especially when he later took her to the local cinema. However, Grimsargh never had a cinema and villagers did not need romantic music or double seats. Indeed, if David Lean had chosen Grimsargh Junction for location shots his film would probably have been given an 'X' certificate! Many late night branch line manoeuvres took place under the eaves of the station shelter after departure of the last train of the day to Whittingham. Not surprisingly the venue is still fondly remem-bered by several of Grimsargh's senior citizens who recalled their courting days and whose identity I must preserve at all costs.

There is also a certain romanticism of those pre-Dr Beeching

The Whittingham train –
known locally as 'Little
Annie' – leaving Grimsargh
Station.
Courtesy of Mrs Frances Wright

days before the railway network of Britain was substantially reduced by his clinical interventions. I knew the village of Grimsargh in the early 1950s when Preston Road was obstructed twice a day by the white level crossing gates situated between the two stations. As the main line engine and a few trucks prepared to show their true colours in tackling the ascent to Longridge, a quaint little steam engine with up to three odd-looking green passenger carriages was gently simmering in Grimsargh's second railway station which served Whittingham Hospital. The locomotives operating on this anachronistic Victorian railway made the main line engines on the Longridge branch look like the equivalent of today's Advanced Passenger Train.

The distance between Grimsargh and Whittingham stations was almost two miles. Undoubtedly unique, it claimed to be the only free railway in the country, as there were no ticket offices and anyone could travel. All they provided on Grimsargh platform was a small shelter next to a waiting room complete with a roaring coal fire and a single electric light bulb. It was a bit like the 'Marie Celeste', a ghost station with no staff. Beneath considerable smoke emissions, an ancient steam engine would suddenly appear around the curve close to Dixon's Farm, working to a non-existent station timetable on a single-track line.

The Junction Station at
Grimsargh on the
Whittingham railway with
Grimsargh LMS station
behind the semaphore signal.
Hospital workers board the
train which is about to be
hauled by one of the two
Barclay engines.
Courtesy of Mr T. Heginbotham

During my visits to the station I witnessed the strange sight
of the train arriving and departing. The late shift slammed the
doors of the carriages, which had been converted from guard's
vans by the hospital's joiners and bore an uncanny resemblance
to three cattle trucks. The ends had been boarded up and about
six windows allowed passengers to savour the pleasant countryside
during the six-minute journey to Whittingham. The patented
Mark Two models even had the luxury of wooden seats around
the sides and gas central heating provided by a Calor gas bottle
which was locked away in its carriage compartment. The entire
staff on the railway comprised of the friendly driver and fireman
who allowed me on the footplate and showed me their shovel
which was placed above the roaring fire to fry bacon eggs and
mushrooms for breakfast. Suddenly, unheralded and unannounced
there would be a jolt as the coupling took the strain followed by
a blow on the engine's whistle as the train eased off from the
platform to trundle back to Whittingham. The railway symbolised
the epitome of the rural railways of bygone Lancashire and on this
line there were no intermediate stations, only a few unscheduled
stops.

It was a bumpy ride at a speed of around fifteen miles per
hour, which was perhaps as well because the carriages had no

brakes. The skills of driver and fireman were synchronised as a team in maintaining momentum over the gradients with a watchful eye from the footplate. The driver had no need to worry about signals because on this railway they did not exist, and who had ever heard of gradient or milepost signs? Even the points were changed by the engine crew who operated hand levers. If the old engine ran out of steam the opportunity arose to gather a few more mushrooms from the fields or collect wild flowers growing profusely in the cutting next to the line. In this haven of rural bliss it was a tradition for the driver to sound his whistle on setting off from Grimsargh Station, particularly if he felt that the wind had an element of westerly origin. This was a signal for Mrs Wild at Dixon's Farm half a mile down the line, to rush out and take her 'Daz white' washing off the line. Former staff at Whittingham have affectionate memories and one ex-nurse told me the driver knew his passengers so well that if anyone missed the train he would reverse the engine back to Whittingham Station

Grimsargh

THE STORY OF A
LANCASHIRE VILLAGE

The Sentinel steam locomotive 'Gradwell' at Grimsargh Station with a single converted passenger carriage epitomises the rural branch line.
Courtesy of Mr T. Heginbotham

to make sure that the night shift coming off duty got their full quota of sleep.

As a boy I was mesmerised by the whole experience of the journey including riding past tumbling lapwings and galloping heifers close to the long curve near Dixon's Farm. The latter had a clear lead over the engine and seemed to be winning an impromptu race. Advancing along a straight stretch the train gained a little speed and may even have reached twenty miles per hour – perish the thought! Close to Savick Brook a family group stood next to a stile and gave us a wave before the train negotiated a right-hander and disappeared into a long cutting, which was gloriously festooned by a colourful mosaic of wild flowers. After the cutting the train emerged onto a high embankment crossing Brabiner Lane where my parents sometimes took me in Dad's old Morris 8 to watch the train crossing the overbridge. The old car complemented the overall scene while we enjoyed a picnic beside the little waterfall at Blundel Brook. From the train the familiar water tower landmark and Whittingham Hospital buildings came into view At the end of a long curvature of the track the train entered Whittingham Station, which was prominent on a high embankment and commanded a good view of the hospital's sewage farm – not a real show-stopper as tourist attractions go! The engine driver now eased off the throttle and the vigorous activity of the engine gained some respite. As the carriages clanked into the station, adorned with a glass roof, there was an opportunity to look beyond the hospital towards the picturesque Bleasdale fells.

Alighting from the train, we walked past the engine shed and around a lake in the hospital grounds. Then, after being attacked by a mute swan it was time to walk back to the railway station and experience the return journey to Grimsargh. After being serviced the engine, 'Gradwell', emerged from the shed and now seemed to be going backwards while propelling its train from the rear – though with this particular push-me-pull-you design of engine it was difficult to be sure. The lack of proper resources at Whittingham for turning the engine once led to two curious bovine milkers aspiring to become roast sirloin after the cows had wandered onto the track near to Dixon's farm; clearly something had to be done to improve the technology. Somebody decided that the driver really needed a clear view of where he was going. The question was, how do you get the engine to gain its rightful place at the head of the train without the luxury of a turntable? All was revealed when the engine crew produced a Hoover-like contraption and pushed the three carriages along the track – this could only happen on the Whittingham Railway – where the superior technology had replaced hauling the carriages into the siding with a cable or simply with the engine propelling the carriages all the way back to Grimsargh. On this most basic of railway lines it seemed to be a question of making use of limited resources which all added to its character and charm – I enjoyed it, but I am not too sure about the cattle!

About a hundred yards to the east of Dixon's Farm the Whittingham Hospital Railway line bisected the farmland. Two level crossings provided access to fields where cattle had to be brought across the track twice daily for milking. One dark morning a train hit two cows on the crossing which were instantly despatched to an eternal grazing land far beyond Grimsargh. Small wonder the people at Dixon's had mixed feelings about the subsequent closure of the line in 1957, that put an end to 'Puffing Billy' discharging copious amounts of black smoke. When Ada Wild was a little girl the kindly engine crew gave her a lift from Grimsargh to an unscheduled halt at Dixon's. This was not the local bus service and there can surely be few places in the country other than Grimsargh where this could have happened. No such service was provided for the gentlemen patients from Whittingham who often 'walked the line' and enjoyed a kind welcome at Dixon's. One gentleman came into the house and made himself comfortable with a cup of tea and asked if he might have a wash before walking back to the hospital. Another regular visitor was an elderly gentleman who had no known family. This lonely figure regularly walked to the 'windmill pit', where he spent many happy hours fishing before rounding off his day with a cup of tea at the farm and a two mile walk back along the track to Whittingham. Gone but not forgotten.

The local children, too, had a fondness for the train and spent their days travelling up and down the line. When they became teenagers they caught the last train of the day on New Year's Eve to attend the Whittingham Ball held in the hospital's ornate and commodious ballroom. In the early hours of the morning young Nell Noblet and Esther Rigby and friends walked back to Grimsargh, via the most direct route, which was along the track of the Hospital Railway. At that time of the night the hoot of the old steam engine's whistle was replaced by the hooting of an occasional tawny owl. The wise old owl guarded over the young ladies and its vocalisations provided them with some comfort. Many other Grimsargh people enjoyed the free rides and reminisce about watching the Christmas pantomimes staged in the ballroom or spending a summer's evening enjoying cricket matches and walking round the lake, whilst having a chat with the friendly patients and staff.

The tranquil railway scene had seen minimal change since construction of the railway began in the late nineteenth century. At the time there was considerable opposition from landowners and farmers, and internal wrangling at the hospital between the Finance and General Purposes Committee and its four-man sub-committee which had been appointed in 1884 to investigate the feasibility of a railway facility. The largest asylum in Europe had been constructed during 1873, 'out in the sticks of the Lancashire countryside' about eight miles from Preston. It was largely self-contained, but supplies – including coal – had to be drawn by horse and cart from Preston or Longridge railway station. The committee came up with an inclusive figure of £12,000 to acquire land and build 2,863 yards of track. This was to include junction facilities at Grimsargh to enable trucks to be shunted onto the proposed Whittingham line. However, the idea of through trains operating from Preston was permanently denied by the operators of the joint L & Y and LNWR companies.

Following protracted exchanges within the hospital's boardroom it was beginning to look like the whole concept of a railway was about to be sidelined. Undaunted, the sub-committee decided to quash internal dissent by applying the full might of the law and in January 1885, the Annual Sessions at Preston presented a bill to Parliament. The proposals were now to be officially acknow-ledged under the title of the proposed 'Whittingham Tramway' and the committee correspondingly became the 'Tramway Sub-Committee'. The so-called tramway was to carry goods to Whittingham and the first sod was cut at Grimsargh in 1887. Traffic began running on the line in 1889 and the permanent way became a permanent feature of the landscape for around seventy years.

When the railway first opened it carried only goods as Smith recounts. "The steam tram to Whittingham Asylum starts from Grimsargh; but costly as the venture has proved to the county ratepayers, the line is not allowed to be utilised by the public

Whittingham Station; a terminus station with a single platform and overhead glass canopy.
Courtesy of Mr T. Heginbotham

for local traffic – a state of affairs which doubtless the County Council will at once rectify".[9] The opportunity to carry passengers was soon mooted and accommodation was first provided for them in six acquired four-wheeled carriages, including a vintage North London Railway third class carriage. During 1921 a 523-yard extension of the line was made from Whittingham's single line station platform. It was for goods trains only and crossed landscaped lawns and gardens, terminating at the buffers beside the new boiler house.

Throughout its entire life the Whittingham Railway only aspired to four hard-working steam locomotives which should have been pensioned off years before their eventual demise. The hospital purchased the first locomotive with a wheel arrangement of 0–4–0 and works number 304, from Andrew Barclay & Sons in 1888 complete with two goods vans to make up its train. A second Barclay locomotive with a slightly different wheel arrangement of 0–4–2 joined its sister engine on the line in 1904. They were identified as County Mental Hospital One and Two and lasted until 1947 and 1952 respectively. When 304 was scrapped in 1947 a replacement engine was urgently required. This was before nationalisation, when many veterans of the 'iron road' were being permanently laid up. Approaches to the companies were made for a suitable machine and only the Southern region responded with an 0–4–2 DI Stroudley No. 2357. The engine even had its southern nameplate of Riddlesdown and should really have been destined for a transport museum. This engine was older than the line, having been manufactured in 1886 for the London, Brighton and South Coast Railway. Not surprisingly it was the sole survivor of its class when purchased by Whittingham for £750 in 1947 for immediate operational use. The engine came north, where it was duly renamed 'James Fryar', in honour of the Chairman of the hospital's visiting committee. Amid clouds of steam Alderman Fryar screwed a nameplate to the engine and took his committee for a ride to Grimsargh. A comment from the engine crew about his namesake's performance was, "all right on the straight, but she grinds a bit on the bends".

A replacement for the second Barclay locomotive was sought in 1952 and a driver was instructed to 'go to Bolton Gas Works to pick up an engine'. The fourth and final engine was a 100 h.p. Sentinel steam locomotive resembling a diesel but with copious amounts of white smoke and still resplendent with the emblem of Bolton Corporation. Not quite so far away from home as its predecessor, this engine named 'Gradwell', works number 9377, operated the service during the last five years of the railway's existence.

The little engine 'Gradwell' is draped with bunting at Grimsargh Station in preparation for the last journey in May 1957. Driver Gilbert Wright is on the footplate together with his crew.
Photograph courtesy of Mrs Frances Wright

In its heyday the train carried about 3,000 passengers a week and more than 12,000 tons of freight per annum. There were twelve daily passenger trains operating in each direction, the first leaving Whittingham at 6.10 a.m. and the final departure from Grimsargh at 9.35 p.m. There was no Sunday service. Despite the withdrawal of passenger services on the Longridge line in 1930 the Whittingham line continued to carry passengers and freight but during the war the infrastructure degenerated and the track had to be re-laid as late as 1947. Passenger numbers began to decline with the provision of a direct bus service from Preston to Whittingham. In its hospital engine shed 'Jimmy Fryar' had been laid up with severe internal boiler problems, preceding an ignominious funeral in 1956. To replace the engine was not conceivable and it was with some sadness and reluctance on the part of the Whittingham Hospital Management Committee that a decision was made to close the line from January 1957. In the event of the petrol crisis of that year the line was given a reprieve but this only stalled the inevitable closure. In June the engine 'Gradwell' was draped with bunting for a ceremonial last run for VIPs and carried a special board in front of the boiler proclaiming its heritage – 'Whittingham Railway 1887 –1957'. There was less ceremony shortly after 7 p.m. on Saturday, 30 June 1957, for the last scheduled train to depart from Grimsargh. The small group of people who watched 'Gradwell' and its three green carriages disappear round the bends close to Dixon's Farm forever included myself, relatives of the train crew and just a few more onlookers. As the Sentinel steam engine chugged away into history a number of warning devices exploded to ceremoniously mark the end of the railway. Indeed, the memory of that hissing green snake writhing away into the sunset was a lasting one and today the memories come flooding back when I attempt to trace the railway.

Even to the trained eye, the old track-bed has almost disappeared. A few public footpaths and occupation crossings are all that is left to mark its former course. The main overbridge on Brabiner Lane has been reduced to a stone buttress and both stations have long since disappeared. The Whittingham line had become one of the last railway curiosities remaining in the country and had it survived it would have become a Mecca for railway enthusiasts from far and wide. The coming of the first railways had prompted many social changes which impacted significantly on the history of Grimsargh-with-Brockholes. Having fulfilled their function it was now time to 'bow out' and yield to the course of progress.

References

1. LRO, DDC1/1183.
2. *Preston Directory* (1840), p. 110.
3. William Dobson, *Rambles by the Ribble* (third series, 1877).
4. *Mannex Directory*, 1851.
5. 'The Preston and Longridge Railway', by Norman Parker, published by the Oakwood Press, 1972.
6. *Lancashire Daily Post*, Monday, 2 June 1930.
7. *Lancashire Evening Post*, January 1936.
8. Article in the *Railway Magazine*, April 1955, by G. Pember, B.Sc.
9. T. Smith, *A History of Longridge*.
   I am grateful for the help of Mrs Frances Wright of Longridge who was the wife of the late Gilbert Wright, the driver of the last train on the Whittingham Railway and the people of Grimsargh for sharing their personal recollections and providing photographs. I acknowledge the sources of information from the following articles featured in the *Railway Magazine*. 'The Whittingham Railway' by T.R. Perkins, April 1934; 'The Whittingham Railway' by H.C. Casserley, May 1957. Affray at Whittingham' by Norman Jones, May 1958.

Grimsargh

THE STORY OF A
LANCASHIRE VILLAGE

CHAPTER THIRTEEN

The Agricultural Landscape

T HE AGRICULTURAL LANDSCAPE of the Ribble Valley is in stark contrast to the arable plains of west Lancashire, where the best soils are to be found. The inventories that often accompanied yeomen's and farmers' wills – detailed in the appendix – and the tithe maps and schedules show that rearing livestock has mainly been the established farming practice in the Grimsargh and Ribble Valley area and important for the local rural economy. Documentary evidence indicates that land use was predominantly pasture and meadowland with some planted and arable holdings from medieval times until the early twentieth century.

In 1914 Brockholes had a fair amount of land devoted to cereal crops such as wheat and oats. During the Napoleonic and Second World Wars, agriculture was predominantly arable with the growing of oats, wheat, turnips, and potatoes to ameliorate national food shortages and provide feed for livestock. Statistics from 1905 show the way in which the agricultural use of the land was then being utilised in both Grimsargh-with-Brockholes and Elston: arable 147 acres; grass 2,367 acres; woodland 251 acres.[1] The twentieth century saw a dramatic decline in the number of working farms throughout Grimsargh and Elston. At the beginning of the twentieth century the principal landowners included: 'Frederick Openshaw, Hother-sall Hall, 1,216 acres; John Mercer, Alston Hall, 482 acres; and William Cross, nephew of Viscount Cross'.[2] They managed their affairs from afar and chose not to live within the township.

It appears there is significant survival of ancient enclosure patterns in the lands of Grimsargh Parish, although more modern land use has sometimes obscured the patterns. Enclosure of land began in earnest in the sixteenth and seventeenth centuries and continued into the nineteenth century. The Enclosure Act meant redundancies for many people lower down the farming scale who lacked title to the land. Copies of all plans and schedules were lodged with the Clerk of the Peace in each county. Enclosure had a significant impact on the landscape, with hedgerows

appearing in the lowlands and stone walls dividing the upland areas. The familiar but disappearing hedgerows are representative of significant periods in history including the beginning of commercial farming during the Georgian and Victorian periods but also having their origins in the medieval, Tudor and Stuart periods. Many of these valuable wildlife refuges have been dug up in line with policies emanating from Europe, though recent legislation aims to redress their indiscriminate removal.

Archived indentures included in the Hoghton deeds reveal clues as to tithe procedures, the nature of farming and the extent of agricultural land during the Tudor and Stuart periods:

> On the 15th August 1579, Richard Hoghton of Parkehall, gent. farmer of the parsonage of Preston leases for £10 to Leonard Hoghton of Grimsarghe the tithes of corn, grain and straw growing upon a tenament in Grimsargh in grantees's tenure, for 40 years at a peppercorn rent. (LRO, DDHO/653)

> 29th August 1615, Writ to the sheriff directing Richard Houghton Kt and Bart. To hold Thomas Cosson to fulfil the covenant made between them concerning 3 messuages, 3 tofts and 3 barns, gardens, orchards and 40 acres land, 20 acres meadow, 40 acres pasture, 6 acres wood, 10 acres moor, 10 acres bog and 100 acres grazing for all kinds of cattle in Grimsargh and to summon Thomas to appear before the Justices. (LRO, DDHO/654).

To the north of Preston Roa between Grimsargh Reservoi and Dixon's Farm (left) are fields of seventeenth and eighteenth century enclosure The fence represents the course of the Whittingham Railway, and is set against a background of Bleasdale and Parlick Fell.
Author's collection

OPPOSITE
Part of the huge 1841 Tith Map showing Grimsargh with Brockholes. The village centre and Longsight Lane can be clearly seen. Each fie was numbered and correspondingly named in the schedules.
Courtesy Lancashire Record Office/Diocese of Blackburn and the G. Loxham, Vicar of Grimsargh

Tithe Maps

The Agricultural Landscape

The Tithe Maps and Tithe Apportionment Schedules produced between 1836 and 1852 yield a fascinating cartographic insight into nineteenth-century parish agriculture as well as other elements of local history. Two maps covered the former townships of Elston (1837) and Grimsargh-with-Brockholes (1841).[3] An examination of the tithe maps and apportionment schedules reveals the names of landowners and occupiers, description of land and premises, the field names including the standard measure of acre, rod and perch, the state of cultivation and the amount payable by the occupier to the vicar and landowner.

The Biblical practice of tithing was enforced by law to provide for one-tenth of a person's accumulated produce and livestock being paid to the rector of a parish. Copies of all plans and

schedules were lodged with the Bishop of each Diocese, the incumbent of each parish and the Tithe Commissioners.

An apportionment rent charge in lieu of tithes payable to the Vicar of Grimsargh, included a miscellany of livestock and agricultural implements:

> For one cow and calf – three half pence; two cows – 6*d*.; 3 cows – 9*d*.; 4 cows; – 1 shilling; 5 cows – ¾*d*.; a plough – 1*d*. a half plough – one halfpenny; a swarm of bees – 1*d*.; a foal – 1*d*.; wool and lambs per score 2*d*.; every seventh goose – 8*d*.

As the old tithe barns filled to capacity the assessment and collection of animate and inanimate tithes was becoming impractical during the nineteenth century. After all, the selling of a swarm of bees and the odd gaggle of geese could not afford to interfere with the rector's pastoral duties in the Parish.

Changes in agriculture and the introduction of new crops led to an increase in tithe disputes and the introduction of the Tithe Commutation Act of 1836. Tithe payments were converted from payment by produce to payment against rent value for every property and piece of land linked to the prevailing price of corn. Surveyors drew up tithe maps and tithe apportionment schedules showing all land within a parish upon which a tithe payment was due. The tithe maps showed land use and the shape of individual fields which were numbered and correspondingly named in the schedules.

The nature of land use is often contained in the several hundred names which were given to the fields in the townships of Elston and Grimsargh-with-Brockholes. Their origin had a meaning to those living and working on the land and gives local historians a better clue to the nature of farming practice, the use of land and the variety of crops grown, the landscape, where buildings once stood, and the establishment of local craft and industries. Some of the names are self-explanatory – a logical explanation for 'long meadow' would be a field of greater length than those within the immediate locality. The origin and derivation of other names were often restricted to particular counties and parishes and where appropriate I have sought clarification by referring to John Field's book on *English Field Names*. The study of field names is fascinating and reveals many more clues reflecting the history of Grimsargh. As it would be tedious to refer to every field I have selected a sample of interesting names.

The 1837 Tithe Map for the Township of Elston indicates both pasture and arable holdings. North of Marsh House Farm two large meadows had been allocated the names 'Flax Croft' and 'Flax Field'. John Field records that the name 'Flax Croft' was unique to Elston and is explained as land on which the flax was grown. The crop was widely grown in the seventeenth and eighteenth centuries, but had declined considerably just before the beginning of the nineteenth century. 'Brick Kiln Field' comprised pasture and was situated alongside Elston New Hall Farm. The name provides a clue to earlier land use when clay was dug as near the building site as possible and kilns were found in many places. The large field situated between The Hermitage, Elston Lane and Longsight Lane was named 'French Meadow'. Here, John Chadwick of The Hermitage paid out the princely sum of 5s. 1d. to Ellen Cross and 7d. to the Vicar.

To the north of Longsight Lane only two reservoirs had been built at the time of the detailed 1841 Tithe Map covering Grimsargh-with-Brockholes. The field adjacent to the reservoir was called 'Smithy Meadow' suggesting land containing or adjoining a forge. At Grimsargh there were plenty of meadows and one of them was named 'Bent Hill', derived from land where the bent grasses grew. This grass is derived from the Agrostis genus of grass and was not considered to be good for grazing. Some field names were prosaic and others romantic with good wholesome-sounding names such as 'Wheat Cake'. By contrast the field name 'Greedy Guts' had nothing to do with eating too many wheat cakes and translated it meant 'land needing much manure'. 'Wheat Cake' was used in the Grimsargh, Greenhalgh and Nateby areas and was a fanciful local field name meaning 'productive land' The productive land in question was situated near the present Three Mile Cross Farm where land use on the tithe map was described as arable. At Red Scar an irregularly shaped field was given the name 'Ranglet', and 'Saw Pit Field' had connotations with nineteenth-century timber exportation. In the days before power saws a two-handed saw would have been laboriously worked in a pit, specially designed for the purpose. Within the hamlet of Brockholes two arable fields are shown below Boilton Wood bearing the name 'Spa Meadow' and 'Spa Field' and owned by Ellen Cross of Red Scar. The existence of land containing or adjacent to a medicinal spring is in all probability a reference to the 'spa well', which was known to Ellen's son, Colonel William

Cross. Close by 'Older Field' was indicated as pasture meaning of 'land on which the alder trees grow'.

The mosaic of fields throughout the township shown on the Tithe Map also included the names of Great and Little Pricton; Barn Field; Potato Croft; Higher Scar Meadow, Cringles, Further Cowhey; Further Boneyworth and many more intriguing names. The field name 'Turf Moss' gives one last insight into the historic nature of the land and diversity of the work carried out when the last peat beds of the valley were being exploited. It also marks the beginning of the Grimsargh Story and tells of ancient forests, and of subsequent ravages of water flooding the valley of Brockholes, thousands of years before it was drained and transformed into a fertile farming area of green fields. I would not be at all surprised if this particular 'good old fossil fuel' had provided a beautiful aroma and welcoming glow within the commodious grates of Red Scar and Higher Brockholes, but alas, I will probably never know.

When they left their firesides the men working out in the pasture and meadows of Grimsargh had to provide Easter dues for the Vicar in accordance with the schedules:

A man and his wife, six pence one halfpenny; a boarder, one penny; a communicant, one penny; a single housekeeper, five pence; a tradesman not a housekeeper, five pence; a widow, a widower, no housekeeper, three pence.

Of Farms and Farming People

At a time when reclaiming the wastes and enclosure were gaining considerable momentum, older sometimes half-timbered farmsteads were replaced by new farms built of stone as finances allowed. In Tudor times Grimsargh farming people were living in the farmsteads of their medieval forefathers, exemplified by today's Grade II listed buildings of Alston Old Hall or the squalid two-bedroomed former house with integral barn and shippon, thirty metres north of Clarkson's Fold Farm at Cow Hill, Haighton. Alston Old Hall is today a private dwelling situated in an elevated position on the banks of the Ribble below Alston Hall College and just within the former township of Alston. Expert opinion suggests certain features could date back to 1290, but beyond conjecture the restored farmhouse is a superb example of medieval architecture. The Clarkson's Fold Farm building is alongside a

Grimsargh

THE STORY OF A
LANCASHIRE VILLAGE

OPPOSITE
The outbuilding at Clarkson
Fold Farm and a close-up of
the original cruck trusses. Still
in use today, this
seventeenth-century building
is Grade II listed.
Author's collection

public footpath, and when seen its historical significance is instantly perceived. This small post-medieval farmstead probably housed farm workers as well as the family. Nowadays it is used as an outbuilding, store and shippon for up to five cattle. Inside three full cruck wooden trusses support the high pitched roof and gable. The house has an intermediate partition of timber framing and wattle and daub. Unfortunately the remains of the thatching have now been covered by a corrugated sheet.

Close to Clarksons's Fold is Old Hall and an account of the origin of its staircase is worthy of mention as it came originally from the rebuilt Samlesbury Lower Hall. When the hall fell into decay the staircase was put in an outbuilding. There Mr H. Mallot, of Grimsargh House and Managing Director of Horrocks Crewdon's, Preston, found it being used as a perch by the hens. Mr Mallot purchased the historic wooden structure and built it into Horrocks' offices in Stanley Street, Preston. When the offices were demolished Mr Harry Horrocks bought the staircase and installed it in Old Hall.

Chapel House Farm latterly belonged to the Church Commissioners and was one of nine working farms situated within close proximity of Elston Lane. It is now a private dwelling and was sympathetically restored during 1997. A section of wattle and daub was exposed from beneath the plasterwork and now makes an interesting framed feature. The true date of construction remains an enigma but there are indications of late medieval construction methods. On the first floor of the east wing there is evidence of a chapel which can be ascertained by indentifying where the reredos used to be by the position of holes in a wooden beam.

Circumstantial evidence would suggest that the name Chapel House could be associated with papists registering small estates at Elston in 1717 and that it was possibly a seat of recusancy. Chapel House was situated close to the site of an ancient cross in a hedgerow, alongside an old footpath, which was later removed and has now disappeared. Mr Clegg, the owner of Chapel House in 1958, is quoted: 'A large stone cross, about 4' 6'' tall, was built into the north wall of our old stone barn. This barn was rebuilt in brick 8 or 9 years ago, and the builders, breaking the cross in taking it down, did not replace it in the new walls, and the fragments disappeared.'[4]

By the sixteenth and seventeenth centuries prosperous yeomen, like John Welchman at Lower Brockholes, were acquiring the rebuilt or enlarged farmsteads of the period. Lower Brockholes Farm was built with mullioned windows and a date stone and coat of arms proclaiming 1634 over the lintel of the front door. In the Grimsargh area many farms were built, reconstructed or enlarged on existing sites as occupiers consolidated land during the eighteenth century. Greater prosperity contributed to the rebuilding of farms typical of Grimsargh including Wood Top Farm (1724), School House Farm (1726) Dixon's Farm (1736), Three Mile Cross Farm (1756), Elston Old Hall Farm (1867) and Grimsargh Hall Farm (1773). Some yeomen and farming families were domiciled in the same farms over several generations and it is perhaps not surprising that several Grimsargh families, particularly of the farming community, are still interrelated. Occupiers often left souvenirs and original artefacts concealed within the structure of the building. Wood Top Farm revealed secrets of its origins when it was converted into a private dwelling and the boot of a three-year-old child was found entombed within the original staircase. This old boot has preserved the historical essence of the building and is today proudly exhibited as a permanent feature.

Boots were made for walking and the effects of enclosure meant that some people were more geographically mobile and seeking pastures new. A percentage of the work force was now to harvest the 'fruits of the Industrial Revolution' with higher wages and their own 'two up, two down' houses in the cotton towns of Lancashire. The exodus into industry began on a large scale in the 1760s and continued throughout the nineteenth century when farm workers including the lesser farmers – the husbandmen and cottagers – left the smaller farms of Grimsargh seeking higher wages and improved social conditions elsewhere. The population of the farming communities of Grimsargh and Elston increased in absolute terms between 1801 and 1821. Mechanisation of the land occurred around 1870 with newly introduced mechanical reapers and steam traction engines. This coincided with further erosions of the workforce of the small farming community of Elston where the population dropped from 53 in 1871 to 43 by the time of the 1881 census.

Two small farms in the hamlet of Elston are now private dwellings and are Grade II listed buildings. The interior of Elston Cottage has been tastefully renovated incorporating the original beams and stout joists in the lounge and the original stone fireplace in the kitchen. Elston Cottage has been home to generations of the farming community and doubtless witnessed many comings and goings since it was built in 1780. It has has been occupied by Mr and Mrs E. Livesey since 1971. The couple are keen gardeners and their beautiful terraced garden of one acre incorporates the original well, constructed in 1780.

Place House Farm is a good example of a late seventeenth-century farm and is approached from Elston Lane by an attractive winding drive descending the valley escarpment. In farming days it was let to Mr James Eccleston who moved into Place House in 1942. Within the farming environment of Place House, young Jim Eccleston learned a lot about his trade from his father and these newly acquired skills were subsequently put into practice when the family moved from Place House Farm to Elston Old Hall farm, in 1966. Elston Old Hall Farm was built in 1767 and to this day Jim Eccleston carries on the traditions of his ancestors.

The road to Elston forks at the top of the steep hill and along the road to the right, just to the west of Place House, is Elston New Hall Farm. Alan Coar is the latest family descendant to carry on the dairy farming tradition at New Hall, where three generations of the Coar family have farmed since grandfather, Edward Coar, moved to New Hall in 1935. Edward's son, another Edward, took over in 1973 and Alan took over completely from his dad in 1995. Both the Old Hall and New Hall farms were advertised as separate lots in the 1955 auction. Most of the farming land around Elston is in the ownership of the Church Commissioners and the farmers at Elston Old and New Hall farms manage 400 and 280 acres respectively of countryside adjoining the Ribble and woodland areas. The farming legacy of Elston is now restricted to only three working farms. The third operational farm, Salisbury House, Elston Lane, has been farmed by John Cowell for over

Long-eared bat. In 1959 Elston cottage was occupied by Mr Bill Peters, his family and a colony of long-eared bats, which were photographed by Geoff Tyrer of the *Lancashire Evening Post.*

The Agricultural Landscape

The bridal party outside Three Mile Cross Farm in 1924 with bride and groom, Richard and Margaret Nelson (centre). The farm had been handed down by Richard's father who moved to Grimsargh from Coventry in 1897. Mrs Gladys Hundziak (née Nelson) was born in 1925 and has lasting memories of life on the farm, especially when the whole family escaped death by inches when a German bomb fell outside the back door.

Courtesy of Mrs G. Hundziak

sixty years. This former dairy-farmer-turned-beef-farmer has been a part of the glory days of farming, whilst witnessing the more recent downward spiral in the industry.

The name of Cowell has been synonymous with farming in the Grimsargh area for many years and today interrelated families farm three farms at Roman Road, Three Mile Cross and Salisbury House Farms. In tracing his own ancestral roots, Philip Cowell of Three Mile Cross Farm recounted that William and Alice Cowell took over the nearby Roman Road Farm in 1902. Their youngest son, Harold, became the last tenants of the Cross family when he took over from the Nelson's at Three Mile Cross Farm in 1942. In 1986 Philip and Nellie Cowell became the present owners of Three Mile Cross. Philip continued the farming traditions whilst Nellie became headmistress of Grimsargh St Michael's Primary School until her retirement in 1997. Three Mile Cross Farm has a plaque with the date 1756 and letters bearing reference to the original name. Richard and Margaret Nelson married in 1924 and farmed here as tenants of the Cross family up to 1942.

Tractors had little effect until the twentieth century although there were many earlier technological developments. It is perhaps quite ironic that a 1902 Burrell steam traction engine named 'General Buller', number 2153, has now returned to Grimsargh. In

pre-tractor days the General used to work in the fields of Grimsargh and played its part in threshing the grain, whilst contracted
out to many local farms. However, it sought pastures new and
was preserved as a fine example of its type near Thetford, Norfolk.
In 2001 it was advertised for sale and was purchased by the Cowell
family at Three Mile Cross Farm who welcomed the General's
homecoming. Both Philip and John Cowell can remember the
engine from the days when they both attended the old Grimsargh
Parochial Church School and were taught by Miss Carbis.

During the Second World War, government guidelines meant
a percentage of farm land had to be for arable use. After the
wheat was harvested, a threshing machine driven by the General
was used. As extra manpower was needed for threshing day,
neighbouring farmers combined forces as the thresher went on a
tour of all the farms in the Grimsargh area. This meant a busy
time in the farmhouse kitchens with the ladies doing extra cooking
for the enlarged workforce and many mouths to feed. Ada Wild
of Dixon's farmhouse was a stalwart member of this team and
was well acquainted with the Iron General. While performing at
the sharp end on the home front and long before semi-retirement,
he clanked across her verdant land with intermittent hisses and
puffs, thus completing the pastoral scene of a bygone age.

Today Dixon's Farmhouse is a Grade II listed building situated
in the parish of Grimsargh close to the boundary with Haighton.
Above the front porch with its panelled pilasters attached to the
wall and moulded pediment above is a date stone panel with the
year of construction given as 1736. It was in 1857 that Richard
Mason leased Dixon's, a 94-acre mixed farm of cattle, pigs and
poultry. In 1889, his son, also Richard Mason, took over a twenty-
one-year lease, paying a yearly rent of £180 and in 1901 he bought
the farm. The farm is still farmed by Mrs Ada Wild and by
the fourth generation, Richard Mason, together with two fifth-
generation nephews.

Ada Wild can remember the days when milk was poured
directly from churns into the customer's jug. Dairy produce was
taken into Preston by pony and trap and a herdsman drove the
cattle into town to be sold on the open market. In the 1920s the
pony and trap was replaced by the first van and the large milk
churns gave way to milk bottles. Meanwhile three beautiful shire
horses maintained something of rural traditions as they continued
to haul all the carts and farm machinery.

Electricity and mains water supplies were installed at the isolated farm around 1945, bringing an end to milking by hand, as well as paraffin lamp installations and cooking on the oven by the side of the coal fire. Prior to this major breakthrough, a well had to be utilised for domestic household supplies and water for the cattle was pumped by a landmark windmill from a pond which was known locally as the windmill pit. It was as late as 1948 that the first Ferguson tractor was purchased and the beasts of burden took a well-earned retirement. Dixons' motley assortment of live-stock was reduced to cattle in 1950 when it became solely a dairy farm and a few years later the milk was sold direct to the Milk Marketing Board and collected by bulk tanker.

Close to the modern St Michael's primary school and tucked away between modern dwellings is School House Farm on Preston Road. This building could easily be overlooked by even the most discerning observer of Grimsargh's history. The aptly named School House Farm was originally a 'Dame School', built in 1726 and the forerunner of Grimsargh Parochial Church School of 1809. At the farm milking was done twice a day by hand and delivered round the village by a lady known as Bessy. The milkman's round was once sacrosanct and the concept of supermarket milk in plastic bottles unheard of. Originally a few farm maidens, including Bessy, used to go out to their customers 'kitting' or distributing the milk with a five-gallon swing can and ladle.

Acquired by the Cross Family, School House and Pinfold Cottages were offered for sale when the freehold farms, land and cottages comprising the estate were auctioned in 1907. The agent described them respectively as Lot 3: situate in Grimsargh, comprising house, outbuilding and closes of land, containing 22a 1r 18p and occupied by Mr Robert Mason, and Lot 4: three cottages and the land occupied therewith, on the East side of the Preston and Longridge highroad, and opposite School House Farm, occupied by Mr Beesley and others, containing 38 perches or thereabouts. Under private ownership School House continued to be used as a farm until 1981, when it became the home of Mr and Mrs Meeson. Close to School House, Fred Wilkinson processed his milk at Nook Farm, said goodbye to 'kitting' and the horse and cart and got himself a van. Fred delivered over a wide area and for many years it was the cream off his pinta that provided early morning sustenance for our resident pair of blue tits.

Church House Farm was typical of the early eighteenth century farms that were built in the Grimsargh area. Today the old farm is a private dwelling which preserves the essence of rural Grimsargh. It may be reached along a picturesque drive lined by eighteen lime trees and is still surrounded by a green oasis of fields close to St Michael's Church. An integral part of the historical package is a large orchard, where enthusiasts pay homage to the dwindling number of traditional farm orchards and the unique Proctor's apple tree said to have originated in the Longridge area.

The present owner, Graham Jones, has no explanation for mysterious occurrences and other paranormal activities at Church House. The farm has clear associations with St Michael's Church and hence the name Church House. Before St Michael's Vicarage was built in 1824, a room was used by visiting clergy, who used to ride up from Preston on Sunday mornings to take church services. The Misses Cross of Red Scar used to walk to the morning service at Grimsargh Church and bring a packed lunch. Between services they spent their time at Church House and taught at Sunday School in the afternoon.

Out in the fields a couple of wonderful shire horses would be hauling the plough. The puzzle of a present-day tombstone for one of the shires show that it was lovingly cared for by a previous occupier of the farm and buried on-site.

Church House Farm was offered for sale by the Cross Family in June, 1907, and described as comprising house, outbuilding and

Grimsargh

THE STORY OF A
LANCASHIRE VILLAGE

closes of land, containing 36 acres, 1 rod and 29 perches or thereabouts, occupied by William Beesley. Farming operations continued for another sixty years. The property and land became subject to compulsory purchase in the 1960s, when many farms in the area ceased production and were demolished. Farmer Croft and his family were the last occupiers before Church House was reprieved and subsequently purchased as a dwelling by a Miss Mary Pegge who bred Arab horses and loved all wild creatures. Today Graham and Gina's two pet donkeys have succeeded Mary Pegge's stallions in the field next to the church and continue to preserve the rural tranquillity of the village and the essence of open countryside.

Throughout the Grimsargh and Elston area many operational farms have ceased production and been converted to dwelling houses while others have been enlarged and amalgamated to maintain viability. Between the old Longridge railway line and the Preston to Longridge road eastwards to Alston there were ten working farms in 1965 employing twenty-eight people. In 2002 only Daniel's Farm and Sudell's Farm survive as working farms, employing a workforce of six. Down in the valley at Brockholes, Lower Brockholes Farm has endured centuries of change. The Brockholes seat of the ailing farming industry survives as the last bastion of farming and a historic reminder of the former hamlet.

Higher and Lower Brockholes are described in *The Victoria County History*, volume 7, page 112:

Higher Brockholes, now a farm house, stands on low ground near

Two of Miss Mary Pegge's lovely horses – Blue Moon and filly – at Church House Farm.
Photograph N. Carbis collection

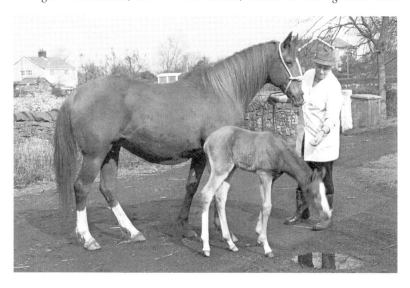

197

the Ribble, below Red Scar. The river here flowing in a south easterly direction on the east side of the house, the front of which faces south. It is a long, low, stuccoed building very much modernised, but retaining for the most part its grey slated roof and some portions of its original timber framing. The timber construction showing externally at the back. The house, however, is architecturally uninteresting except for a portion at the east end now disused. This is a good example of seventeenth-century black and white work on a stone base, with overhanging upper floor and gable. The work is simple in detail, consisting of the structural framework filled in with straight and diagonal pieces and quatrefoils. The interior has been almost entirely modernised, but contains old oak stairs and thick oak doors. A carved oak panel bears the date of 1643 and the initials R.E.A. probably those of Robert Elston and Ann his wife.

Lower Brockholes is now a farm house, positioned close to the bend of the Ribble near Brockholes Bridge, and facing south east towards Samlesbury. It is a small two-storey building, having been modernised and the exterior covered with roughcast. The windows are modern, but the roof retains its grey stone slates, and the north wing, which has a separate gabled roof at right angles to that of the rest of the house, preserves its old timber construction above the ground floor, though much of the timber has been removed. There is a wide-open gabled porch of two stories over which is a stone dated 1634, with the initials and arms of Francis Bindloss.

Mr Joseph Wright and his wife Alice (née Cowell) became the last occupiers of Higher Brockholes in 1926. They traditionally farmed this beautiful section of Ribblesdale for over fifty years. After they had moved out a fire brought dereliction and an undetermined future to the ancient farmstead. Its fate was decided in August 1979, when Higher Brockholes, which had passed unscathed through the turmoils of Civil War and two World Wars, met an undignified end and was reduced to a pile of rubble.

Today Lower Brockholes farm is the seventeenth-century Grade II listed home of Mr and Mrs Leonard Redmayne, where beef farmer Leonard owns about eighty acres. An earlier occupant, John Welchman, yeoman farmer at Lower Brockholes, died suddenly on 7 November, 1693. The splendidly detailed inventory of his goods and chattels is reproduced in the appendix. The first item includes wheat, oats, beans, barley, rye and hay to the value of £136 – an astonishing amount in those days, perhaps enough to supply the whole of Preston. Other items including

OPPOSITE
At Higher Brockholes Farm the haymaking wagons and shire horses hauling the plough in the pastoral countryside of yesteryear were replaced by tractors and trailers. The picture at the bottom shows the vista before the demolition of the house. Today the former hamlet is the site of extensive gravel workings known as Brockhall Quarry, and has been divided by the M6 motorway.
Courtesy of Phillip Cowell

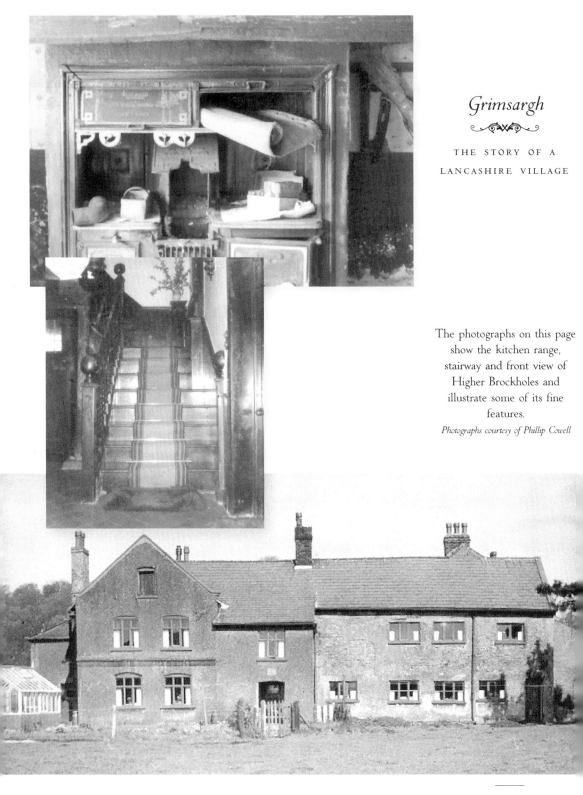

Grimsargh

THE STORY OF A LANCASHIRE VILLAGE

The photographs on this page show the kitchen range, stairway and front view of Higher Brockholes and illustrate some of its fine features.

Photographs courtesy of Phillip Cowell

two guns, a crossbow and a pistol, contrast with an inventory of basic household items and provide us with clues to his lifestyle.

The date 1634 over the porch probably belies the fact that parts of the building are of earlier construction. Three much-eroded badgers carved in stone are fading away into oblivion just like memories of a bygone age and a picturesque riverine landscape. It also serves as a reminder that badgers have for centuries made their brockholes or setts in the steeply wooded escarpments and that the first known family to reside in the locality was known as Brochole way back in 1212.

Long gone are the corncrakes, ancient farmsteads, and lush meadows of the annexed Brockholes with their appropriately named fields – Grey Bank, Margaret Acre, Boat-field, Holme, Eases, Oldhouse, and Brewhouse – and more is the pity! Long before mechanisation and the first traction engines the pastoral scene would have been complemented during haymaking time with a workforce armed with swishing scythes and plenty of muscle and energy. Labourers digging drainage ditches and search-ing for natural land resources occasionally unearthed archaeological artefacts from deep below the surface of the waste. A natural treasure was marl, lime-rich clay, which was present throughout Grimsargh-with-Brockholes.

The Agricultural Landscape

Lower Brockholes Farm. Over the main door are three badgers carved in stone.
Author's collection

During the seventeenth century farmers found that the lime spread on the fields could reduce the soil's acidity and aid fertility. However, local farmers abandoned marl as commercial lime dropped in price and the economic viability of the ponds diminished through higher labour costs. Many marl pits are shown on the first edition Ordnance Survey maps of the 1840s and 1850s, outlining the unspoilt and pristine landscape of the Ribble valley during the reign of Queen Victoria. By contrast modern Ordnance Survey maps show that housing developments have obliterated many of the old marl pits. Sadly, any surviving ponds have often become rubbish dumps or a source of conflict between developers and conservationists. Current conservation priorities lean towards the management of these surviving ponds for wildlife, whilst their historic origins should not be forgotten.

The scenario of the plough and the dogcart eventually gave way to modern tractors, farm machinery and motor cars and new roads. A wooden bridge across the Ribble replaced the ferry when a new road was built in 1824. A stone bridge constructed in 1861 (on the A59) linked Preston with Blackburn. Brockholes Bridge was more familiarly known as Ha'penny Bridge owing to a toll of one halfpenny being levied to all pedestrians crossing over it, though there were those that did not want the new road and river crossing.

The road proposals were at first opposed by the landowners and farmers of Brockholes who were evidently not of the 'free trade' fraternity. The indigenous population sensed competition from the farmers of Samlesbury insofar as the new super highway would give them the means of competing with them by supplying milk and butter to Preston. This must have been serious business for they went to the length of petitioning Parliament against the Bill. However, their contention met with little sympathy and the highway was built. One of the opposing factions to the new road probably resided below the steep slopes of Boilton Wood at another long-lost farmhouse known as Lower Boilton House, situated between Boilton and Brockholes Woods.

Almost a century after the A59 was reconstructed, compulsory purchase of Lower Boilton Farm would have been necessary in order to build the Preston by-pass which was opened by Harold Macmillan in 1957. Significantly the first motorway to be built in the country completely altered the tranquillity of Brockholes by cutting a broad swathe through the woodlands, burying the site

Grimsargh

THE STORY OF A
LANCASHIRE VILLAGE

An interior downstairs room of Lower Brockholes Hall has fourteenth-century style, sandstone mullion windows of two cusped lights and a quatrefoil, which suggest it may have been a chapel.
Author's collection

of Lower Boilton Farm under thousands of tons of construction material, and segmenting the area of Brockholes into two. Unlike the eight-lane carriageway of today, with its accompanying constant roar of the volume of heavy traffic, the original by-pass was of modest dual carriageway proportions and carried little traffic by today's standards.

Grimsargh Hall – The Legend
of the Rib and Cow Hill

The name Grimsargh Hall formerly related to the medieval seat described in Chapter Two. The present building known as Grimsargh Hall dates from 1773 and is situated to the south of Preston Road near Grimsargh Church. Mr Thomas Alston farmed at Grimsargh Hall for over thirty years until his sudden death in June 1895, aged 72 years. He was a successful dairy farmer and was said to be widely known and esteemed in Grimsargh and Ribblesdale.

Grimsargh Hall was Lot 6 when the Cross family sold off their estate by auction in 1907. Since 1991 the former farm has been the home and work base of Mr Ian Rankin, the company Chairman of John Turner and Sons Ltd., Building and Civil Engineering Contractors.

Externally above the door a rectangular date stone is inscribed, 'F.H.H. 1773'. Original features have bestowed Grade II listing on the property and restoration work has been carried out by Mr Rankin. The removal of plaster between the second storey and the garret revealed original oak vertical timber, which has been preserved as a feature along with original oak beams. Outside the owner aims to restore thirty acres of farmland comprising natural woodlands, meadows and hedgerows to engender a richer biodiversity. An additional twenty-four acres is managed in association with a local farmer who rents the grazing and has introduced organic farming.

A surprising addition to the inventory at Grimsargh Hall was a large bone reputed to be the rib of a wonderful cow. The story of the Grimsargh Dun Cow has captured the imagination and is associated with the locally named Cow Hill. Legend has it that in times of great famine the cow exercised her udder and prolifically filled the pails of all and sundry. The unlimited supply saved the inhabitants from death. This aroused the envy of a certain Pendle Witch who just happened to fly over on her broomstick to fully exploit the situation and milk the cow dry. The witch began to milk the cow into a sieve, which, of course, never became full. As the obliging creature tried her best to fill it her strength failed and she died (presumably of exhaustion) whereupon the witch gave out a characteristically evil chuckle and used her broomstick to fly back to Pendle. Hardwick states, 'A locality is still pointed out, named "Cow Hill", where gossips aver that, in relatively recent times, the huge bones of the said cow were disinterred" – a rib of a story if you ask me![5]

Grimsargh

THE STORY OF A
LANCASHIRE VILLAGE

The 'rib' is exhibited proudly
outside Grimsargh Hall Farm.
The plaque gives construction
of the farm as 1773.
N. Carbis collection

Sold to the Highest Bidder

During the twentieth century there were two significant sales of Grimsargh's farms and land. On Tuesday 18 June 1907 the first of these was held when the Cross family began to fragment their estate by auctioning some of their freehold farms, land, and cottages at Ribbleton and Grimsargh. It was stated that 'several of the lots have good frontage to the Preston and Longridge highway, and offer admirable opportunity for development as building land'.

On 31 October 1918 an inventory of farms and land comprising the Red Scar Estate showed that it was still a considerable holding. It is reproduced in the appendix showing details of the occupiers and names of farms, government and private valuations, the extent of land including tithe and yearly rent payable.

The Agricultural Landscape

Pinfold Cottages and schoolhouse farm were offered for sale by the Cross family on Tuesday, 18 June 1907, as lots 3 and 4 in accordance with the plan.
Courtesy of Anthony Cross

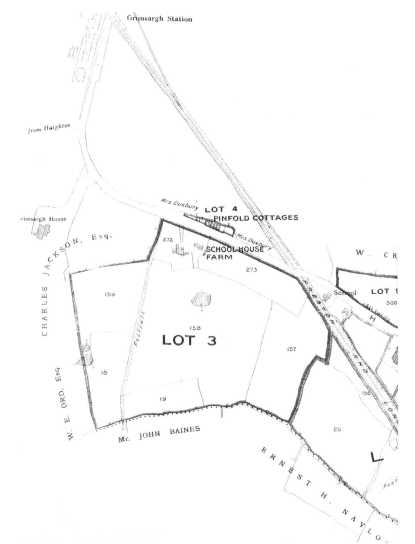

During the nineteenth century William Cross and the trustees of Bushell's Hospital at Goosnargh owned portions of the estate in Elston. In 1924 it was mostly the property of Preston cotton magnate, William Birtwistle who subsequently sold a large portion to the Church Commissioners. Mr Birtwistle was the owner of several Preston mills and at one time resided at Alston Hall, before it became a college.

According to the Barretts 1924 Guide there were no shops or tradesmen when the township of Elston comprised eleven farms. In 1955, Mr Birtwistle was firmly in control of the Alston Estate, which comprised many farms in Grimsargh and Elston and neighbouring Alston. The second 'sale of the century' took place at the Bull and Royal Hotel, Preston, on 7 October, 1955 when Mr Birtwistle instructed Messrs John D. Wood and Co., Auctioneers, to let to an established tenantry the fine agricultural Alston block of the Estate, comprising about 1,368 acres. On offer was 'the freehold of 42 lots comprising 17 well-equipped dairy farms and holdings, accommodation land and sites, nine substantial cottages, and valuable well timbered woodlands and over four miles of salmon and other fishing in the River Ribble, producing at present a gross income of £3,545 5s. 4d. per annum.

The Alston Estate was said to 'present an excellent opportunity to investors and others of acquiring a security in agricultural land of first order in a much sought-after area, with the possibility of future capital appreciation. The farms and holdings are at present in a high state of productivity and the auctioneers desire to draw particular attention to the generally exceptional condition of the residences and fixed equipment. The Estate includes much valuable timber. The auctioneers are prepared to consider reasonable requests to amalgamate lots to suit the requirements of larger investing buyers'. The outgoings included the Tithe Redemption Annuity which had been apportioned over the various lots for the guidance of purchasers only. Property and land for sale included Alston Old Hall Farm, Marsh House Farm, Chapel House Farm and many more.

Since 1955 there has been a gradual reduction of agricultural activity and the pattern of diminishing farms and farming amalgamations in the Grimsargh area has continued into the twenty-first century, where the established practice is now almost entirely beef and dairy farming with some produce grown for cattle feed. Regrettably the foot and mouth crisis is just the latest turn in

Grimsargh

THE STORY OF A
LANCASHIRE VILLAGE

The Agricultural Landscape

the downward spiral of British agriculture. Indeed in historical terms foot and mouth may be crucial in the history of agriculture. Pesticides and herbicides used on the land to spray verges have adversely affected a whole range of flora and fauna. Problems emanating from the Common Agricultural Policy of Europe need to be redressed with greater emphasis on sustainable environmentally sensitive farming and less on mass food production. Greater control of rural planning could also counter the decline of biodiversity and remnant pristine countryside still to be found around Grimsargh.

References

1. *Victoria County History*, vol. 1, p. 79. Statistics from Board of Agriculture, 1905.
2. Smith, *A History of Longridge*.
3. Tithe Map for Grimsargh (LRO, DRB 1/89); Tithe Map for Elston (LRO, DRB 1/74 and DX2048/3.
4. Lancashire County Council, Sites and Monuments Record.
5. The history of the 'Grimsargh Dun Cow' is contained in Charles Hardwick's antiquarian book of *Traditions, Superstitions, and Folklore* and Smith's *History of Longridge*, p. 216; LRO, WRW/A 1694.

CHAPTER FOURTEEN

Recollections of Moss Nook: A Vanished Grimsargh Farmstead

AT THE TIME OF THE SALE of the Red Scar Estate by the Cross family in 1907, one old farm which had seen better days was advertised thus: 'Moss Nook Cottage is a stone-built cottage north of Grimsargh Hall Farm, with bad and long access from the main road at Grimsargh School. The cottage has no water or electricity, has been unoccupied and is in a bad state of repair and unlettable. We value the property at £25 all agri-cultural. The last occupier was a farm worker'. The building's history is humble yet romantic and well worthy of inclusion as part of 'The Grimsargh Story'.

The origins of lonely Moss Nook are obscure. It is not shown on the Grimsargh maps until 1893 and at the time of the 1871 census it was occupied by Richard Dewhurst, a gamekeeper, his wife and two sons. It was then an integral part of the Red Scar Estate and Grimsargh's pleasant countryside and at that time was leased by the Cross family to tenants. Moss Nook featured in the valuations of the properties of Miss Kathleen Cross when offered for sale by Auction as Lot 8 on 18 June 1907. On 31 October 1918 it was being leased to the County Police and Mrs Annie Whiteside resided there with her policeman father, William Cadwelleder. William was also employed as the gardener for his boss, William Trubshaw the Chief Constable who resided across the fields at Grimsargh House. The tithe payable was 2s 10d and the yearly rent was £39 12s. 8d.

In her personal recollections Mrs Whiteside spoke with great affection of her childhood at Moss Nook.[1]

> When I lived there it was an old farmhouse, built of stone. The only way to reach it was across two fields, down a cart track. In wet weather we had to wear goloshes over our shoes; these we would discard on reaching the road; we would hide them under the hedge

until we returned and then slip them on again.

Open a five-barred gate, walk down a path to the front door which had a trellis porch covered with rambler roses, and into the comfortable living room. We had a big open range on which we burned huge logs in winter, as it was difficult for the coalman to come often, due to the poor access. A winding staircase led to the upstairs rooms. One bedroom would have housed four double beds, but we used it for storing apples, all laid out on paper, also onions and pears – what an aroma when the door was opened!

My bedroom had a wide window-seat; I loved to sit there and gaze out on miles of fields, hedges and trees, and to be able to touch the roses which climbed so high; to be awakened by the dawn chorus of birds; sheep baaing, contented cows lowing and our own hens and one supercilious cock crowing to show his ladies who was the boss. These memories I cherish dearly.

Although Moss Nook had been a farmhouse we only kept poultry, two rabbits for me, a dog called Ben, and a cat known as Jimmy. At one side of the house we had a well; such clear, cold water. There would be twenty or thirty bright green frogs round the well, but my father would tell us that frogs only lived near pure water.

There was a barn adjoining the house with a hayloft and this was used as a roosting place for the poultry. We had white leghorns and buff Orpingtons and Wyandots; also a very fierce cock which woke us up in the mornings with its cock-a-doodle-doo! My father had made very comfortable nest boxes lined with straw and it was my job to gather the eggs. I went groping under the warm feathers to see if there was an egg – the hens didn't seem to like it.

My father loved gardening; we always had plenty of fruit and vegetables. There was a kitchen garden, a strawberry patch, raspberry, blackcurrant and gooseberry bushes, and an orchard with apples, pears, plums and damsons. The blossom in spring was so lovely – pink, red, and white. Our friends would come to see the blossom and later to pick the fruit. The damsons were most prolific, and it was from these that my father made damson gin; a strong concoction containing more gin that damson juice, or so I thought. When everyone had picked baskets full we would finish off with a picnic on the lawn and for after, of course, there was loads of fresh fruit. Then our visitors would stagger off under the weight of their full baskets to try out the jams, jellies and wines from swapping recipes.

The front garden was a riot of sweet-smelling flowers and plants, and there is nothing to beat wallflowers, night scented stock and mignonette to this day for fragrance. On summer nights we all liked to sit out on our rustic seat and enjoy the perfume of the flowers. At haymaking time the scent of new-mown hay would be wafted on the air from the surrounding fields, adding to our enjoyment. We must have sat for hours, content to enjoy the summer evenings and to listen to the lovely song of the blackbirds – they seemed to keep very late hours compared with other birds. It must have been like a bird sanctuary at that time – we had so many birds' nests in our hedges.

In winter it was a different story. I can remember now a time when I was unable to go to school. This was no hardship to me. The view from all our windows was like a Christmas card – pure driven snow – only the footprints of birds, rabbits, or a vole, the church spire, and a few cottages in the distance. What lovely winter evenings we had if our friends ventured out to see us. We had a piano and my mother played quite well, and we would all gather round to sing. My father liked to render 'If you were the only girl in the world' and the popular tunes I remember were 'Tea for two', 'One Alone' and excerpts from 'The Merry Widow. Lots of harmonising, whether good or bad, no one worried. There was always a huge log fire and we would have roasted chestnuts, potatoes covered in their jackets, or toast. Even Jimmy the cat was forced to retreat from the heat of the fire. We had oil lamps, sending a soft glow over my mother's beautifully polished brasses. A copper kettle stood on the hob ready to make a warming drink, and for those who desired something stronger there were our home-made wines.

We played card games, rummy, old maid and donkey. This was a rather rough game in which one had to get four cards of one suit, then grab a bobbin and the other who didn't succeed in getting a bobbin was the donkey. There were some scratched fingers at the end

Gone but not entirely forgotten – the pile of masonry is all that is left of Moss Nook in 2001. Houses close to Ribblesdale Drive are just visible through the trees.

Author's collection

Recollections of Moss Nook

Young Vera Beesley seen here with her mum Nellie during the 1930s outside the same masonry which then constituted Moss Nook. This is believed to be the only photograph of Moss Nook.
Courtesy of Mrs V. Raby

of this game. We played Ludo and snakes and ladders, probably for my benefit.

We felt so sorry for our friends when the time came to make their departure, to have to go out of the warmth of our house into the freezing cold. No doubt they acquired an inner glow, for they never seemed to come to any harm. When we went out to church or friends we were always so glad to reach home and throw a log on to the fire. Even as we marched home we could detect that nostalgic aroma of a wood fire. To this day, if you take a walk off the beaten track in the Lake District you can discern the open fires by their spiral of smoke and the smell of wood burning.

There was one severe winter at Moss Nook, when my father was returning from work, and found a heron which had been grounded, probably due to the weather. He carried it home and found it had a broken wing, so he made a splint and with the help of my mother and me, managed to apply it. The wingspan of a heron is about 40 inches, so it was no mean task and we did not think it would survive in captivity. For days it would not eat, just stood with its head sunk on its shoulders, then mother mixed some mash she used for the poultry with some leftover fish, put it in a bowl and placed it near the heron. We were delighted when it started to feed. It was nearly six weeks before it took to the air; it never became tame, but sort of put up with us. The tamest birds, I think, are robins, and although ours only seemed to put in an appearance in winter, we always had a robin. When my father was digging the garden he would follow him and pick up the odd worm, which had been turned over in the soil. Naturally we had a barn owl from time to time and his familiar call could be heard all night.

A mention must be made about our dog Ben. He was a mixture of collie and terrier and was absolutely no good at all at protecting us. He would wag his tail at every visitor, roll over and expect to have his tummy tickled. The cock was a much better home guard. He would be out at the front gate, wings a-flutter and his squawking was so loud our dog would fly inside and guests dare not venture through the gate; my father would have to poke him with a stick to allow anyone through to the house. In the end he had to become a chicken dinner! The cat Jimmy was very much a household pet; he had a habit of fetching mice, voles and a young rabbit on the doorstep every morning. We thought it was his way of bringing a gift.

We were all very sad when we had to leave Moss Nook due to my father's work. We moved to another village but not in a house with oak beams, thick stone walls, large open fireplace, and well-rooted plants and trees like Moss Nook. This was my home. I once paid a nostalgic visit to see it again, but alas, the building had been pulled down and the surrounding fields were filled with houses and bungalows, and it was hard to tell where Moss Nook had actually been.

Pure nostalgia, reflecting the times of the early twentieth century and perhaps typical of lifestyles in a rural community like Grimsargh. Sadly, Mrs Whiteside has now passed away but in February 2002, I spoke to the last tenant of Moss Nook, Mrs Vera Raby (née Beesley). Vera Beesley was born at Moss Nook in 1932 and resided there with her mother, Nellie, until 1951. Thereafter Moss Nook degenerated into oblivion before the landscape changed dramatically with modern housing developments based on Ribblesdale Drive. Vera reflected on the loneliness of the place. There was no access road and the coal delivery man, Jim Wilkinson, had to wait for a dry day to drive his heavy wagon across the fields to reach Moss Nook. Because of its isolation, mains supplies were never installed and as daylight faded the glow of the fire and improvised candles and paraffin lamps provided minimal creature comforts. Water for domestic use was taken from an on-site well and drinking water was collected in a pail from her Uncle John Beesley who was the school caretaker and lived about half a mile away at School House on Preston Road. When Vera was in her early twenties she put on her wellingtons to walk across the wet fields to School House to change into her fashionable clothing before enjoying a night out in Preston. On returning she again changed, collected the water and trudged home to Moss Nook in total darkness.

Reference

1. Mrs Anne Whiteside was a good friend of Miss Carbis to whom she told her childhood memories of Moss Nook. I am very grateful to William Whiteside and Marian Roberts for the privilege of being allowed to record for posterity these personal recollections of bygone Grimsargh. Thanks also to the last tenant, Vera Raby, who kindly supplied the rare photograph of Moss Nook together with herself and her mum.

CHAPTER FIFTEEN

'A Lark Ascending': A Natural History Miscellany

I N 1979 THE NATURE CONSERVANCY COUNCIL (now English Nature), scheduled the Red Scar and Tun Brook woodlands a Site of Special Scientific Interest (SSSI). This was at the suggestion of the Lancashire Wildlife Trust. In the early 1980s the Trust contacted the various owners, who at that time included Preston Borough Council, the Church Commissioners, Courtaulds and the Central Lancashire Development Corporation (CLDC) in order to try and establish a nature reserve. The Trust was able to buy the land owned by Courtaulds and some of that owned by CLDC. It has licences with Preston Borough Council and the Church Commissioners to manage their land as a Nature Reserve. Being woodland it does not need much active management but alas, there have been problems with the poaching of roe deer, vandalism, pollution and despoliation of the woodlands by unlawful motorcycling and car abandonment. Luckily there are several local people who are keen to stop this vandalism, though it is not easy. Education and environmental appreciation may, in the longer term, be the answer. As a member of a committee that oversees the management of the woodlands I acknowledge the help and dedication of Dr Janet Edmunds who has made a significant contribution to the establishment of this fine nature reserve.

Boilton Wood is part of the Red Scar Nature Reserve and SSSI.
Courtesy of Mr P. Cowell

Historical references to the flora of Brockholes in 1883 are contained in Dobson's *Rambles by the Ribble*. 'In the weed, by the wayside, there grows very plentifully and very luxuriantly, the handsomest of the fern tribe, indigenous to these islands, the royal fern (*Osmunda Regalis*). In the same wood the clinging corydalis is very abundant, and is scarely to be met with elsewhere in the district. The scarce carex pseudo cyperus grows in a ditch by the side of a wood near here, and the moneywort is very abundant upon a bank near Lower Brockholes. The hemp agri‚ mony is not infrequent in wet places about the sides of the woods in both Higher and Lower Brockholes. The rare broad leaved ragwort grows by the Ribbleside beyond Red Scar and is reported also in some places higher up the stream. The whole valley about here is good ground for the botanist.'

That scene has long gone and several of the plants referred to including the royal fern are now extinct in the area. In springtime the woods are still clothed in white blossom of the gean or wild cherry and give a fine display as you come up the M6 from Junction 31. In the woods themselves, the ground is covered with a mosaic of colour. There are great swathes of fragrant bluebells contrasting with the pungent smell of clumps of white ramsons. Elsewhere early purple orchids stand proudly against the less spectacular dog's mercury and enchanter's nightshade. A profusion of the differing shades of yellow lesser celandines, golden saxifrage and primroses contrast with the beautiful spring violets and delicate white petals of wood anemone and wood sorrel.

On the river bank at Elston the first wild snowdrops bravely emerge from receding patches of snow but an isolated cluster of the rare yellow Star of Bethlehem (*Gagea lutea*) is no more. It

A baby roe deer.
Author's collection

was a strange irony that a large tree fell on the site and the ample trunk ensured that this endangered plant would never again see the light of day and henceforth be confined to the annals of botanical history. Later in the season the greater bellflower and yellow archangel may still be found at the confluence of Tun Brook and the River Ribble. This latter species is at its most northerly occurrence in Great Britain and there is also a clump of the rare green hellebore. The vanilla-like scent of sweet woodruff makes further appeal to the senses and characterises the ancient woodlands.

The trees include ash, some oak, sycamore, alder and wych elm, which has suffered much from Dutch elm disease. The understorey consists of holly, some hazel and a little field maple, a shrub that is commoner in the south on limy soil. There are several species of mammal, many species of birds, and quite a few interesting invertebrates, including the rare white letter hair-streak butterfly, which is on the wing in July and August, after the larvae have fed on the leaves and flowers of the diminishing wych elms. The speckled wood butterfly has recently expanded northwards and is now regular in the woodlands where the sup-porting cast includes an impressive list of moths: the angle shades, the snout, mottled beauty, silver ground carpet, the twin spot carpet, the barred straw, and the clouded magpie and – yes, we are still talking about moths! The oak bush cricket is a notable species associated with the woods. However, many invertebrate groups have not yet been properly surveyed. At the other extreme the mammalian contingent ranges from the timid roe deer to the diminutive common shrew.

The lead role is taken, however, by my favourite beast of the wood, 'meles meles', better known as the nocturnal badger. Over the years I have enjoyed watching the nocturnal activities of badgers in one of the vast woodlands that skirt the Ribble about a mile from my home. The glories of the place where I saw my first wild badger on 18 April 1959 still lie in quietness. On that night I described the weather conditions as mild with a slight easterly breeze and a bright half moon to provide some lighting.

At dusk in springtime the last vestige of daylight was enjoyed by a solitary vocal robin. As it wound up its rusty monotonous song cycle a 'roding woodcock', silhouetted just above the tree line, carried out its territorial flight across the wooded ravine. Quite oblivious to my presence three or four roe deer tripped through the bluebells, providing an impromptu interval, before the main performance of the evening. As the sun disappeared below the silhouettes of impressive beech and wych elm trees, standing against the skyline like guardian sentinels of the wood, twilight gave way to inky black woodland. Suddenly something rustled at the entrance to the badger's sett about twenty feet below. In eager anticipation I scrutinised the sett and was surprised that the magnified sound was only a humble wood mouse going about its business rustling the foliage. It paused for a moment on the sand like some time served maestro on his podium and then suddenly ran up the bank.

Suddenly without warning a black and white striped head appeared at the entrance, silently moving in a circular manner as it scented the night air. A tawny owl nesting in a beech tree flew by and in stringent vocal terms screamed kee wak. This seemed to convey the right message to the badger for it disappeared back into its labyrinth of subterranean tunnels. The time was 20:08 hours and I meticulously recorded the events in my notebook. At 20:10 hours the head pattern revealed a large grey grizzled back as the full form of a boar badger emerged. The endearing beast had a good scratch before it commenced to walk towards me. Suddenly it made a grunt and glanced towards the sett as if to be saying to the wife, 'It's all right lass, you can come out.' A second face appeared at the entrance and then promptly disappeared back down the hole. The boar ambled off into the murky depths of the woodland along his own well trodden path to attend to ablutions and forage for bluebells. After waiting nearly an hour with no activity I duly wrote, 'Badgers seen at last', and returned to civilisation. I have staggered out of the same wood on many occasions since and find it reprehensible that the so called sport of unlawful badger digging and baiting is still practised, for clearly it is cruel and sadistic in the extreme. Grimsargh with Brockholes contains a clear reference to its long association with badgers. For centuries they have lived in the wooded ravines of the Ribble Valley in harmony with titled landowners and successive generations of the farming community. It is tragic that this carnage is allowed to continue and one must now fear for the future of sustainable populations.

There have been isolated reports of otter sightings in recent years and it may be making a comeback to the Ribble and Hodder Valleys. It is unfortunate that the alien mink is now well

A Natural History Miscellany

established and may compete with native otters for the Ribble's chub, dace, roach, barbel, pike, perch, eels, carp, bream, gudgeon and minnows. Elsewhere ancient marl pits in the fields have been filled in and deprived waterhens, teal and reed buntings, colourful dragonflies, frogs, toads and endangered great crested newts of their natural home.

In the Grimsargh area the refreshing aerial song of skylarks ascending and dropping like a stone is now being consigned to history. Not to be outdone lapwings used to call in the same fields and performed an unsurpassed tumbling display flight. It is sad they are no longer such a quintessential element and embodiment of all that was pure in the English countryside. Charismatic species such as these are obvious metaphors for the vulnerability of our farmland birds. Nationally, skylark numbers have plunged by over a million in the past three decades and many countryside birds have declined by almost half.

Music often reflects the glories of nature and the rich tapestry of Grimsargh's countryside and wildlife has helped to inspire my own musical appreciation. Recalling a more ecologically rich countryside I am reminded of Vaughan Williams' *The Lark Ascending*, but wonder how much longer this species will be the prima donna of the fields of England. The children of Grimsargh School were motivated by Miss Carbis to take an interest in all aspects of natural history. On a calendar they meticulously recorded the dates of seeing the first emergent spring wild flowers and dates of arrival of the first swallow and cuckoo. Swallows are not so common now and whilst the occasional lowland cuckoo may still be heard the prospects of coming across a nightingale singing around Grimsargh are just about as remote as finding one singing in Berkeley Square. Since the end of the Second World War there has been a significant regional and national decline in biodiversity mainly due to the intensification and mechanisation of agriculture.

Nowadays the dearth of birds makes a compelling environmental statement. Breeding pairs of songbirds such as the song thrush are estimated to have dropped by over 50 per cent between 1979 and 1989. In the Grimsargh countryside the yellow wagtail, corncrake and yellowhammer are but a memory; while the last vestiges of nationally-important populations of threatened species including the grey partridge, skylark, linnet, song thrush, reed bunting, tree sparrow, spotted flycatcher and lapwing cling on. There is no

The corncrake, now extinct in the Grimsargh area and much of Britain.
Photograph by Steve Young

better example of loss than the catastrophic decline of the corn-crake from the fields of mainland Britain. A century ago this primitive bird was well established in the meadows of Grimsargh but has now retreated to the Outer Hebrides. Nevertheless, in 1971 I was delighted to hear the rasping of a solitary corncrake from deep within a field above Gib Holme Wood. The quail is another rare visitor to Grimsargh and in May 1996, one gave out its call sounding like wet-my-lips from fields close to Tun Brook.

The Ribble Way footpath provides good viewing of Horse Shoe Bend and the wooded valley of Tun Brook before the walker is taken across a large field onto Elston Lane and past Marsh House Farm to Ribchester. Throughout the seasons the footpath provides for an interesting and varied walk and opportunities to see flocks of fieldfare, redwing and brambling. During the Summer months the woodlands are a haven for numerous breeding species including chiffchaff, willow warbler, blackcap, garden warbler, whitethroat, lesser whitethroat, kestrel, sparrowhawk, tawny owl, little owl, woodcock, tree creeper, the rare hawfinch and all three species of woodpecker.

Nearer to home the 'dawn chorus' brings a wide variety of birds to the listener's notice. How fortunate it is that one of Grimsargh's finest songsters, the blackbird, is also one of our commonest British birds. The song thrush and robin often compete with one another at first light in spring, but the latter is vocal throughout most of the year. I still hear the murmurings of starlings and before daybreak the familiar call of a tawny owl before it goes to roost, sometimes in an ivy-covered alder, at the bottom of my garden. A skein of twenty-five Canada geese are extremely vocal as they leave their reservoir roost and seek a quiet stretch of the Ribble for the day before returning at dusk. Nowadays that Asiatic invader of the late 1960s, the collared dove makes its incessant calls in the early morning. This species extended its range across Europe from the early 1930s. The first British sighting was in Lincolnshire in 1952. It first bred in Lancashire in 1961 and is now well established in the Grimsargh area.

It is becoming increasingly evident that the copious supply of nuts fed to the resident blue, great, coal and long tail tits in turn provide bait for the increasing numbers of sparrowhawks which regularly patrol the area. This predator seems to be more common than the kestrel, which still hovers over the rough industrial land at Red Scar looking for small voles and mice. Legislation and enlightenment over the past fifty years have brought about a return of some birds of prey species to the Ribble valley. The peregrine falcon can now be seen flying over the fields of Grimsargh once again. In all probability peregrines would have been no strangers to the knights and squires of the ancient parish of Grimsargh-with-Brockholes. It is not too unusual to see a soaring buzzard over the extensive woodlands of the valley. I got my biggest surprise in August 1997, when a red kite flew from the direction of the Ribble and over my back garden. On seeing me sunbathing it twisted its long rusty red forked tail to the right and flew off east towards Bowland, and who can blame it! The variety of birds at Grimsargh is not so good as it used to be. Magpies live in my back garden all year where I have observed them devouring fledglings. Together with rogue felines and alien grey squirrels from North America, they are definitely not welcome! The raucous calls of that other member of the crow family, the rook, can no longer be heard at the former rookery in the tops of the tall beech trees lining the drive at Grimsargh House. The colourful jay hides its acorns in caches throughout the woodlands and is not such a rogue as its larger relatives.

In May flocks of whimbrel still gather in the fields of Elston and at Grimsargh adjacent to the reservoir near Dam House Farm, whilst en route from their wintering quarters in Africa to breeding grounds in Shetland and Scandinavia. On warm summer evenings the sound of a snipe tumbling to earth with vibrating spread tail feathers producing a drumming sound is no longer a part of the scene and belies the name 'common snipe'. On a beautiful December day in 2001 with the sun shining on the fells of Bowland and crisp hoarfrost adorning the trees and fields I walked the footpath alongside Savick brook. As I trampled on ice crystals a diminutive jacksnipe flew up from my feet and I was left to wonder precisely where this rare winter visitor had commenced its long migratory flight.

Grimsargh's reservoir banks consist of unimproved grasslands representative of a different era. Here is one of the biggest colonies of delightful early purple orchids in Lancashire as well as a profusion of primroses and other associated meadowland flora totalling over fifty species of wildflowers. The smaller mammalian contingent comprises of pygmy and common shrew and the ubiquitous wood mouse. At dusk noctule bats fly over the banks

Kingfisher.
By John Leedal

and are joined by Daubentons (water) bats skimming the surface of the water and pipistrelle and long-eared bats.

All three Grimsargh Reservoirs have regular flocks of Canada geese, mallard, tufted duck, pochard, widgeon, cormorant, lapwing, curlew, oyster catcher and smaller numbers of common sandpiper, meadow pipits, grey and pied wagtails, sedge warbler and reed bunting. Great crested and little grebe, tufted duck, waterhen and coot have bred in the aquatic vegetation and tawny and little owl utilise the trees lining its banks for their nest sites. During springtime a cacophony of birdsong heralds the territories of garden warbler, lesser whitethroat, willow warbler and chiffchaff. The wetlands are also acknowledged by ornithologists as a habitat for unusual passage migrants. During mid-April or early June the scarce osprey and delightful flocks of black terns have been seen flying over the reservoirs. Other vagrant visitors have included an immature long-tailed duck, a female smew, ruddy shelduck, ruddy duck, whooper swan, black-necked grebe, common scoter, black tern, brent goose, turnstone, kittiwake and a long-staying scaup. Most of these birds are migrants, stopping off for a rest, but the flash of blue provided by a kingfisher is not so irregular and is always a delight to see. During high summer vast numbers of swallows, swifts, sand martins and house martins fly relentlessly over its waters catching abundant insects and make a spectacular sight in late evening. They are replaced in winter with flocks of redwing and fieldfare from Scandinavia and mixed parties of siskin, chaffinch, goldfinch, greenfinch, long tailed tits, tree creeper and wren which may be seen from the reservoir causeway feeding on alders and in the adjacent fields.

Angling first came to Grimsargh Reservoir in 1967 when Court-aulds Angling Association obtained the lease of the three

An immature, long-tailed duck was a rare visitor to Grimsargh reservoir in 1999
Photograph by David Pye

reservoirs. At first only fly-fishing was allowed but with the closure of Courtaulds, Red Scar Anglers was constituted and coarse fishing was authorised. The Preston Water Board was grouped within the North West Water Authority in 1974 and today the reservoirs are managed by United Utilities who lease the fishing rights to the angling club. The idyllic environment is compatible with both natural heritage and recreational use and the facility is considered to be one of the best of the local fisheries. A public footpath crosses the causeway of Grimsargh Reservoir and affords good public access.

During the mid-nineteenth century Charles Dickens was a frequent visitor to Preston and is said to have gained inspiration for some of his writings there. In those days there would have been many larks ascending and his evocation of the countryside indicate evidence of early conservation awareness. Writing of Dullborough Town in *The Uncommercial Traveller* Dickens says, 'It was gone. The two beautiful hawthorn trees, the hedge, the turf and all those buttercups and daises, had given place to the stoniest of jolting roads, while, beyond the station, an ugly dark monster of a tunnel kept its jaws open, as if it had swallowed them and were ravenous for more destruction. I looked over the low wall at the scene of departed glories …' – a theme which sounds all too familiar and he was only talking about the coming of the railway.

As the EU expands in Eastern Europe, can we afford to continue to run the gauntlet of the Common Agricultural Policy? A lark ascending is a symbol of a healthy environment and their loss may symbolically herald the extinction of many birds not just from the landscape of Grimsargh but throughout Europe. Even the familiar starling and humble house sparrow are endangered. Many species face extinction in a mere instant of time of man's relentless progress and well-established track record of environ-mental damage. The flora and fauna go back long before the beginning of the Grimsargh Story and are the product of thirty million centuries and three thousand million years of evolution since life on earth began – give or take a year or two, of course!

CHAPTER SIXTEEN

Victorian and Edwardian Grimsargh-with-Brockholes

Grimsargh Reservoir

THE VICTORIAN RESERVOIRS are important as a biological site and perhaps worthy of consideration as a local nature reserve and amenity to be enjoyed by the public and local school children alike.

As we have seen, the construction of Grimsargh reservoirs and the first railway line changed the social fabric of Grimsargh in Victorian times. The reservoirs became an important water resource for Preston and in later years the Courtaulds factory, while today they are disused.

In medieval times the majority of the population, including children, drank weak beer although water from the upper reaches of the Ribble and certain springs was said to be unpolluted. Centuries later, Hewitson's *History of Preston* records the existence of a well near to Red Scar which was reputed to be medicinal in that its water cured consumption. It went by the name of 'Boilton Spa' and was in the form of a double trough at the foot of six steps. The water came out of a chalybeate spring and entered the well through the mouth of a sculpture of a human head. It has been estimated that thousands of gallons of excellent drinking water had been carried to Preston and given to the sick before the well was demolished in 1850. The stone trough and ornamental head were removed to the home of Colonel Cross at Red Scar. During the latter half of the nineteenth century water obtained from private wells was polluted and responsible for epidemic water-borne diseases including cholera, typhoid and dysentery.

Throughout Preston and its environs private resources had become inadequate to meet a growing population of 35,000 in 1831. Preston Waterworks was constituted by an Act of Parliament in 1832. The preamble to the Parliamentary Bill mentioned several springs of water or wells in the townships of Alston with Hothersall and Grimsargh-with-Brockholes and recognised the need to provide a constant supply of water into proper reservoirs and from there into the houses and premises of inhabitants. A small reservoir had been constructed at Ribbleton on the south side of Longridge Road near the junction with Gamull Lane and this was known as Fulwood Reservoir. Water from this increasingly inadequate source flowed into the Borough by means of gravitation.

Preston's population had doubled in the years from 1831 to 1851, from approximately 35,000 to 70,000 people. Progressive measures had included the abandonment of Fulwood Reservoir to be re-placed by the two service reservoirs at Grimsargh. On 1 November 1834, a contract was placed with a local stonemason – James Wilkie of Preston – to undertake construction of two storage reservoirs at Grimsargh opposite the Grimsargh Mill at a cost of £1,600 and for completion against penalty on 1 June 1835. After construction the depth at Grimsargh was increased to 12 feet and a smaller reservoir was added at the eastern end. These additions increased the total storage to 53 million gallons and covered 21.94 acres.[1]

The old Preston Waterworks Company was taken over by the Corporation of Preston in 1853. In 1857 it was proposed to construct three sets of filter beds adjoining Grimsargh Reservoir near to

A frozen Grimsargh reservoir shortly after dawn of 2002, with the moon about to sink below Dam House Farm.
Author's collection

Dam House Farm. Work on the intended filter beds was commenced but only one was completed and it is doubtful if it was ever used by the authority. In wintertime it was let to Preston Curling Club and used by local skaters, including a certain young Nick Swarbrick who gave virtuoso performances on the ice (which he told me about when I saw him at Grimsargh House in 2001 and he was then a sprightly 102 years).

At Alston Chapel and School the conditions were still primitive in 1910. The following year Father Coupe spoke of the conditions:

> There was no fresh water. The farm collected water off its own buildings. The bigger boys got 3*d.* a week for bringing two buckets of water for the teachers, from a well up Suddell's Lane. For washing their hands when necessary the boys used the brook in the lane which was dammed sufficiently to call it a well.

In 1935 the newly built Courtaulds Factory drew water from a separate pipe which was independent of the supply to Preston Borough. When the Preston and District Water Board took over in 1959 they found that Grimsargh reservoirs were becoming surplus to requirements; and this brought cessation of domestic supplies for the borough. The reservoirs continued to be a resource for Courtaulds, however, up to the closure of that factory in 1980. Grimsargh Reservoirs have now ceased to have any operational function and their use is purely recreational. The filter bed has long been filled in and the old red screening house constructed in 1909 has also disappeared.

Grimsargh Parish Council

In December 1894 the first democratically elected Grimsargh-with-Brockholes Parish Council came into being under the jurisdiction of Preston Rural District Council. The Parish Council held its first meeting on 13 December 1894. The interests of local democracy were then served by Messrs. William Blackhurst, William Dagger, Thomas Thornton, John Hothersall, and John Margerison. It was resolved that William Blackhurst be Chairman for the coming year – clearly there was important business on the Council agenda.

There were even traffic problems in Grimsargh in the early 1900s. In December 1904, the motion before the Council resolved 'That the clerk write to the railway company pointing out the delay to traffic through closing the gates on the level crossing

Grimsargh

THE STORY OF A
LANCASHIRE VILLAGE

adjoining Grimsargh Station and the measure of time taken by the collection of tickets and shunting operations on the asylum railway and that some attention be given to stop what at present is a great public nuisance'. The poor state of the main road between Ribbleton and Grimsargh School occupied Council business in November 1907, when the motion was carried that Councillor Nicholas Swarbrick (senior) should write to the Rural District Council. In June 1926, the Council presided over incidences of smoke and coal dust from the Whittingham Asylum train, as it idled in the bay platform of Grimsargh railway station. Complaints had been received about black smudges on whiter-than-white sheets floating on washing lines and the clerk was asked to write to ask those in charge to, 'fire the train up outside the station'.

The new bus companies serving Grimsargh were the Empress and Claremont bus services. At the old Preston bus station the facilities were apparently less than adequate and in May 1927 the motion was carried that the Preston Town Clerk should be asked to provide equal facilities for the buses serving Grimsargh and Longridge which were given to others.

Motion 589 of 22 September 1922 resolved that a letter be sent to the Rural District Council concerning the dangerous state of Grimsargh's railway bridge. It was considered (even then) to be too narrow for present-day traffic. The bridge was not widened because somebody thought it would be a good idea to build a Grimsargh by-pass road. On 8 January 1925, the proposal was to build a road which would commence near to Grimsargh School and rejoin Longsight Lane near to Kitchen Terrace, thus avoiding the railway bridge and level crossing. There have been several proposals for a Grimsargh by-pass but none of them have come to fruition. In 1939, pedestrians including children en route to St Michael's Church and School still had to 'breathe in' against the parapet whilst crossing the railway bridge. A teacher stood at either side of the bridge and the children crossed over in a single line. A footbridge provided the answer and the iron construction arrived just before war broke out for installation in the same year.

In 1946 the Council was renamed Grimsargh Parish Council. The effect of Local Government reform in 1974 was to abolish the rural district and urban district councils and the parish council then came under the control of Preston Borough Council. The original minutes are housed in the Lancashire Record Office (LRO, RDP 20/2).

The Real Essence of Victorian Grimsargh

Newspaper reports in the days of Queen Victoria were predictably long and involved. The reporting of contrasting events have necessarily been abridged to mirror the times and atmosphere of late nineteenth-century Grimsargh.

Grimsargh even had its own Temperance Society and a meeting was convened in January 1878:

An annual tea meeting in connection with the society was celebrated on Wednesday evening in a part of the barn belonging to Nook Farm, which Mr Bamber who tends the premises, has at great expense, fitted up for preaching purposes on Sunday evenings. The place was neatly and tastefully decorated with strings of evergreens and a very substantial tea was provided. About 200 sat down to tea; after the tables had been cleared, a meeting and entertainment was given, after which Mr Hartley of Preston presided and in a speech well adapted for the younger portion of his audience, opened the meeting. Mr Leadbeater of Southport said that he had not addressed a Temperance meeting for many years, yet he was greatly in favour of total abstinence. He could not conceive how a believer who was told that whatsoever he doeth, he do it to the glory of God, could dabble in strong drink which was the cause of so much crime throughout the land.

Perfect sobriety did not always prevail and provided some vindication for the Temperance movements. The plight of a Preston woman found dying on the Grimsargh highway was a victim of the evil drink. The sad, almost unbelievable chain of events was reported on 26 March 1881:

Yesterday the coroner received information from the police at Grimsargh that on Thursday night about o'clock two boys found a woman lying helplessly drunk in a ditch on the side of the highway in that township. A man pulled her out and sent for the police. P.C. Bennett reached the woman at 8 o'clock and found her moaning on the roadside. She could not speak and the constable assisted her into a milk cart and took her to the Plough Inn, Grimsargh, where he was told that there was no room for the woman, excepting in the barn. A Preston gentleman came up and suggested that she be taken to the Fulwood Police Station. He at once proceeded to Fulwood and on reaching the police station, P.S. Kinlock felt at the woman and found that she was cold. She was then driven to the Fulwood Workhouse and on lifting her out of the cart it was found that she was dead. Inquiries were made and it was ascertained that the woman

was *Mary Kellett*, aged 48, a widow and servant at the Bath's Hotel, Saul Street, Preston. She had been to Longridge with two women, one a landlady and on returning was left on the road-side as the women could not get her further.

Dixon's farm, Grimsargh was the scene of a suicide, which carried a report on 25 April 1883. Interestingly the Plough Inn was the venue where HM Coroner held the inquest.

On Saturday morning Thomas Turner of Dixon's farm, Grimsargh, committed suicide by hanging. He rose early and assisted in milking the cows. At 8 o'clock his son went into the house to get breakfast, leaving his father in the yard. On returning shortly after 8 he missed his father who was subsequently found hanging by a rope from a beam. Life was extinct. An inquest was held on the body on Saturday at the Plough Inn, Grimsargh, by Mr Gilbertson. It was stated that the deceased had been failing in health for two or three years and had been seriously ill for about 3 weeks. His medical attendant was Dr Eccles of Longridge. Verdict: Committed suicide whilst in an unsound state of mind.

On a much happier note in October, 1881, members of the Cross family joined, Mr H. Bramwell, school master, for a concert at Grimsargh School:

On Thursday evening a very successful concert was given in Grimsargh School room by members of the Glee class which is conducted by

Mr H. Bramwell, the school master and others. There was a crowded attendance amongst the audience, which numbered 160 persons, being a number of ladies and gentlemen from Preston. The platform was carpeted and was profusely decorated wth exotic plants which had been kindly lent by Colonel Cross of Redscar. Mrs J. Brown kindly lent the pianoforte at which Miss Cicely Cross presided with great ability. A lengthy programme was gone through in a most creditable manner, the executants being in turn warmly applauded.

In August 1895 there was a definite waft in the air, which had more to do with the local sewage farm than the flavour of Victorian Grimsargh:

> Correspondence from the railway company concerned the flooding of the Longridge railway: 'The Council Surveyor has investigated the matter and after discussion it was decided better, before deciding anything definite, to visit the place'. A further complaint was made about the stopping of a drain betwixt the 6 and 6.25 mile post.[2]

The scouring of old newspapers now on microfilm in Preston reference library undoubtedly yields fascinating results. The following reports provide further insight into the nature of crime during the same era.[3]

> A very bold robbery was perpetrated yesterday morning at the dwelling of Mr James Burns, farmer to Mr Cross of 'Red Scar'. Burns lives near the Chapel of Grimsargh and on Thursday evening went to retire to rest as usual. Between 3 and 4 in the morning, however, he was awoke from his slumbers by a noise, which at first appeared to him like a scratching of mice, but on drawing his curtains aside he was disagreeably surprised to find a light in the apartment and a man busy at his desk. The burglar sprang through the chamber window and disappeared, carrying away with him about £7 in gold and silver, and Burns' watch.

I have it on good authority that the local constable commenced his reports with the clichéd words of the music hall comedians of the period – 'I was proceeding in an easterly direction when my attention was drawn to a serious farm fire at Grimsargh …'

> Supposed incendiarism: About 7.30 p.m. on Thursday fire broke out in the rick yard of Higher Brockholes Farm, Grimsargh, occupied by Mrs Balshaw and sons. Three stacks consisting of beans, rye and wheatstraw were burned to the ground. P.C. Almond arrived from Samlesbury and took steps to prevent the blaze spreading. A loose stack was only five yards from one of the three on fire, two yards

THE STORY OF A
LANCASHIRE VILLAGE

from a Dutch barn and about five yards from a stack twenty yards long. Showers of sparks were falling upon it and the Dutch barn and under the direction of the officer, buckets of water carried from the pond were thrown upon the site nearest the conflagration.

During May 1842 the Reverend Cowban took a rare leave of absence from the presbytery at Alston Roman Catholic Church for the night. Alas, he chose the wrong night for this was when the burglars found their way from Newton Street, Preston, to the wilds of rural Grimsargh. The house was burgled by three men who viciously assaulted his housekeeper and his niece. During the commission of the crime the burglar's candle went out. Mr Cowban's niece seized the opportunity to escape to Woodfold Farm for help. The burglars escaped with a few shillings of her personal money and were arrested the following day.

An important consideration of landowners in north-west England has always been the protection of game and this applied equally to the Cross Estate.

More game cases – At the Magistrates Court on Saturday, [January, 30th 1859] a youth named Thomas Walmsley of Alston, pleaded guilty to a charge of having on the 22nd ultimo, illegally used gins for the purpose of taking game on the preserves of Major Cross. Hood, the gamekeeper, proved that he saw the prisoner in a field at Alston, near to three gins, one of which contained a Hare. In reply to the bench it was stated that Walmsley had borne a very good character, and the Magistrates taking this into consideration fined him five shillings. Three other youths named Henry Walmsley, James Wearing and William Brown, all factory operatives, also pleaded guilty to using snares and trespassing in pursuit of coneys. The defendants were found in a field belonging to Lady Shelley, the game on which is preserved by Major Cross at Brockholes, with a dog and a ferret and three rabbit snares in their possession. The property was produced in Court.' After conviction came the punch line as Brown addressed the Bench. 'Please Sir, if we pay th'money [20 shillings] con we hev we'r tackle back agin'?

References

1. E.C. Oakes, *A Centenary Handbook – Water Supplies of Three Centuries*, Preston.
2. Jane Smyth, *A Step Back in Time – A Chronicle of Village Life in and around Longridge*.
3. *Preston Guardian* reports.

CHAPTER SEVENTEEN

The People and Places of Twentieth-century Grimsargh

MAPS HAVE LONG PROVIDED many clues to historians and periodic revisions demonstrate the changing landscape of Grimsargh. However, social change cannot be reproduced by enterprising cartographical expertise and throughout this chapter the changing social scene is illustrated by the people and places of Grimsargh over the last century.

A Remarkable Centenarian: Nicholas's Exciting Twentieth Century

Grimsargh House is the home of Grimsargh's oldest resident, the lively and scientifically orientated Mr Nicholas Swarbrick. I was privileged to meet the venerable gentleman during his 103rd year when he gave me a good historical account of his native Grimsargh and eloquently related his passion for science.

Mr Swarbrick's father, Nicholas Swarbrick (senior) was a former member of Grimsargh Parish Council. During a lifetime spanning three centuries 'young' Nick Swarbrick has seen it all. The family farmed at Blackrock Farm which formerly occupied the site of the modern Brown's garage complex on Preston Road. This used to be situated opposite Grimsargh Railway Station where young Nick caught the train to Preston.

As a young farmer working in Grimsargh Mr Swarbrick developed a specialised knowledge of the scientific aspects of animal husbandry. Always at the forefront of agriculture and science in farming, he has long had the foresight to predict trends and was a founder committee member of the British Cattle Breeders' club at Cambridge University. He speaks with enthusiasm and pride of research projects and consultations with a Dr John Hammond and the teams who pioneered animal surrogacy and artificial insemination over fifty years ago. On reaching his centenary he met Professor Peter Sharpe of the Roslin Institute at Edinburgh who is a leading protagonist on the cloning of farm animals. On the subject of the cloning of Dolly the sheep Nicholas elaborated further, whilst drawing a parallel and speaking with undoubted authority about the coming of the motor car. 'I remind you of what happened when the motor cars first appeared. People were so alarmed by them that a man with a red flag ran ahead to warn other road users of the potential danger. Fifty-five years ago a farmer said to me that we were interfering with nature. I pointed out to him that all scientific animal intervention is interfering with nature and the process of evolution. Nowadays evolution itself is firmly in our grasp.'

I never ceased to be amazed about the ideologies of Mr Nicholas Swarbrick and who could not admire his lively mind and expressed eloquence. He ended our discussion by succinctly informing me that 'during the twentieth century the human race made more progress and achievement than the sum total of previous recorded history and where Einstein alive today there would exist a moral imperative of the highest order that he be cloned' – now there is food for thought!

The Plough Inn at the Hub of the Village Community

The Plough Inn of today was first constructed in 1785 and was originally a coaching house and combined farm under the control of the squire until 1831. Landlords in those days had to deposit ten golden guineas with the squire as an assurance they would keep good behaviour at the inn. Another stipulation to be met was the provision of a loose box for a travelling stallion, and accommodation for the grooms. In Victorian times the landlord donned their second caps and went farming in the fields. Even inquests into sudden deaths were held regularly at the multi-purpose pub.

The first trains of the Longridge line stopped outside the Plough where facilities inside the pub included a booking office. With the opening of a new Grimsargh railway station across the road the former booking office was converted and the slotted shelves which used to hold railway tickets are today concealed behind the plaster. The Plough Inn and its lush bowling green have long been a focus of village social life. Its walls have witnessed many comings and goings of local tradesmen, farmers and a succession of 'mine hosts'. Like many village pubs it has helped to shape the social and cultural history of the village. The arrival of the first horse-drawn train in 1840 later provided some incentives for the formation of modern Grimsargh.

The 1841 census shows Mary and William Walmsley, as mine hosts and six family members whose ages ranged from four years to twenty-four years. In 1922 the landlord, Thomas Brown, was advertising the proximity of the railway station facility as well as 'refreshments, billiards, wines and spirits of the best quality, cyclists and picnic parties catered for'. Cyclists would perhaps have time for a quick cuppa before embarking on a voyage of discovery beyond the extremities of Grimsargh-with-Brockhole. Tom managed the Plough as a 'free house', before selling it to Matthew Brown of the Blackburn-based Lion Brewery. In the good old days before the establishment of the large Blackburn breweries, horses and drays used to pull from the yard, for in addition to sustaining their own alcoholic beverage, the Plough

Blacksmith Joseph Walmsley in his shop about 1920. The blacksmith, and wheelwright, Bob Noblet, co-ordinated their work manufacturing cart wheels and affixing the metal rims.
Courtesy of Mrs Nell Noblet

Grandpa Noblet in his
workshop, where he also
made coffins to order. Bob
died in 1956, aged 87 years.
Courtesy of Mrs Nell Noblet

also supplied beer to hotels in Preston. Next door, on Longsight
Terrace, Esther Rigby (née Finch) was born in 1911 and her younger
sister, Margaret Jackson was born in the same house. Remarkably
both these senior Grimsargh ladies are together again in retirement
in exactly the same residence, enjoying the 'longsight' along
Longsight Lane (now Preston Road.) Their grandparents had been
former licensees at the Plough and worked in an adjoining building,
brewing their own ale, as strong as barley wine and on tap, from
the barrel.

In 1919 Joseph and Martha Walmsley and daughter Nell (Nell
Noblet) moved from Tarleton to Grimsargh. The Walmsley family
had strong family ties with Grimsargh and took up occupation
of the School Cottage at Alston Church, before Martha took
over as landlady from Tom Brown in 1928.

School Cottage was situated below the school classroom of the
old Roman Catholic Church building at Alston. As a five-year-old
it was convenient for little Nell Noblet (née Walmsley) to walk
out of her house and go up the external steps to her classroom

within the same building. Occasionally she could have retreated down the same steps to escape the wrath of her black-smocked teacher when she wielded the cane. In those days they were not averse to caning girls as well as boys and according to Nell, 'it was all in a day to be late and be caned through birdnesting.'

In the early 1920s Grimsargh was bustling with local trades people going about their business. Nicholas Swarbrick lived at Blackrock Farm and farmed the land between the Plough and what is now the village green. The Swarbricks leased their juxta-posed farm building to Joseph Walmsley to work in the smithy. Robert Noblet (senior) worked in another workshop, as a joiner and wheelwright, where the Plough car park is now situated. The Grimsargh village blacksmith and wheelwright co-ordinated their work in manufacturing cartwheels and affixing the metal rims. Their range of skills was in great demand by the rural farming community where farming had been a way of life for centuries. Occasionally Bob Noblet had the sombre duty of undertaker to perform and made his coffins to order.

Taking to the roads in an open-top charabanc was a real adventure and oilskins, rugs and umbrellas were part of the inventory and merriment. With a bit of luck it might make Longridge, but Blackpool was likened to a major expedition. The Walmsleys enjoyed the occasional trip into Grimsargh on an old charabanc/goods carrier. During the week it was the latter but on special occasions a frame with seats was placed on the carrier and the 'toastrack' conversion carried people. In 1928 when Nell was thirteen years old the family boarded the charabanc with a one-way ticket from School Cottage at Alston Lane Church to the Plough Inn, Grimsargh. Nell Noblet's mum took over as landlady of the Plough Inn and young Nell was destined to become Bob Noblet's daughter-in-law.

After working at the furnace all day Mr Walmsley went into the pub at half past five for a well-earned pint and joined his wife to play dominoes or a 'sing along' with the local farmers. Martha made sure that everything was nice and clean at the 'local' and scrubbed the flag floors of the public areas twice a day. In 1929, Joe Walmsley managed to talk his own way into the bar permanently alongside his wife, Martha 'the management'. During the tenancy of the Walmsleys the Plough Inn became officially known as the Plough Hotel but after the Walmsleys finally called last orders in 1942 it reverted back to the Plough Inn. In later

Grimsargh

THE STORY OF A
LANCASHIRE VILLAGE

President's Day at the
Bowling Club, Grimsargh.
Courtesy of Mrs Nell Noblet

Anyone order a carriage? The Plough Inn was still advertising brewed ales at the time of this 1929 photograph.

Grandpa Noblet outside his workshop in the 1930s.
Courtesy of Mrs Nell Noblet

years the blacksmith's workshop became a combined petrol station/garage and village shop. Many of today's villagers will remember the garage complex that incorporated the former Blackrock Farm. It was demolished in 1998 to make way for Brown's Garage and car showroom. After the war, Robert Noblet's son, Bob Noblet (junior) carried on his father's business below a room used by the village boxing club. Clearly there was no shortage of eligible young men in Grimsargh but romance blossomed when Nell married Bob, the young joiner. The couple resided on Longsight Terrace for over half a century and next door to their lifelong friend Esther Rigby. Over many years of the twentieth century these two families witnessed social change embraced by a complete transformation of the serenity of Grimsargh.

During 2001 three senior ladies of Grimsargh, Nell Noblet, Esther Rigby and her sister Margaret Jackson kindly shared their memories. Esther did escape from Grimsargh to Ribbleton in 1934, before returning to Longsight Terrace twelve years later. The attractive young woman loved horse riding and ventured to Ribbleton Hall Farm with her newly married husband, Fred, to join him in his riding school. This farm was in the shadow of Ribbleton Hall, a fine mansion built in 1865 for Thomas Birchall, a former mayor and local solicitor, which had been converted for the use of the ATS and US troops during the Second World War. Whilst on horseback she discovered Higher Boilton, Moorside and Moor Nook Farms, in a rich tapestry of countryside and pasture. After the Second World War the couple began to witness the swan song of Ribbleton's countryside as many farms to the east of Preston were engulfed by housing estates and Ribbleton Hall became a part of that legacy when it was demolished in 1950. For reasons of a domestic nature they returned to Esther's birthplace in Longsight Terrace, Grimsargh in 1946.

Social change is captured within the memories of many people who have been interesting characters and have played an essential part in 'the Grimsargh Story'. In his latter years old Bob Noblet was ailing and Mrs Nell Noblet affectionately recalled her father-in-law's misjudged anticipated demise.

> In retirement the elderly joiner and undertaker had not been too well and thought he was on his deathbed. He was, after all, an expert on such matters! A farewell party of friends and relatives were there to give him comfort and support, particularly when he warned them, 'Tek that piller, I'm gonne dee.' Father Horrocks was telephoned and advised that the pillow be taken away, if that was what he wanted and hastily made his way to Longsight Terrace, to join in the prayers. All the family was gathered round him saying prayers. The group was resigned to the inevitable and no allowance for divine intervention had been contemplated. 'Will someone send for the doctor?' 'There's no point in sending for't doctor you might as well send for't bloody

Young Bob Noblet with his sisters. Bob later became Nell Walmsley's husband.
Courtesy of Mrs Nell Noblet

undertaker,' came the reply. It was therefore to everyone's delight when 'old Bob' did a U-turn on dying. He suddenly perked up and instructed them to 'Fetch my pipe.' Nellie put away her handkerchief for a minute and was pleased to accede to his next words of command, 'I think you 'ad better gimmee that piller I'm not gonne dee!' The patient was given his pillow along with some appropriate advice from his caring daughter. 'I think you had better start eating some proper food,' she told him. Bob had been a long time a-dying and ate nothing but chocolate. One day he had a change of mind when he raised himself up and said, 'Martha! Is that a bit of 'am I can smell cooking? Ah could fancy a bit o' that fer me tay!' 'That's fer t' buryin,' she said. Bathing too became a problem when he asked for 'time' whilst having his feet washed. 'Come on, you haven't finished washing yer feet.' The old gentleman thought different and told his carer, 'I'll do t'other tamarraw.'

Grandpa Noblet put the Lancashire custom of 'burying with ham' on hold until 1956, when the death of this fine old Lancastrian symbolically marked the end of an era. Unlike his generation, village children could no longer play games and skip in the middle of the road outside the Plough. In the 1920s Esther Rigby and her friends did just that before walking to school along the centre of Preston Road. The children dodged the early motor cars and the occasional steam traction engine or roller making up the road. Small cars were now being mass-produced and the motor car was no longer the exclusive preserve of the rich. This was the dawn of the commuter age, although in Grimsargh you would never have guessed, for time had stood still. Everyone had to watch out for the 'carriers' which came down from Longridge. If villagers needed anything from town they had to tie a ribbon on their gates (and perhaps even the old oak tree) in order to alert the driver to stop and receive instructions. Great herds of cattle and flocks of sheep were driven all the way from Chipping to Preston Cattle Market and the official advice was 'keep your garden gates closed'. The morning and evening milk run consisted of beautiful shire horses hauling carts with heavily laden milk churns from the local farms to and from Grimsargh Railway Station. As part of this 'wagon train' farmers would tie up their horses to the rings which may still be seen outside the front door of the Plough Hotel. Small wonder that the legislators saw fit to create the offence of being drunk in charge of a horse or carriage, a sort of pre-cursor to the breathalyser.

There were impromptu performances too on the 'straights' of Longsight Lane with Esther and Fred Rigby and Margaret trying out Fred's brand new motorbike and sidecar and even performing a few stunts. (In those days the Road Traffic Act of 1930 had yet to receive the Royal Assent, and of course there were none of the speed cameras now installed on Preston Road close to where she still lives.) Things were really getting out of hand in Grimsargh and it was high time to blame the vintage train for making a dirty mess of clean washing hanging on the line! Not everyone agreed and some local tradesmen capitalised on the railway. At the Plough, business prospered and Martha made sandwiches for the hospital's visitors and staff before they embarked on the wondrous train journey to Whittingham. The first rural bus services from Preston to Longridge were established during the 1920s to take over from the carriers' carts. In 1930 Grimsargh Station closed to passengers during a year of significant national branch line closures. Since the early 1950s falling cinema and theatre audiences in Preston and the introduction of television instigated further change to the rural way of life and a declining demand for rural bus services.

Post-war Grimsargh and a New Landlord at The Plough

Following hostilities there was a resumption of normality and it was as though time had stood still in the immediate post-war years. Grimsargh's own version of the *Last of the Summer Wine* team of Foggy, Compo and Clegg team kept one another company on the wooden bench opposite the Plough. From this strategic position they had been watching the world go by since, it seemed, time began. Matters of all sorts were debated at length and judgements handed down, the person or persons being discussed going about their daily lives in blissful ignorance of the 'rulings from the bench'. One day in 1948 they had a matter of extreme gravity to cope with. They had heard a whisper that a new landlord, Tony Parker and his family, were about to move into the Plough. My informant must have been recording the minutes and their conversation was noted for posterity. 'Dus't know owt about new folk as comin' in?' 'No, norra thing.' 'Waint make any bloody difference – weel at' buggers to keep waint we?' Next on the Court agenda was the important issue of the Parkers' religious

convictions. It was decided that their spokesman should tackle Mr Parker with a face-to-face in the bar. 'Dus't go up t'road or down t'road?' which, translated, means 'Are you Catholic or Protestant?' This benign gossip used to be the essence of village life and where better for it than that grand old English institution, the village pub.

The landlord under discussion, Councillor Tony Parker, was both Chairman of Preston Rural District Council and the District Councils Association and represented the interests of the local community on several other committees. This was only possible because of the unflagging support of his wife, Peggy Parker, who ensured that a good pub atmosphere of conviviality and pleasance flowed as freely as the pints. In the late 1940s Grimsargh's roads were pitch black at night and one of the first things Councillor Parker did was to have an adequate system of street lighting installed. After all, the genial Landlord was an original traffic 'courtesy cop' in the Lancashire Constabulary and knew about the importance of road safety issues. When road traffic accidents occurred outside the pub he would take charge at the scene and instruct his daughter, Eileen, to direct traffic until the arrival of the police. It is perhaps not surprising that after twenty years of being brought up at 'the hub of the village', that the young trainee followed in her father's footsteps. In 1968 Eileen Parker decided that 'there were constabulary duties to be done' and as it transpired, I was to share some of these duties with her at Fulwood Police Station.

As a child Eileen made thousands of salmon sandwiches in the pub and consequently now loathes salmon. The experience was worse than the rigours of the classroom environment of St Michael's Parochial School, where the austere persona of Miss Nellie Carbis was beginning to mellow. Dad was the archetypal landlord and mum made the best soup with dumplings in the north-west. The 1950s pub grub at the Plough preceded the universal adoption of 'bar snacks' and included a fare of delicious hot pies with bowls of pickles, red cabbage and salad strategically placed on the sideboard. The idea was for patrons to purchase a pie and help themselves to the red cabbage. At lunchtime a few local labourers constructing the new Spade Mill reservoir at Longridge brought in their own bread and helped themselves to the nibbles and pickles. If mine host sensed impending trouble he would say to their foreman, "If there is any trouble I expect you to deal with it and take him off the premises". On the rare occasions when there was trouble at the Plough mine host had his team of

Grimsargh

THE STORY OF A
LANCASHIRE VILLAGE

New landlord Tony Parker
and wife Peggy.
Courtesy of Miss E. Parker

The Plough Inn at the time of the Parkers' tenure.

Courtesy of Miss E. Parker

tough farmers to deal effectively with the situation. The unfortunate miscreant was politely asked to leave and if he refused he was passed along a human conveyor belt with a one-way ticket to the outside world.

The accents of the Fab Four were once heard at the Plough Inn. Imagine mine host, Tony Parker behind the bar, one summer lunchtime when a large car drew up outside. A certain aspiring group and a woman with long blonde hair purchased several gills and a pint at the bar. The men drank the gills and the woman the pint before they asked for directions to The Hermitage, which at that time was on the market. Tony later told his daughter, PC Eileen Parker, that he believed that the Beatles had just dropped in at lunchtime. As a result of diligent enquiries it was ascertained that the group appeared at Preston's Public Hall in August 1962, and a visit to Grimsargh could have been on their agenda before the gig and indeed before they achieved world fame.

A sobering touch of human kindness was extended to an old man who lived in a wooden hen cabin with no sanitation. Peg Parker treated his sore thumb, afforded him the luxury of a bath,

and the hospitality even extended to a roof over his head with copious supplies of soup. Across the road the free soup kitchen was extended to the elderly on cold winter days in their own kitchens at Kitchen Terrace. At 5.30 p.m. the pub doors were open for business and if you wanted a seat for the evening you had to be there before seven. In the early evening it was a focal point for people travelling home to Longridge and beyond and the clientele included representation from most of the professions. The card and domino schools were quick to grab a table, and a pint of mixed or a G & T was placed on the table in anticipation for regular clients who arrived bang on schedule. Lancashire dialect flowed as fast as the beer and the trick was to engage a man who had a 'reet good' Lancashire accent in conversation to learn the local vernacular. In 1977 after meticulously cleaning out the cellar and pipes for the last time the Parkers retired to a house on Preston Road but sadly, Tony Parker enjoyed only nine years of retirement.

Following a complete refurbishment of the Plough in 2002 by Scottish and Newscatle Pub Enterprieses, the high standards and traditions set by the landlords of yesteryear look set to continue. Once again it has become the focus of village life serving tradi⸗

Does it always snow in Grimsargh? The railway station gable, crossing gates and station garage, which used to be part of Blackrock farm, epitomise Grimsargh after the war and into the early 1970s.
Courtesy of Miss E. Parker

tional food in a very pleasant heritage atmosphere under the watchful eye of convivial hosts Karen and Francis McGrath.

Entertainment in Grimsargh

In the field between Grimsargh Reservoir and the main road were two tennis courts and a wooden construction known as the Recreation Hall or the Grimsargh Association Rooms. The rooms known as the Pavilion were used by the tennis club and the local population also enjoyed the social functions, whist drives, billiards and indoor games. An advert in the *Lancashire Daily Post* of 13 December 1899, announced a significant event: 'Recreation Hall at Grimsargh. Dance every Saturday to the largest electric piano in England,' and 'only a five minute walk from Grimsargh Railway Station.' The following year the *Preston Guardian* stated: 'Recreation Hall, Grimsargh will re-open for the season on Saturday next. Classes every Saturday evening. Socials, weddings, birthday or funeral parties catered for. Proprietor J.C. Broughton.' The humble Pavilion assumed the role of the original community village hall and preceded another entertainment hot spot known as the Grimsargh Assembly Rooms which opened in 1913, situated in Grimsargh's 'West End', right next to the railway station.

Members of the tennis club were ordered 'off court' to make way for the official celebrations for the Coronation of King George V and Queen Mary. This was probably the first Grimsargh Field Day and thereafter followed Council business on 23 July 1923, when the provision of a recreation field for Grimsargh was broached. On 24 June 1939 it was reported in the *Preston Guardian* that the wooden structure known as Grimsargh Association Rooms was to be replaced by a brick one – all right in theory but it took another forty-four years before the village hall finally became a reality! The old Recreation Hall was acquired by William Dagger who had been the gentleman farmer at Marsh House Farm since at least 1885. Use of the hall changed from accommodating the tennis club and their whist drives to housing William's prized pedigree pigs, which he proudly sold at auction. William walked up the half-mile country lane (which today forms part of the Ribble Way) onto Elston Lane often wearing his plus fours, to attend meetings of Grimsargh Parish Council. In those days he would have had the company of the resident pairs of yellowhammers, singing their piece which is likened to 'A little bit of bread and no cheese'. Forty years ago I trod the same route and well remember the friendly Rich family who took over Marsh House Farm. George Rich was proud of his yellowhammers 'down t'lane' which, alas, are now extinct in the area and have joined the long list of diminishing farmland bird species.

Little Jimmie Elliott spent his childhood in Grimsargh and from being a five-year-old developed his gift of being able to imitate the natural sounds of birds and animals. After entering theological college he decided to develop his gift of mimicry and go into show business. Mr Elliott brought his vast repertoire to the audiences of the music halls of London and the Provinces and appeared on the same bill as Laurel and Hardy and Morecambe and Wise. Thousands will remember him for his simulation of a dogfight and over 1,000 radio appearances. He still found time to be a church warden at Grimsargh St Michael's Church and in June, 1934 he featured in the parish magazine performing his duties with fellow churchwarden, Mr Myerscough from the village shop and sidesman, Mr Latham the former stationmaster. In 1970 he returned to the lanes and farms of his native county when he retired to live in Garstang.

The original Congregational Mission hut closed its doors to worship in 1913 and moved up Longsight to a brand new church.

Aladdin was the panto staged
in the Assembly Room at
Christmas 1928, featuring Nell
Noblet (right).
Courtesy of Mrs Nell Noblet

The Mission became Grimsargh Assembly Rooms and later still an early version of the present Grimsargh Social club which today occupies the same site. The *Preston Guardian* gives a clue as to the diverse entertainment on offer at Grimsargh Assembly Rooms, which I am told was not quite up to the standard of the London Palladium. There were dances and whist drives and Grimsargh Lawn Tennis Club held their annual dance on 18 April 1925, to the accompaniment of the Nashdown's Orchestra. The Chairman introduced musical trios and locals who recited poems and proudly proclaimed their Lancashire dialect. Cinema type seating meant that the Grimsargh Players could stage their first amateur dramatic productions and the annual Christmas pantomime delighted the children.

The Reverend George Rubie brought along his cinematograph on 18 March 1939 and presented a show in aid of the Lifeboat Fund, and in May 1939, the Assembly Rooms welcomed St Wilfrid's Band from Longridge, who played in celebration of Father O'Sullivan's jubilee. After the Second World War the old Mission hut Assembly Rooms finally bowed out whilst it was being used as a Licensed Men's Club. Unknown forces probably decided that activities were getting too hot to handle and the former place of worship was destroyed by a gale – the Lord works in mysterious ways! Following the demise of the old Assembly Rooms and Licensed Club the committee moved into the outdated Co-op village grocery store. Since the Swinging Sixties, Grimsargh Club has provided a focal point for villagers and has ample facilities for snooker, conferences, entertainment and social functions.

Shopkeepers and Delivery Men

Grimsargh's shopkeepers and tradesmen have served the village well. According to Barrett's Trade Directory for 1936, Todd and Eccles occupied the premises of Yew Tree House near to Longsight Terrace. Their speciality was the making of delicious confectionery including oatcakes and crumpets which were sold from a van in Grimsargh and Longridge. Harry Eccles was affectionately known as 'the oatcake man', but he was not the only confectioner in Grimsargh.

Mr Myerscough offered some competition to 'the oatcake man', when in 1936 his business premises had become a grocery and confectioner's shop, with Mildred Myerscough working in the shop and three ladies working in the bakery. At the bakery the smell of new-baked loaves and confectionery tempted those cus-

About the time of the Great War Grimsargh Post Office and village shop was managed by James Myerscough, who also looked after the Assembly Rooms. Today the building is Grimsargh Social Club.
Photograph by Mr J. Myerscough

The People and Places of Twentieth-century Grimsargh

Mrs B. Smith and son at Grimsargh level crossing. The Co-op store (left) was then still in use.
Courtesy of Miss E. Parker

tomers who enjoyed an early morning cuppa in the café. One can imagine that the hot pies attracted the village blacksmith and farrier, Ralph Ireland, who had taken over from Joseph Walmsley, or Sid Horam from the garage. Robert Noblet was still the joiner and wheelwright in 1936 and his home is listed as 3, Longsight Terrace. The village Post Office by that time had moved to premises across the road and Mr Irvine Rotheray is listed as the postmaster. Mr Myerscough's village shop was taken over by the Pullen family and eventually became the Co-operative grocers where the popular 1960s 'Co-op divvy' ensured sales until the advent of urban supermarkets which in turn led to the old Co-op being given a new lease of life as the present Grimsargh Social Club.

The quaint tradition of the 'oil deliveryman' continued at Grimsargh until the Second World War. Paraffin oil was still used for lighting and cooking at some houses and the 'oil man' ambled up from Preston with his cart hauled by two lovely horses. At the farms he often received fresh eggs in lieu of payment. Eggs were also collected by the people of Grimsargh and delivered to local hospitals in the 1930s. Hospitals depended on voluntary subscriptions and it was the custom for country schools to hold an egg collection at the time of the year when eggs were plentiful. Thousands of eggs were handed over to the ambulance men and were put into pickle for use in diets; surely a thoroughly worthwhile gesture by the people of Grimsargh.

Messrs Robert and James Wilkinson were in business delivering

'Operation egg yolk'. Hannah Butler, May Rhodes, Joyce Rhodes, Betty Dicken, Esther Clegg and Margaret Toppin collecting eggs.
Parish records

coal from the British Railways sidings. The coal wagons from Preston were shunted into the goods sidings and the burly brothers transferred it to their own classic commercial vehicles for local delivery. Both brothers worked very hard and tried their best to provide a service to the public in the days of coal dependency. Nothing was too much trouble when the telephone rang and the caller informed them that 'I have run out of coal'. At personal sacrifice they went down to the yard and loaded up two or three bags onto a three-ton Morris lorry which was purchased new in 1933, and like its drivers was no stranger to hard work. During thirty years of active service it covered over half a million miles carrying 40,000 tons of coal. Customers on the rural patch were served at Longridge, Chipping, Ribchester and many villages in between. The regular driver, James Wilkinson, proudly drove this lorry to isolated farms such as Moss Nook, Grimsargh, where they was no hard road at all – only a field – and up and down the hills and dales of Bowland whilst delivering good old fossil fuel to the local community.

In those days there was a real need for coal, especially so during the harsh winters of 1940 and 1947. During the 'big freeze-up' of 1940, snowbound Grimsargh was cut off from the outside world

TOP

our men who freed the coal lorry from the snow: left to right, Bill Coupe, Jim Coupe ocal farmers), Norman Hunt and Bob Wilkinson.

BOTTOM

The vehicles of the brothers Wilkinson at their home base behind the station in 1964.

Courtesy Mr D. Wilkinson

and transformed into a winter wonderland, but this, the epitome of many a Christmas card scene, was not all that it seemed. On 2 February 1940, Bob and Jim and their assistant loaded up copious supplies to sustain the domestic energy resources of Inglewhite and Whitechapel. On the return run from Whitechapel, they came across something resembling Antarctica and had little choice but to abandon their vehicle or risk being buried in snow blown by the howling winds. They might have been 'gone for some time' but for a brave rescue party who managed to reach the spot along a single track cut through the snow where telephone

Grimsargh

THE STORY OF A
LANCASHIRE VILLAGE

wires and poles had collapsed. Nine days later a second expedition
to Whitechapel eventually managed to free the Morris lorry from
its icy tomb and miraculously the engine was to roar once more.
The coalyard site and Grimsargh Station have now been replaced
by the bungalows for the elderly in Old Station Close. Several
occupants can remember those days and when, before the comforts
of gas central heating, the oil man came to Grimsargh.

TOP
The heavily laden 1933 classic
Morris lorry pictured in 1960
retaining many of the original
features.
BOTTOM
Grimsargh Wilkinson Bros.
coalyard but where is the
coal? This was taken during
the particularly hard winter
of 1940.
Courtesy Mr D. Wilkinson

CHAPTER EIGHTEEN

Grimsargh in Wartime

T HE UNDAUNTED Grimsargh community spirit prevailed throughout two world wars, and the local Assembly Rooms was a focal point of activity. A fundraising event on 28 November 1914 featured 'The Frolics Concert Party'. A long and varied programme was presented in aid of the local needlework party for supplying comforts to the troops by Miss L. Cummins (soprano), Miss L. Rigby (contralto) Mr W. McTaggart, (tenor) Mr F. Ward (baritone) and Mr R. Goodburn (piano). The Frolic went down well and the large appreciative audience expressed demands for encores, which were acceded to. On 15 January 1916, Grimsargh farmers brought forward their social so that several men who had been called up could attend and enjoy the musical trio of Miss Woodruff on piano and Messrs Carter and Coupe playing violins.

Following the Great War, it was proposed by Grimsargh Parish Council to call a public meeting concerning the restoration of Three Mile Cross, as a War Memorial. On a Saturday evening in April 1920, the ceremony took place in the presence of a large gathering and was performed by Major General T.H. Shoubridge, who unveiled the cross draped with the Union Jack. There was a combined parade of Boy Scouts and St Thomas's Band, Preston. Mr Marcus Rea, chairman of the local committee presided over the proceedings, and was supported by the Reverend T. Buzzard, Vicar of Grimsargh, Father Harris, the Reverend W. Machin, Mr T. Harrison Myres and others. Mr Rea gave a short history of the movement that had led to the erection of the cross. Their one great object was to show the honour and respect they felt for those who have given their lives for them.

The Major General read out the names of the fallen with the devout injunction, 'Let their names never be forgotten.' After standing at the salute for a moment before the memorial he delivered a short address, reminding the children present that if it had not been for these gallant men who died for them their chances of a full life would have been small: they would have been downtrodden; their education would have been neglected;

and they might have been put under the heel of the Hun for good. Major General Shoubridge concluded his address by trying to provide some comfort for the relatives of the badly wounded, and of those who had died. "Let me tell you this, that during four and a half years of war it has been my fate to go onto many battlefields … I can say to those relatives who are here – and I speak with experience – that absolutely their last words and thoughts are, in almost every instance, about those people they are leaving behind at home. They will always try and send messages to those dear ones who are living in a nice country village like Grimsargh, just to let them know that they have not forgotten them, when the time comes for them to go away" The proceedings were brought to a close with the national anthem and the sounding of the Last Post by a party of buglers.

Today the War Memorial cross is a Grade II listed structure standing about three metres high and mounted on a pedestal, believed to be of late medieval origin. It has long been a local roadside landmark on the western outskirts of the village commemorating those who died for their country. The inset metal plate has the following inscription together with the names of the gallant men of Grimsargh who paid the supreme sacrifice.

'The Glorious Dead'

This cross was restored by the inhabitants of Grimsargh and District in Memory of local sailors and soldiers who fell in the Great War 1914–1919 [followed by the following fifteen names]:
William Banks, Albert Carr, James Chew, Charles Finch, Roger James Finch, John Garlick, Richard Holden, James Hoyle, John Howard Vincent Latham, William Henry Lofthouse, John Mason, Ernest Park, John James Park, William Henry Morris Park, James Willasey Stevenson.

With the outbreak of the Second World War gas masks arrived and villagers were given instructions by the Air Raid Wardens. There was an emphasis on food production and farms in the area became arable, growing vegetables, including potatoes, turnips, cereals and root crops for the cattle. Even Bob Noblet's workshop was commandeered by the authorities for the storage and repair of agricultural machinery.

Grimsargh played a part in the evacuation of hundreds of thousands of urban children to the countryside of Britain. On

Grimsargh in Wartime

The commemorative unveiling of the War Memorial in 1920, built from the medieval base of the Three Mile Cross.
The neighbouring eighteenth-century farm is known as Three Mile Cross Farm – like the cross, it is approximately three miles from the centre of Preston.
Courtesy of Mr P. Cowell

August 28 1939, evacuees from Withington were processed at the old Assembly Rooms and allocated by the WVS to their billets. Tom Heginbotham can remember the day, when he was only seven, that a special train hauling many carriages steamed into the closed Grimsargh station, only two weeks after the outbreak of war. Tom recalled those early days of the war with affection:

> The evacuees from the Manchester area had labels on their collars with their names on so that brothers and sisters would not be separated. Each had a gas mask in a box tied with string around their neck. They were met at the station by the families who were prepared to take them. Some of the bigger farms would take two or three children but after only three weeks some of the homesick children went back to Manchester, while others settled and attended the local schools. Because of classroom overcrowding, part of each day's work had to be taken in the open air or elsewhere at other premises in the village. I became a part-time scholar, going to school in the morning one week and in the afternoon the next.

Some of the evacuee children were taught in the Assembly Hall and PE lessons were held there to relieve the restricted capacity at the Old School. Football and cricket matches were organised with the evacuees' team playing against the local children. On 30 December 1939 the children's party included a special treat with the Reverend Rubie showing his Charlie Chaplin films.

The unfolding drama did not stop the visit from the school nurse and it is small tribute that on more mundane yet important matters the 'nit nurse' reported 'all heads clean'. The children knitted extra comfortable clothing for the Army, Navy, Air Force and Merchant Navy. Local boys and girls spent their limited pocket money to purchase wool and knitted hundreds of garments for the 'men at the sharp end'. Today, Hannah Fisher resides at Haighton but during the Second World War she was a pupil at Grimsargh School knitting pairs of seaboot stockings for the Royal Navy.

The children were supplied with luminous badges by the vicar to wear in the blackout and strips of muslin were pasted over panes of glass. They also received instruction in first aid and became the proud recipients of St John Ambulance certificates.

Miss Carbis told me about her wartime memories and how she complied with the procedures listed in her rule book.

School was closed for the arrival of the evacuees. We waited in Grimsargh Assembly Rooms. WVS had lists of homes to which children would be allocated. They arrived by bus from Preston railway station, all with name labels in their lapels, clothes in a variety of containers, and, of course, gas masks. Mothers and babies came too. It was night before they were all sorted out. Numbers on roll were now 161. Old forms from the playground were scrubbed and brought into school, but in the senior school three children occupied each dual desk. Later, desks arrived by lorry from Manchester, and all had to be entered on stock and accounted for, with much shifting from one school to another as the number of evacuees fluctuated. The school contributed to the war effort by making and sending large parcels of knitted garments to the services. Fire practice was held at intervals. When I blew the whistle (a long blow) and each class filed out of its own door and walked to the church, teachers carrying registers and checking numbers, and myself carrying the log book, admission registers and stock book all sacred. During October 1940 there were frequent air raid warnings and Mr Rubie the vicar provided a stirrup pump and practices were held in the yard in accordance with the rules: air raid practice involved each infant being allocated to a senior. 'The infant room will not be used during a raid because of the risk of fire in the wooden building; 135 children and 4 teachers will be spread over the two main rooms and their cloakrooms; gas mask drill is being taken regularly and senior children are given simple instruction as to what to do in emergency.

Miss Carbis remembered the invasion in May 1940 of Holland

'Comfort for the Forces':
Hannah Butler exhibits a pair
of seaboot stockings, just like
a top model.
N. Carbis collection

Grimsargh in Wartime

and Belgium and that as each country joined the allies, teachers were advised by the Ministry of Education to study the country's national anthem and history played on the BBC every Sunday night. In May 1940 – long before every packet carried a Government health warning – King George VI asked the children to send money to the Overseas League to buy cigarettes for the troops. The sum of £4 was sent and it was a sad irony that the King would eventually die of cancer, which may have been related to smoking.

During late autumn 1940, nightly air raid warnings pierced the darkness of Grimsargh's night sky. The reality of war is grim and the vicar was asked to fill in a Government return stating how many burial places he could provide in the churchyard. The Reverend G. Rubie had a good relationship with the Local Defence Volunteers or Home Guard, which was under the command of Colonel Potter who served in the Great War. Checkpoints were set up near the village boundary at the White Bull and bus passengers were asked to produce their identity cards. Reservoirs and key water installations including the pipeline from Thirlmere

Close to the ruins of Lower Hall, a fine Victorian iron aqueduct carries the four conduits of water supply across the Ribble and was once guarded by the local 'Dad's Army'.

Author's collection

to Manchester were guarded by the volunteer soldiers. One senior Grimsargh citizen performed his duties armed with an old gun on Beacon Fell and was dedicated to the cause of capturing hordes of German parachutists who, we are told, were about to descend on England's green and pleasant land. Mrs Ada Wild of Dixon's Farm remembers the Italian prisoners of war who constructed a 'tank trap' alongside Savick Brook and a reinforced concrete gun house in the nearby field. Thankfully, neither of these proved necessary.

Mr and Mrs Mallot at Grimsargh House both toiled for good causes and made a substantial contribution to the war effort in Grimsargh. Their mansion became the headquarters of the local WVS and the base for the ambulance which was driven by Mrs Potter, the wife of Colonel C. Potter, of the Home Guard. A room was allocated to be manned by first aid and fire watching volunteers each night. Mrs Mallott was said to be a natural leader of the WVS and with about thirty active members had responsibility as billeting and evacuation officer. The WVS met at Grimsargh House once a fortnight to make clothes for evacuees and netting for the troops and on alternate weeks enjoyed a social evening organised by Mrs Mallott. At Christmas time the Grimsargh Mothers' Union sent a gift to over forty young men from the village who had joined the services. The parcel contained a ten-shilling note, woollen comforts and cigarettes. Also at Christmas more than 150 Grimsargh schoolchildren and evacuees enjoyed their party organised by Mrs Mallott and Mrs Potter together with many willing helpers. The children enjoyed their Christmas fare in the gaily-decorated Assembly Room and after the meal, a Punch and Judy show was given by Professor Green of Blackpool. This was followed by community singing and yet another cinematograph performance provided by the vicar, Reverend Rubie. The celluloid images got the kids laughing before they finally joined in with the chorus of 'Auld Lang Syne'.

Mr Mallott handed over his study for the use of the night shift on fire watch. Adults received instruction in Civil Defence and were supplied with a shovel and stirrup pump to augment the frequently held fire drills. All signposts were removed, place names obliterated, roadblocks implemented, and concrete pillboxes and shelters erected. Compared with Liverpool and the major cities the Preston area escaped relentless bombing. However, it is probable that Courtaulds factory was within the bomber's sights when mis-directed bombs descended on Grimsargh during the early 1940s. At the Courtaulds factory, an annex had been acquired by the Ministry of Defence and local women, including my mother, working on the night shift, contributed to the industrial war effort. I am informed that morale on the production line was high and at the dead of night morale-boosting songs spontaneously echoed across the shop floor, oblivious to Hitler's bombs narrowly missing the factory.

After a German bomb realigned the landscape at Cow Hill with a massive crater there followed an isolated bombing of properties near to Stone Cross and Higher Brockholes. About 9.30 p.m. on a Saturday evening in September the sirens at Courtaulds pierced the night sky. The lone German night raider may have been targeting the factory but instead succeeded in badly damaging two houses at Stone Cross on Longridge Road and narrowly missing Higher Brockholes Farm. Luckily no one was killed during the attack but it was definitely a close one for the Nelson family at Three Mile Cross Farm. Sixty years later Mrs Gladys Hundziak (née Nelson) related the events to me.

At nine o'clock dad sent us five children to bed. Twenty minutes later we heard the air raid warning and the drone of a German bomber. Within seconds of dad's exclamation, 'That sounds like a Jerry', we heard a whoosh and the house literally rocked. We lay in bed scared and motionless and the following morning saw that the edge of the bomb crater was about six feet from the back door. The coal shed had been demolished and miraculously we all survived, shocked but unscathed. Two of the new semis on Longridge Road had been badly damaged and we were very relieved to know that no one was seriously injured. Dad thought Jerry was either targeting Courtaulds or being chased by the RAF and decided to jettison his bombs on us! Coal was scattered across the farm and fields and nearby at Grimsargh Hall Farm a high explosive landed right in the middle of a midden filled with manure. The consequential mess 'when the stuff hit the fan' did not deter an army of sightseers from Ribbleton visiting us on the Sunday morning. My mum, Margaret Nelson, put out a collection box in the yard. The proceeds were donated to the War Office to fund the next Spitfire and help prevent further trauma at Grimsargh.

The *Lancashire Evening Post* reported on the air attack on both Grimsargh and Brockholes:

The raider flew straight across the town dropping incendiary bombs at intervals across the most thickly populated part and high explosive bombs on the suburbs. One of the high explosives that dropped in the suburbs landed between two semi-detached houses on Longridge Road, near the stone cross memorial. It left a 15 foot deep crater in the garden and severely damaged both houses. The only casualty was one of the occupiers, a Mr Joseph Hodgson who sustained a cut wrist. He was in the bathroom cleaning his teeth when the explosion happened.

The heat got too close for comfort at Higher Brockholes. Farmer Joseph Wright told the *Post*, 'I remember being awakened one night by a German plane circling the area. I went downstairs and everywhere outside seemed to be enveloped in flames. Incendiary bombs appeared to have dropped in several places but luckily they had just missed the house and the barns which were filled with the harvest.' The next day Civil Defence workers came to the farm and told Mr Wright they had collected the remains of about 400 incendiary bombs, which had fallen in the area during the night. In later years, Mr Wright still came across the odd incendiary when he was ploughing and believed there could still be more bomb relics to be located.

After all the turmoil of war, a Service of Thanksgiving was held in St Michael's Church for VE Day on 7 May 1945 and this was followed by a well-deserved two-day holiday. However, it was not only German bombs that changed the face of Grimsargh as we will see in the next chapter.

Grimsargh

THE STORY OF A
LANCASHIRE VILLAGE

258

CHAPTER NINETEEN

The Changing Face
of Grimsargh

AJOR DEVELOPMENT was planned for a new town for Central Lancashire based on Preston, Chorley and Leyland and a 1965 Act of Parliament drew up policy on new town planning. In December 1968, the extent of the new town was defined and many areas took exception including Grimsargh and Longridge. Originally the expansion was to go eastwards beyond Longridge and embrace Grimsargh within the urban sprawl. The Corporation's plans for the district were the subject of two public enquiries, the first of which was opened in Preston on 12 May 1969. The main objections from Longridge concerned the inclusion of the socalled 'Longridge Spur'. There was opposition from the new town proponents who stated, 'If the Longridge Spur were omitted, or cut back to a Grimsargh/Elston line, this would reduce the population capacity of the town and so inhibit the prospects of achieving the aim of a centre of growth.' Local Grimsargh people were opposed to the loss of green fields. The campaign was led by Councillor Geoff Swarbrick who became Preston's First Citizen during the Millennium and the most recent Grimsargh resident to have had the honour of being Mayor of Preston bestowed upon him.

The Minister's decision came on 24 March 1970. He decided to exclude most of the Longridge spur and other land amounting to almost 5,600 acres but the area east of the M6 motorway as far as the Grimsargh to Goosnargh road and land at Elston was to be designated for the new town. In December 1972 the Central Lancashire Development Corporation (CLDC) announced that it proposed to make compulsory purchase orders on over 3,000 acres of land in the Grimsargh area. The shock news revealed in the outline plan published by the CLDC was that the population of Grimsargh was to rise from its population of 1,600 to 20,000 by 1986 and 52,000 by 2001.[1] The report stated that 'Grimsargh of ancient origin, has avoided the worse aspects of nineteenthcentury development which characterised so many parts of the area, but has outgrown its compact form in a series of suburban developments from the inter-war period to the present day. The township as a whole has very great potential for future development. The topography is varied with gently undulating pasture alternating with deeply incised and well-wooded stream valleys such as Savick Brook and the tributaries of the Ribble, together with the dramatic escarpment of the Ribble itself.' Not everyone agreed — a Grimsargh and Haighton Action Committee was formed to fight the new town boundary and they presented strong opposition at a public inquiry in August, 1973 into the Compulsory Purchase Orders. In June 1974 it was revealed that Haighton was to be developed before Grimsargh and at the end of 1974 a further public enquiry was held at Preston into the CLDC's Outline Plan. There were further cutbacks but large-scale expansion around the peripheral areas of Grimsargh has continued.

The railway provided a ticket for change in the nineteenth century and helped to spawn Grimsargh's development. Over 150 years later there have been at least four major housing developments and a planned Redrow development of 200 dwellings will significantly transform village life when work commences early in 2003. More greenfield sites, woodland and ancient field systems behind the village hall will now have to be sacrificed. This seems a familiar story throughout the country despite the ramifications of the 1947 Town and Country Planning Act, which first legislated for changes to the use of land by implementing requirements for planning permission by the appropriate planning authorities.

Centuries after some Grimsargh people moved out of their rural homes to find work in swelling towns like Preston, the movement is being reversed. The consequential infrastructure of new road networks and industrial and housing developments has led to loss of hedgerows, felled trees, dwindling ponds and a general loss of habitat for wildlife. Planned developments close to the boundary of the Red Scar and Tun Brook woodland site are likely to cause some degradation of this sensitive Site of Special Scientific Interest through misuse and general disturbance. It is evident that the conservation debate of sustaining the village character is losing out to the bulldozers. Grimsargh village will now gain the whole paraphernalia of a new infrastructure. The course of so-called progress, it seems, must march relentlessly on with unabated momentum.

After the *laissez-faire* ribbon development of villages such as Grimsargh there now seems too little scope for compromise. The fields of Preston East have currently been sacrificed to the latest phase of extensive industrial development and at the time of writing developments continue to devour the pleasant countryside with its diminishing bird populations. People and employment matter but future generations should not be denied opportunities for leisure and a rich biodiversity of wildlife. We will have to wait and see if the ramifications of housing and industrial developments contained in existing and future proposals of Lancashire County and Preston Borough Councils grandiose plans will be welcomed by tomorrow's children. As we have seen there have been certain triumphs for local democracy due to the commitment of local people who dare to speak out. It reminds me of the philosophy of a certain George Bernard Shaw: 'The reasonable man adapts himself to the world: the unreasonable man persists in trying to adapt the world to himself. Therefore all progress depends on the unreasonable man.'

With the proposals to construct 200 new houses to supplement Grimsargh's 900-plus homes, the population could rise to around 3,000 people. Rowan and Mary Harty brought their shop into the twenty-first century by doubling its size and giving it a contemporary supermarket image. The Post Office moved to its present location in a semi-detached house before the last war. Business enterprise led to a combined Post Office/village store by taking over the adjoining semi. The shop's pivotal role for the Grimsargh community has since been managed by a succession of owners culminating in the arrival of Mr and Mrs Rowan Harty in 1997. Grimsargh Post Office and convenience store now has a considerable range of stock tightly managed on their computer systems. Their enterprise combines the best of the old with the new and the smell of freshly baked bread resurrects a Grimsargh tradition dating back to the days of James Myerscough's original village shop.

Demographics have changed a great deal in recent years and Grimsargh, like so many other villages, is rapidly becoming a commuter zone for Preston and further afield. Lancashire's major towns and cities are easily reached by a convenient link with the M6 motorway less than two miles away. Dairy and beef farmers still earn a living, but many farms have now been converted into dwelling houses. Even the old terrace names on Preston Road including Longsight Terrace, Kitchen Terrace, Sunny Bank, Myrtle Bank and Lynwood Villas on Whittingham Lane have plunged into obscurity with the introduction of new postcodes and now serve as a reminder of Grimsargh's nostalgic past.

Not surprisingly local and national beaurocracy often comes in for a certain amount of chaff, for despite the rhetoric of politicians it is difficult to turn the clock back on a damaged environment. The changing landscape is ongoing and landscape historians will probably have a field day with their research in the next century.

As to how it will look then boggles the imagination in view of current radical proposals, and clearly anything can happen. Fortunately some researchers will be blissfully ignorant of what might have faced them and how much head-scratching they were spared. A comedian friend of mine, Peter Brown from Penwortham, told me that one member of a local council suggested erecting a Cromwellian Millenium Dome on the banks of the Ribble at Horse Shoe Bend – doubtless following the lead set by central government with the dome at Greenwich. Fortuitously, the council had more sense than money and the folly was scuppered. At the commencement of the next financial year on 1 April the proposer was summoned to appear before his colleagues and prescribed twelve months' counselling forthwith!

St Michael's Church of England Primary School

Throughout its history the old village school invariably remained a happy and secure haven for the country child. Time marches on and so does progress, and computer technology has been installed in the modern Grimsargh St Michael's School. Mr J.W.R. Lister from St Thomas's School, Lytham, succeeded Miss Carbis in 1964 and together with his staff facilitated the move from the redundant old school to the brand new Grimsargh St Michael's Church of England Primary School in 1968. Mr Lister maintained traditonal values and also propagated the seeds of responsible citizenship in the minds of Grimsargh's young people in the traditional and well-disciplined classroom environment.

The dream of a modern school for the village became reality when the first children walked across the threshold of the new building on 21 October 1968. Mr Lister, very well respected by children and colleagues alike, died in office and was succeeded as headteacher by Mr Geoff Bond and Mrs Nellie Cowell

respectively. Mrs Cowell taught at the new school for twenty-five years and was headmistress between 1990 and 1997. The present headteacher, Mrs Janet Butterworth, has led a team of seven teachers and support staff into the twenty-first century, whilst providing for the educational needs of 176 children from the Grimsargh area, whose ages range from four to eleven years.

The Vicar of Grimsargh, the Reverend Geoffrey Loxham, is Chairman of the Governing Body. The joint responsibilities of the Governing Body include the content of the secular and religious curriculum, the admission of pupils, regular communication with parents, and the appointment of staff with whom they work in close consultation. The teaching of Religious Education is governed by the Blackburn Diocese who ensure that the Parochial Church Council contribute fifteen per cent towards the upkeep of the building. Each Monday morning the Reverend Loxham follows the time-honoured tradition of taking the short walk from the Vicarage to the school to take morning assembly and share prayers with children and staff. Mrs Butterworth still wields the original school cane as an anachronistic exhibit in the history lesson and definitely not to the dread of naughty children!

The Mission statement of Grimsargh St Michael's School maintains the best of the old worthy traditions with new educational policy and philosophy and reads: 'The School's aim is to develop the children intellectually, socially, morally, spiritually, physically and culturally within a caring, supportive, and stimulating environment, based on the values of the Christian faith, taking into consideration each child's needs, abilities, and interests' – I suspect at least one venerable former teacher would have been pleased with the statement and awarded it full marks!

The Village Hall

Grimsargh is catering for the expanding population of well over 2,000 people and the village hall provides for an eclectic mix of interests. Its existence is a tribute to the resolve and campaigning spirit of villagers. The vision of a new village hall was conceived to improve the quality of life and provide better facilities for all. Forty years after the demise of the old Assembly Hall it was felt there was an urgent need for a new village hall. In May 1971 the Parish Council called a meeting to form a committee to 'undertake the provision of a community centre in the village'. Thirteen people offered their names and became founder member of what became known as GRAFT – Grimsargh Village Area Foundation Team – led by Dr Douglas Watt as Chairman and his wife Helen, who became Secretary.

Graft it certainly was and it seemed like there were endless delays in obtaining support from official bodies. Great ingenuity was shown in fund raising by the indefatigable team. Events included taking over the Field Day from the Old People's Welfare Committee, parties and draws, dances, a Christmas Fayre, a '200 Club', 'It's a Knockout' contests, daffodil teas, sunflower-growing contests – anything to raise money.

Councillor Geoff Swarbrick built a train called 'The Grimsargh Flyer' which was really an old Austin Mini car in disguise. Kids of all ages welcomed the arrival of the green fun train during the fund raising years. Instead of raising steam it raised hundreds of pounds for the kitty when it led the Field Day processions complete with an amplifier and military band tapes. A major hurdle was overcome in April 1980, when Central Lancashire New Town offered a plot on the former Fulwood Amateurs' football ground for the sum of £4,222. Building began in 1982, with the cost of the new hall put at £107,200.

A total of 150 meetings were held in the homes of members

The almost-completed village hall. It was purpose-built and now serves the village for a variety of functions.
Courtesy of Councillor G. Swarbrick

The Changing Face of Grimsargh

Dr Douglas Watt and Councillor Geoff Swarbrick at the official opening of the village hall.
Courtesy of Councillor G. Swarbrick

in Grimsargh and Longridge. On the agenda in June 1982 was an advert in the *Lancashire Evening Post*. It concerned the sale of 19,000 wooden flooring blocks from the floor of the then-defunct Courtaulds canteen. It was decided to purchase them and considerable work went into their removal and storage. A valiant group set about the slow and tedious task of scraping off hardened bitumen from the blocks in preparation for relaying. Local magistrate Vic Moores had a brilliant idea to alleviate the trials and tribulations and provide some help for the team. The results of real-life trials to employ youths on community service could be utilised and the probation service was approached. A gang of youths duly arrived and under supervision set about their punishment task. Surprisingly, the job lasted only a few days and the blocks were stored ready for laying. A week before the flooring specialist was due the blocks were tipped out of their bags. Surprise, surprise – bitumen deposits still adhered to most of the blocks. It was discovered that the youths had only cleaned a few blocks and put them on top of each bag, which brings one back to the old adage: if you want a job doing right, do it yourself. The bogus team could not be recalled and it now had to be all hands to the pumps with volunteers working till their hands ached and became ingrained with the bitumen dust in order to complete the tight work schedule.

On Saturday 8 October 1983, the culmination of twelve years' work by village residents rose triumphant over all obstacles and finally became a reality. The purpose-built village hall and car park adjoining Preston Road was officially opened by Mr Harold Bridges OBE, whose trust donated £5,000 to purchase the old football pitch. Mr Bridges said, 'I would like to thank the committee for the opportunity to open this magnificent village hall. This is the twenty-first village hall that the Foundation has given support to in north-west Lancashire. Village halls are going to have far greater importance than they have had in the past and such a project depended on support from the community. Village halls will take their place.' Mr Bridges was presented with a silver tray and a bouquet on behalf of the committee to commemorate 'this wonderful day in the history of Grimsargh'. A plaque was unveiled and a tree planted and the public viewed the facilities. Most people found it to be a homely place and very welcoming.

The building comprises a main hall with a stage and bar, a smaller hall ideal for meetings of thirty to forty people, kitchen, boiler room and storage. At the opening Dr Watt wrote a feature article in the magazine published by the Community Council of Lancashire.

> The opening of the hall has enabled the formation of the playgroup, youth club, gardening club, badminton, club, all of which are thriving. In addition the hall is used by the WI, ladies' forum, parish council and further education classes. A luncheon club has been set up and a sequence dancing club meets regularly. A very successful school of dancing and ballet uses the hall as its headquarters. This proliferation of activities shows how great the need was for this facility. There were times when the problems of fund raising and persuading the Central Lancashire Development Association to release the land seemed insurmountable. There is no doubt that the building would never have got off the ground but for the dedication of Dr Watt and his committee. Our forefathers will probably find it difficult to believe that there was ever a time when the village did not have its own hall, or indeed other well-founded institutions.

An Audience with the Grimsargh Players

The Society can trace its roots from some of the earliest dramatic efforts in Grimsargh village. It was in December 1927 when the group that was soon to become the Grimsargh Players first took to the stage. They produced two children's plays at the Grimsargh Assembly Rooms featuring many familiar names. The Assembly Rooms remained the home of the players for their formative years. Refreshments and dressing facilities were provided by court-esy of Myerscough's Bakery.

Following the war the Society as we know it today was properly constituted in 1947. Those founding members could hardly have expected their humble club to celebrate its Golden Jubilee in 1997. It is thanks to them that the Grimsargh Players continue to flourish into the new Millennium with two full-length plays staged at the Preston Playhouse each year. Alston Hall has been the longstanding home to the players' rehearsal periods held between September and March. Combined with the presentation of numerous evenings of drama and the involvement of several members in the provision of drama course,s the Grimsargh Players have become a familiar part of Alston Hall's activities.

Since 1947 the Society has been an integral part of village life and, of course, they always welcome new members who may be budding thespians or just want to participate in some other way.

Two Centuries Not Out

Grimsargh has maintained the joyousness of the old country festivals that were beginning to die out. Generations of children from St Michael's School have been dancing round the Maypole, at the annual Vicarage Garden Party, for almost a century and long may the rustic rites continue. The village green has been at the heart of the local community since Herbert Mallott was in residence at Grimsargh House in 1938.

The tradition of schoolchildren from St Michael's dancing round the Maypole at the Vicarage Garden Party goes back over many years.
Parish records

Nellie Carbis (centre) opene the Field Day in 1970.
Parish records

Mrs Brindle crowning the Rose Queen, Gillian Thoma in 1970.
Parish records

The village green is seen at its best on the occasion of the Grimsargh Field Day. In June 1972, the tradition was resurrected as a means of fund raising for the new village hall. After a few lapsed years the annual event has been reinstated by a dedicated committee of supporters who formed the Grimsargh Field Day Committee. The Rose Queen, her retinue, floats and brass bands help to create a carnival atmosphere and it is testament to the dedication of the committee, generous sponsorship from large organisations, small businesses and individuals that everything runs smoothly on the day.

Traditionally no village green is complete without certain institutions and top of my agenda would be a game of cricket on a summer's evening; though nowadays I am more inclined to watch. In 1949, Herbert Mallott along with Jack Wild, Ted Melling and Arthur Barnforth were anxious to put Grimsargh on the cricket map and formed Grimsargh Cricket Club. The home games were played on the Grimsargh playing fields and the club enjoyed its best season in 1952, when it reached the final of the

The young people of Grimsargh with Nellie Carbis at the 1970 Field Day.
Parish records

The procession of the Rose
Queen heads towards the
Field Day Celebrations in 20▪
led by Reverend Geoffrey
Loxham, PC Yvette Ashton
and Father Harry Doyle.
Author's collection

Makinson cup playing in front of 3,000 spectators. Sadly, the club
was disbanded in 1957, due to a lack of players but was reformed
in 1978. In the early days, changing facilities consisted of a tent
on the green. Seven years of fund raising and help from the
Harold Bridges Foundation culminated in the opening of a brand
new cricket pavilion in 1995. The team has since gone from
strength to strength and is now well established in various leagues.
There is also a junior team made up of Grimsargh's aspiring
cricketers.

The teams may even gain some inspiration from the club's
hard-working officers including secretary, Marie Wallbank and
her husband, Bob, an ex-Lancashire Schoolboys player and former
club chairman. Stalwart team members include Grimsargh photo-
grapher, Phil Garlington, who bowled the rest of the team over
with his plans for a cheeky and raunchy WI Rylestone-style

calendar. The 2002 calendar features the lads in various poses and all the proceeds will help to raise funds for Manchester Children's Hospital. Certainly, there was no shortage of members lining up to feature in the calendar and it is due to their fans and a degree of media coverage – or should that be media exposure? – that the calendar has been a success.

The Nellie Carbis Millennium Woodland

Miss Carbis nurtured the school garden long after her retirement as headmistress but with advancing years the garden became neglected. The land was subsequently purchased by Grimsargh Parish Council for £1 from the New Town Commission. In 1998 a feasibility study decreed that it could be restored and the project was launched as the 'Nellie Carbis Millennium Woodland'. Restoration of Grimsargh's secret garden began in January 1999. Miss Carbis continued to oversee the work and gave her blessing to new features such as footpaths and a bridge over a mini-lake.

The Nellie Carbis
Millennium Woodland.
Courtesy of D. Leech

She toured the revitalised woodland only days before her death on 20 November 1999, and was delighted with what she saw.

The on-going propagation process has been implemented by a project team and a nucleus of devoted and hard-working villagers led by Mr David Leech. The overgrown vegetation was cleared and the original stock preserved. The pond was rebuilt with an integral fine new bridge. The focus was on easier access for the disabled and wide new paths and a new entrance gate has helped to meet this need. To a certain extent, the course of events has gone full circle with children from the two local schools again working in the garden. In keeping with the traditions of the old Parochial School the Nellie Carbis Millennium Woodland is still a valuable educational resource, appropriate for the biological science component of the National Curriculum. The transformation has been greatly enhanced by generous funding provided by industry and several organisations. The supplementation of many new bulbs, plants, and trees have once again made the garden interesting throughout the year both as a haven for nature and a peaceful woodland which is a mass of colour in Summer. The Nellie Carbis Millennium Woodland was formally opened by the Mayor of Preston, Councillor Geoff Swarbrick (also a resident of Grimsargh) as the village's Millennium Project. During the same year a tree was planted on behalf of the project team in remembrance of Miss Carbis and was later dedicated by the Vicar of Grimsargh, the Reverend Geoffrey Loxham, during a special ceremony. The woodland is open during daylight hours and entry is free. It has its own web site at www.nellsgarden.fsnet.co.uk and now attracts visitors from afar.

Reference

1. CLDC Outline Plan – published November 1973 and a report contained in the *Longridge News*, dated 4 January 1979.

CHAPTER TWENTY

Lancashire Chaff

I N 1992 Miss Carbis recounted that 'I am now playing on injury time and the whistle could blow at any minute. What can I do? Like the old chap "I sits and thinks and sometimes I just sits." Thoughts jostle up and down like midges on a summer's evening and they take me back to people and places I have known and loved.' Nellie still lived in the age of the dollytub, the posser and the mangle and had neither the will nor the wish to cope with modern technology.[1] In 1935 Miss Carbis 'flitted to Grimsargh – my father and mother and our elderly cat, and all our elderly furniture. Tib settled into his new home and lived to enjoy a few years of country life. My father and mother settled just as well and found many kind friends in Grimsargh.'[2] This quotation encapsulates her humour and feelings for Grimsargh. Unquestionably, the tall headmistress struck more than a chord with some of her pupils whom she told in a deep voice, 'I will have you know that I will not tolerate bad behaviour.' Mere presence and a degree of eye contact was enough to maintain discipline for infinite school terms.

I remember my first encounter with her in 1957 when I joined the former Preston Scientific Society, which met in Ellesmere Chambers next to The Empire Theatre in Church Street, Preston. A well-informed society it certainly was, but never dull or boring. The weekly lectures by experts in their own particular field included those given by Miss Carbis, who was also a venerable member and officer of this historic Society founded in 1876. My initial perception was of a tall woman with a serious look, until you saw the twinkle in her eye and the way her expression changed to a smile that radiated kindness and warmth of personality. Possessed with a range of talents Miss Carbis was always willing to share her knowledge with anyone, and as a radio broadcaster and author her distinctive dulcet tones reached a much wider audience. While entertaining her audiences with frequent anecdotes, it was heartening to know that she was raising money for Imperial Cancer Research.

I know that Nellie Carbis was no stranger to impish and at

times risqué humour and clearly her spirit of bouncing back and helping others was again to the fore with her booklet, *Lancashire Chaff*, the proceeds of which were donated to the *Lancashire Evening Post*'s Magic Million Appeal fund. In it she recalled that

> Our entertainments were home-made – we played card games by lamplight in the evening and went to bed by candle light, half-scared by the long flickering shadows that danced up and down the walls. Any work that had to be done outside at night was done by the light of a storm lantern. The knocker-up came round in the morning rattling his bundle of canes against the bedroom windows. Mr Kenny came round in his trap, with a large 'kit' of milk and we carried out our jugs to have our pint or quart ladled into them. When I came to Grimsargh in 1935, Bessy from the farm across the road came round twice a day holding half a dozen 'kits' in each hand, her red flannel petticoat drooping below her skirt, chewing over to herself the items of news she had picked up on her way round the houses.
>
> Babies were not discussed openly until they had actually arrived. I was surprised once when asking a boy about a baby, which I thought had arrived, to be told, It's there alright, but it hasn't come out yet. Expectant mothers didn't go out in public but were taken for a discreet walk in the dusk, when their husbands came home from work. Some children were rather naïve about the birds and the bees – a small boy refused to wear a V-necked pullover that his granny had knitted for him. 'My teacher at school wears one of those and when she bends down you can see her lungs.'

Away from the professional stage there were one or two comedians and raconteurs who shared their anecdotes with great enthusiasm and Miss Nell Carbis was a star player.

A vicar, exhorting his congregation, said, 'And when the time comes, will you be found watching the wise virgins or sleeping with the foolish ones?' (According to Nell the curate thought that they could not have been all that foolish if they were still virgins!)

Many of her tales concerned farmers. A boy who was about to leave school fancied a job on a farm. He went to a farmer and asked if he was thinking of taking anybody on. 'Hasta getten thi character?' asked the farmer. 'No,' said the lad. 'Then gerroff back to thi school master and ask 'im fer one. Then come and see me again.' A week later the farmer met the boy in the village. 'Neh then, asta gettin thi character?' 'No,' said the lad, 'but ah've getten thine, an'm noan coming.'

Another young farmer had been courting and was showing his

Grimsargh

THE STORY OF A
LANCASHIRE VILLAGE

young lady round the farm. He was a bit backward about coming forward and the young lady was losing patience. They were leaning over a gate looking into a field where a cow and its calf were licking noses. The lad nudged the girl and said, 'Seein' them two as set me thinkin' o' doing' summat of same miself.' 'Well,' said the girl, 'get on with it there's nowt stopping thee, it's thi cow!' A buxom woman was asking her way to the farm; 'Can I get through this gate?' she asked a young lad. 'Ah should think so,' he said. 'A load of hay went through it an hour ago.'

Or how about taking the pig for a ride? During the last war, when petrol was strictly rationed, farmers were allowed an extra amount to be used for farm purposes only. The result was that a custom grew up known as 'taking the pig for a ride'. The farmer who wanted to meet his cronies would hitch up the trailer to his car. The pigs became so knowing that they would jump up into the trailer without any encouragement. One local farmer was stopped in Clithereroe by the police and found to be under the influence of drink. He was told that he would not be allowed to drive his car to get home to Grimsargh. 'Tha can keep thi car,' he said, 'but a'mus take t'triler home – t'pig's got to get me ter t'auction tomorrow.'

Lancashire dialect was expressed in a variety of ways and one old chap who fell out with his neighbour's wife sought out the venerable Miss Carbis to vent his spleen. 'Ah caun't think what made 'im wed 'er. She's one o' them women as'd look for lice in a bald 'ead – she's got a mouth like a 'em's bottom and she skens like a Ribble fluke.'

On a trip to the local vet another elderly gentleman eloquently summarised the condition of his dog. 'Ah cawn't mek owt wot's wrong wi' er. She's off her food, an' she doesn't seem to have any life in er.' The same gentleman was a gasbag and proceeded to give the vet a full account of what the doctor said about his wife's ailments. Trying to break in on this, the vet said. 'Tell me, have you noticed her dragging herself along the ground and trying to grind her bottom into the carpet?' 'Eh no,' said the man, 'there's nowt like that – ah don't know as ah've ever ...' Then it dawned on him. 'Oh, tha means t'dog!'

References

1. N. Carbis, *Lancashire Chaff* (1992).
2. N. Carbis, *Nellie Carbis Looks Back.*

CHAPTER TWENTY-ONE

Grimsargh Remembered

The Swinging Sixties

A FEW YEARS AGO I decided to embark on some genea‑ logical research. In endeavouring to trace the origin of the name of Hindle I discovered that the name Hindhull was common in the Whalley area of Lancashire as long ago as the early 1400s. After quite a lot of water had flowed under the bridge it changed to de Hyndill. 'Hindle Wakes' serves as a further reminder of my own ancestors in industrial Lancashire and that there is no justification whatsoever to fly the de Hyndill family banner!

I was born in the penultimate year of World War II in St Joseph's Hospital, Mount Street, Preston, and as a war babe, lived at Ribbleton within view of Grimsargh St Michael's Church spire. In between mature beech trees at Grimsargh, 'a host of golden daffodils' now beautifies St Michael's churchyard in the spring. 'When 'oft upon my couch I lie' I am reminded of Wordsworth's immortal poem and my own early recollections and perceived images of the Grimsargh area. In spring it was a delight to experience the sights of the countryside and be bombarded by early migrant birdsong from the riverine woodlands above the Horse Shoe Bend. For me this awakening of the senses helped to stimulate a lifelong interest of all things natural and appreciation of our countryside heritage.

My childhood memories include watching the legendary Tom Finney outclassing all his opponents on the field of Preston North End, and pillion rides with my grandfather on his BSA Bantam. Grandad Bowman introduced me to the delights of the Ribble Valley in the early 1950s and from his Bantam's pillion seat one could see curlews and lapwings in the fields and the quaint hamlets of Elston or Alston Bottoms on the banks of the Ribble. At Grimsargh a walk onto the station platform of the Whittingham Hospital Railway to look at the antiquated steam train was a compulsory stop for us both. Invariably the kindly engine crew invited me onto the footplate to look at the fiery furnace which was at the heart of the veteran locomotive. Much to my surprise, the driver proceeded to fry his breakfast on the shovel and asked me if I wanted a bacon buttie – thanks but no thanks – before grasping the regulator to take the nurses to work. My father's green Morris 8 often broke down and walking became the preferred option. As a family we enjoyed long walks, some planned, some not, for the reliability of cars was pretty unpredictable. We wandered through Squire Anderton's Wood, past Cow Hill and Grimsargh village green or through Red Scar and Brockhole Woods at the top of Horse Shoe Bend. At Tun Brook numerous steps descended a steep woodland bank leading to a footbridge across the clear and fast-flowing stream.

On leaving school and commencing employment at Whittingham Hospital, work was shared with a young nurse, Dorothy Shorrock, with whom I was destined to share a lifetime. As teenagers we caught the Number 8 Ribble bus to the Palace at Longridge. There was method in my madness because Longridge Palace had the added attraction of double seats for courting couples. Whittingham Hospital was a self-sufficient institution, which had its own farms, church, beautiful gardens and anachronistic transport fleet. This had included the steam railway to Grimsargh, a vintage fire engine and a horse-drawn hearse, which was still in regular use for hospital funerals. On these occasions staff swapped their brown work coats for a black topper and suddenly became reverent. On certain weekdays young Whittingham employees became students and were conveyed to Alston Hall on the hospital's Bedford Charabanc. The fifteen-minute ride on the old coach seemed to stimulate youthful exuberance and may even have raised a few eyebrows in Grimsargh.

Alston Hall was meant to further enrich our education in the science subjects but, alas, some students sustained an appalling lack of commitment! The college skeleton went on regular walkabouts to the rose garden or to take a comfortable seat in the conservatory. Memorable college lecturers included the venerable Miss Barbara Clegg whose presence maintained discipline within this hallowed seat of learning. The Principal, Mr J. Shemilt, took a professional and affectionate interest in each and every one of us. Inspirational and charismatic, there was no subject that failed to engage his superior intelligence and wit. During the excellent lunch we joined students on similar day-release schemes and afterwards followed the sounds of Cliff Richard's 'Move it' and 'Living Doll' to the cellar dance floor. Shades of the famous Liverpool Cavern, perhaps, but in 1960 nobody had heard of the Beatles. The Swinging Sixties at Alston had been launched and the sight of girls dressed fashionably in mini-skirts dancing their lunch hour away, immediately springs to mind.

Away from the confines of the cellar at Alston Hall the resident pair of spotted flycatchers returning to their nest on the imposing ivy-clad building provided a welcome interlude from the cellar and a time for contemplation. After twelve months at Whittingham I decided to become a police cadet at Blackburn with GCE 'O' levels acquired at Alston Hall.

Living in Blackburn did not stop my walks along the Ribble in the Swinging Sixties. Downstream, Higher Brockholes House loomed out of the swirl of the Ribble's early morning mist. Outside, the soil was rich and crops and garden flowers flourished. Vocal bumble-bees foraged over a wealth of wild flowers and the last occupiers of the neglected building performed a ghostly screaming as the sun sank just below the horizon. As twilight dimmed a pair of rare barn owls re-energised their nightly rituals within the historic structure. Symbolically this declining species heralded the passing of Higher Brockholes and in total darkness would have been good soulmates for any spectral visions of the atmospheric seventeenth-century house.

A lonesome pine tree at the side of the Ribble Way today marks the site of Higher Brockholes. Lonesome indeed, for it has endured a major transformation of the landscape of the Ribble valley. Perhaps it was an omen that the buckets of pure water drawn from a well from the gravel beds below Higher Brockholes would one day lead to further exploitation of the site. The newly created gravel workings at Brockholes Quarry wetlands have pro-duced an impressive list of birds. In birding nomenclature the site is today visited by serious 'twitchers' from neighbouring towns, with regulation telescopes mounted on tripods, who often greet each other with the crucial question, 'Anything about?' The closing scene in the history of Brockholes may yet see the establishment of an important and picturesque nature reserve – watch this space!

Quite a few years on from the Swinging Sixties I feel fortunate to be enjoying retirement in Grimsargh. The village has retained something of its rural charm and there are still undefinable

Sunny Bank and Victorian residents shortly after it was built. (No. 8 was the house on the extreme right.)
T. Heginbotham collection

qualities in the appearance of the village green, the backcloth of hills of Longridge and Bowland or the beauty of Ribblesdale with its unspoilt countryside that please the eye. Although Grimsargh's old cottages are outnumbered by modern houses and many of its senior citizens with a tale to tell, have passed on, the village has retained an entity of its own. The friendliness of the villagers is a part of this entity and I am grateful for all those who shared their experiences with a splendid knack of making me feel at home.

Young Alan Wilding was a transient visitor to Sunny Bank in the 1930s and kindly shared his memories of those halcyon days with me.

Memories of a Grimsargh Childhood by Alan Wilding

'My great aunts moved to Grimsargh from No. 82, Stephenson Terrace, Deepdale Road, Preston, in 1932. Their new home in Grimsargh, No. 8, Sunny Bank (now re-numbered) was the last at the end of a terrace of red brick houses on the left of the road to Longridge. It was bought and owned by my great uncle Bert, the funeral director, Herbert Blacow, whose premises were at No. 1, Garstang Road, Preston. Uncle Bert lived at Sunny Bank with his wife Emily, his daughter Dorothy, a vivacious young lady, my two other great-aunts, and uncle John Atkinson.

'My earliest memory of No. 8 at Grimsargh was the slightly winding path through lovely rose beds to the front door. Uncle Bert was an expert with roses and even got a contract to sell them for extra income. On one occasion I remember, as a small boy, he cut one for me for my buttonhole as we set off for a trip on the small steam train, 'Little Annie', which then plied between Grimsargh and Whittingham Mental Hospital, for a walk in the hospital's grounds. This was my first ever train ride and the train trip was the real object of the visit. I seem to recall we walked to the railway terminus in Grimsargh and that the service was used for only a few passengers and bulk freight to the hospital.

'My memory of the house at Sunny Bank was its elegance, with comfortable furniture, probably a continuation of the ambience of the Preston house. There was a huge grandfather clock just inside the front door to the left, near the door to the sitting room and a smaller grandmother clock in a landing part way up the stairs. They never chimed quite in unison and I used to wonder if they ever would. Victorian lifestyle prevailed because most in that household had been born in the late nineteenth century. So we would have afternoon tea off willow-patterned crockery with silver teaspoons and cube sugar using sugar tongs, with which my siblings would threaten to pinch my nose! My great-aunts would always do their own baking and there was ever the delicious smell of baked pastry in the kitchen. There was a room between the hall and the kitchen, which was their 'day room', usually with a warm fire. The elegant sitting room with its chintz furniture, deep pile carpet, ornate fireplace, and highly polished grand piano was treated as the traditional 'parlour' and used mainly for visitors. So I felt deeply honoured as a boy to be allowed into that 'Holy of Holies', during visits with my mother, their niece Kathleen.

'A wide track ran behind all the houses of Sunny Bank Terrace. Beyond was what seemed a huge area of, I think, still more rose beds, with a lawn beyond. At the far end of this area was an extended summerhouse, with a pigeon loft at the left end. Uncle Bert was a great pigeon fancier and would rejoice in flying his pigeons and seeing them return to their loft. There was also a 'swing settee' in a frame and at the height of summer my aunts

Grimsargh

THE STORY OF A
LANCASHIRE VILLAGE

Grimsargh Remembered

would sit out and take afternoon tea there, wearing flowered summer dresses as a change from their usual long dark, rather mournful Victorian wear. Living in the busy town of Preston as we did, a visit to my great-aunts and uncles at Grimsargh was always a special occasion. Time seemed endless and to go more slowly on those visits. It was my first acquaintance with the sort of gracious comfort I was later to experience while living in RAF Officers' messes. On the way I watched the new Courtaulds factory being built with its two red brick chimneys, said to be among the highest in Britain and I remember hoping such industry would not get nearer my beloved Grimsargh.

'I never actually saw one of Uncle Bert's funerals, but I understand he carried on the tradition of his father, in having the hearse pulled by black horses with purple plumes in their head-bands. He thus got most of the big funerals in the Preston area since in the local parlance it was a 'gradely do' and the deceased was 'buried with ham', an expensive delicacy in those days.

'Grimsargh seemed quite a long village and a fairly open airy sort of place, stretched out along the Longridge road. Sixty years after the time I visited Grimsargh as a ten-year-old boy it seemed much as I remembered it. I called on the present occupant of the house in Sunny Bank and explained my visit. I gave her a copy of my book, *Memories of a Preston Childhood*, as a memento, featuring my memories of the house. It was a joy once again to sit by that fire in the day room – it was as if nothing had passed in between. So ended a memorable and very formative period of my life. I've not been back since; though even now, when I hear the music of Lehars's 'Merry Widow', a piece of music which I often heard played on an old wind-up gramophone in my Aunts' house, my mind goes back to those heady days of my dear great-aunts and uncles at Grimsargh, and I let myself wallow in waves of delicious nostalgia.'

Acknowledgements

The following firms have generously sponsored the production of this book:

Mondi Board Ltd
Mitie Property Services (North West) Ltd
T. W. Fabrications Ltd
John Turner and Sons Ltd.
Bako (North West)
Pakawaste Group

I acknowledge the support of the following who have contributed in many different ways

Mr Peter Brown
Dr Stephen Bull
Mr Jack Billington MBE
Mrs Janet Butterworth
Miss Nellie Carbis
Mr Alan Coar
Miss Kirsty Connor
Mr P. Croft
Dr Alan Crosby
Mr Anthony Cross
Mr and Mrs Philip and Nellie Cowell
Mr John Cowell
Father Harry Doyle
Mr Wilfrid Eccles
Mr Jim Ecclestone
Dr Janet Edmunds
Mr Ben Edwards
Mrs Anna Fisher
Mr Phil Garlington
Mr and Mrs Wilfrid and Betty Gornall
Father Philip Graystone
Dr Andrew Gritt
Mr and Mrs Rowan and Mary Harty
Mr Frank Harrison
Mr Jonathan Heaton
Mr Tom Heginbotham
Mr G. Hothersall

Acknowledgements

Dr John and Mrs Enid Houghton
Mrs Gladys Hundziak
Mr Peter Isles
Mrs Margaret Jackson
Mr Michael Jackson
Mr Graham Jones
Mr Gareth Lazell
Reverend Geoffrey Loxham
Mr and Mrs Francis and Karen McGrath
Mr Nigel Morgan
Mrs Nell Noblet
Mr Tom Nuttall
Miss Eileen Parker
Mr and Mrs M. Pattinson
Mrs Frances Potter
Mr Ian Rankin
Mr Leonard Redmayne
Mrs Marian Roberts
Mrs Esther Rigby
Miss Olive Sim
Councillor Geoff Swarbrick
Mr Nicholas J. Swarbrick
Dr Frank Salter
Mr Peter Vickers
Mrs Nellie Willett
Mrs Ada Wild
Wing Commander Alan Wilding
Mr David Wilkinson
Mr Brian Woodburn
Mrs Evelyn Woods
Mrs Frances Wright
Ann Dennison and staff at Harris Reference Library
Elaine Hargreaves and staff at the office of the Diocese of
    Blackburn
Mrs Jayne Woollam and the Grimsargh Field Day Committee
Staff at the Lancashire Record Office
The Longridge News
Lancashire Evening Post

Appendices

List of non-Jurors in 1715

The History of Longridge by Tom Smith (1888), contains a list of non-Jurors in 1715 which reflects the nature of employment.

	£	s.	d.
Paul Charnley, yeoman, freehold estate and at Elston, subject to annuities to his mother and Anne, his sister	30	7	6
John Coseing, husbandman, leasehold estate	9	17	6
Robert Hummer, miller			
Richard Fishwick, carpenter			
Clarkson, husbandman			
James Rogerson, yeoman			
John Newsham, of Brockhull, 7 houses and 16 acres at Fulwood, and freehold estate at Whittingham	26	15	0
Gilbert Slater, husbandman, son of Thomas Slater, leasehold there and at Haighton, part tenanted by Thomas Slater, charge with £20 to his sister and £4 to his mother	11	0	0
Elizabeth Hull, widow, estate at Magnes, in Kirkham, left to her by her husband W. Hull for the maintenance of her children	23	0	0
Thomas Slater, yeoman, leasehold	13	0	0
Alice Charnley, of Elston, widow, annuity of £5 and leasehold land	6	5	0
Ann Charnley, spinster, amount out of land at Elston in possession of Paul Charnley	5	0	0
Henry Crumaleach, Elston, yeoman, 32 acres in fee tail, charged with £4 to his sister, and bequeathed by his father-in-law, John Walmsley, Elston, tanner			

I have studied many wills and probate inventories of the people of Grimsargh-with-Brockholes, which are archived at the Lancashire Record Office. Legible probate inventries provide an essential insight into what life was like in the seventeenth- and eighteenth-century township. Every item in all rooms, as well as agricultural implements, was meticulously listed by the appraisers and the inventory of John Welchman is chosen as a particularly interesting one. Arable farming was clearly very important to John Welchman, who died suddenly on 7 November 1693.

Inventory of John Welchman

	£	s.	d.
Inprimis [First] in wheat, oates, beans, barley, rye and hay	136		
Item in wheat growing	4	3	4
Item in 18 geldings, mares and colts	53	0	
Item 10 cowes, one heffer and a bull	43	0	
Item 6 bullocks, 5 stirks and 8 calves	40	0	
Item 9 sheep and two swine	3	10	
Item geese, ducks, turkeys and hens	1	0	
Item in arks in the barnes	3	10	
Item in wheels and carts	6	0	
Item in sacks, ridles, skutles, fans, pickforks and window sheet	1	0	
Item plows, harrows, sleds, cart saddles, strappings, singletrees, one wheelbarrow and 2 new yates	1	18	4
Item teames iron traces collars and halters	1	0	
Item in new iron, old iron, wimbles, chisells, iron axletree pins		15	
Item spades, forks, muckcrooks yokes and bowes		15	6
Item in wood over the swinecoats and in the worke house		6	8
Item in wood on the green at barn end, in cart house and in the woods	2	0	
Item in the milne, cart chests, an old wane, 2 old chists an Arke, have hook nets, with other old goods	1	10	
Item the haireing on the kilne, boards and wood in the new stable	1	10	
Item in the garner ash boards, oake board with other wood	8	0	
Item pack sadles, orleys, seedhopper with other old goods in the garner	6		
Item in the barkhouse 2 chists, 2 salting tubbs with other odd goods	8		
Item in boarded roome 3 chists, an old cupboard, shelves, one web of lead, hemp and other old goods	1	6	8
Item in the flaggd chamber 2 pair of bestocks with bedding hangings, 6 chaires, fire iron with other goods	3	10	0
Item in the buttery chamber a pair of bedstocks with beddinge and hangings, one little table one chist in the stare case with other old goodes	1	10	0
Item in the red chamber 2 paire of bedstocks with feather beds,			

bedcloaths, hangings, six chairs, one table, one chist, and 4 quishons	9	8	6
Item in the porch chamber in bedstocks feather bed, bedcloaths, hangings, one table, one chaire and carpet	3	0	0
Item in the white chamber one paire of bedstocks with dawne bed, bedcloaths, hangings, 2 tables, 2 stands with some other old goods	8	10	6
Item in the wenches chamber 3 pairs of bedstocks with all bedding and bedstocks thereunto belonging	4	8	6
Item in the buttery chamber one paire of bedstocks, one feather bed, bedcloaths hangings, one press, 2 chists, one fire iron, two covered stools with other goods	6	5	0
Item one watch and silver plate	5	0	0
Item in the clossett one seeing glass, one cupboard, white metle lasses and some other goods of small value		12	
Item one old brass clock		15	
Item in the servants chamber in bedstocks and bedding and two chists	2	0	0
Item in the parlour one oval table one chist of drawers, two other tables, 7 cahaires, 5 stooles, one fire iron with other old goods	2	13	4
Item in the day house, one great Arke one flowers chist, 5 old tresls, 12 cheesfatts with basons, treys, barrells, muggs and some other old goods	2	10	0
Item in malt meal butter and cheese	5	6	0
Item in the seller 4 barrells and 3 shelves with other odd goods		15	
Item in the hall 4 tables with formes, 7 chaires, one paire of Virginalls with frame, 6 Quishons, 5 voiders with some other goods	1	7	0
Item in the buttery oneold cupboard and a table with shelves pewder brass and linnen	15	0	0
Item in the kitchen one setle one cupboard, one plate cupboard, stooles, foure chaires, two tresls with trenchers and other goods	1	7	0
Item the fire iron in the kitching with tongs fire shovel, girdle, spitts, withall other iron utensills and tinn goods	1	10	0
Item 2 gunns a cross bow and a pistol	1	5	0
Item in ladders and cart ropes		12	
Item in the brew house one lead one Arke two old chists with wooden vessell	2	18	
Item in turfe and coals		10	
Item one bull hide and some other leather		12	
Item the decedants apparrell	7	0	
total £402		9	4

Valued and apprised by Ri: Graton, Ric: Kellett, John Alker.

The Administration Bond stated that 'Know all men by these presents that Ellana Welchman of Brockhall in the County of Lancaster, widow, and Richard Pollard of Walton le Dale in the same county, gentleman are firmly bound by this obligation to the Reverend John Cartwright, Commissary in the Archdeaconry of Richmond in the diocese of Chester in £1,000 on 3rd October 1694.'

Appendices

Red Scar Estate: Particulars of Farms etc. Comprising the Whole Estate 31 October 1918

Name of farm	Occupier	Valuation			Tithe payable			Yearly rent			Gov. val.	Private val.
		a.	r.	p.	£	s.	d.	£	s.	d.		
Woodtop Farm	Richard Bibby	55	0	35		2	9	90			1,970	2,500
Higher Boilton	George Birketts Exs	100	1	14		4	10	150			4,080	
Church House	Farm William Beesley	36	1	27		2	11	81			2,050	2,500
Elston Hall farm	Joshua Burrow	150	0	24		6	3	140			4,130	
Grimsargh Hall farm	Edward Coar	174	3	25		10	4	260			7,000	9,500
School House farm	Arthur Carr	22	1	17		1	9	40			1,310	1,550
Sandbank Farm	Mrs Clegg	61	0	6		4	11	127			3,420	
Roman Road Farm	William Cowell	68	2	35		3	9	130			3,385	3,900
Bank House + land	James Cross						9	25				
Dixon's Farm	Rd. Dewhurst	33	1	16		2	10	70			1,870	2,100
Richie's Farm	Bilsborough	89	0	3		13	0	210	10		5,260	
Tun Brook Head Farm	Wm. Margerison	75	1	29		3	8	125	14		3,430	
Pedder House Farm	W.J. Margerison	68	3	1	2	7	9	140			3,760	4,000
Three Mile Cross Fm	J.T. Nelson	62	3	7		4	4	134			3,600	4,250
Pinfold cottages	Miss Beesley											
W.A. Proctor												
Mrs Lofthouse												
Moss Nook Cottage						2	10	39	12	8		
County Police												
Grimsargh School House												
Red scar and shooting		48	0	21		3	6	100				
Woodland 120 (estimated)												
Bailiff's cottage												
	TOTAL	1,066	2	10	5	16	2	1,862	16	8		

List of Subscribers

Pamela and Matthias Woerfel,
   Grimsargh
Kim Molnar, Grimsargh
Tony and Dianne Cookson,
   Grimsargh
John Batty, Grimsargh
H. F. Brownrigg, Grimsargh
Mr Wilfrid A. Eccles, Grimsargh
Susan Higham, Grimsargh
Mr and Mrs RJ Birch, Grimsargh
Norman Ridding, Grimsargh
Mr G. and Mrs L. C. Bell,
   Grimsargh
Mr N. and Mrs A. Sanderson,
   Grimsargh
Susan Proctor, Alston
Harry Coar, Longridge
Mrs Pauline Speak, Goosnargh
John and Pat Tucker, Grimsargh
Mr and Mrs J. Longworth,
   Grimsargh
Jenny and Richard Coulston,
   Grimsargh
Peter Brown, Penwortham
John and Mary Almond,
   Fulwood
Mr William and Mrs Constance
   Taylor, Grimsargh
Dr and Mrs D. A. L. Watt,
   Morvern
Mr D. A. Lee, Grimsargh
Mrs I. Joynt, Grimsargh
Vic Johnson, Grimsargh
Mrs D. Ryding, Grimsargh

Mr and Mrs Nickless, Grimsargh
Mr and Mrs George Reavley,
   Grimsargh
Mr Peter Uttley, Grimsargh
Melvyn Croasdale, Longridge
Annie Webb, Grimsargh
Chris C. Dover, Longridge
J. A. and L. I. Eccleston,
   Grimsargh
Brenda and Peter Croft,
   Grimsargh
J. and V. Garstang, Grimsargh
L. and M. McKevitt, Grimsargh
Mr P. B. Kenyon, Higher Walton
Brian Woodburn, Alston
Frank Harrison, Huby
Lilian Worrell, Grimsargh
Mr A. Brown, Ashton
John Pinder, Grimsargh
Andrew Shackleton, Fulwood
Brian C. Charnley, Grimsargh
Mr and Mrs Sommerville,
   Grimsargh
Mr and Mrs C. B. Nevett,
   Grimsargh
Capt. J. K. Hall Munday,
   Grimsargh
Mr Anthony F. Bamber,
   Grimsargh
Anthony Coppin, Garstang
Christopher Turner, Grimsargh
Peter B. Williams, Grimsargh
Longridge and District Local
   History Society

William Routledge, Grimsargh

St Michael's C. of E. School,
  Grimsargh

University of Central Lancashire
  Library

Alan Edington, Grimsargh

Mr and Mrs G. Murry,
  Grimsargh

Mr and Mrs K. G. Willan,
  Longridge

Mrs M. Spencer, Grimsargh

Mrs H. Millington, Grimsargh

Ian and Debbie Liptrot,
  Grimsargh

Alan and Rena Eastwood,
  Grimsargh

Mr J. A. Lander, Grimsargh

Charles M. Connor, Longridge

David R. Banks, Longridge

Mr and Mrs P. Cowell,
  Grimsargh

Mr and Mrs A. P. Cowell,
  Grimsargh

Mr and Mrs M. A. Cowell,
  Longridge

Mr and Mrs N. J. Cowell,
  Longridge

Miss Emma Wilton, Grimsargh

Miss Rebecca Wilton,
  Grimsargh

Joseph Wilton, Grimsargh

Mr J. E. Hodgson, Grimsargh

Mr J. Collinson, Grimsargh

Claire Wilby and Scott Nelson,
  Grimsargh

John and Janet Wilby, Grimsargh

J. C. Leach, Grimsargh

A. L. Leach, Grimsargh

Simon Smith, Chipping

Bob Smith, Grimsargh

Mrs Annie Webb, Grimsargh

Lance and Marie Gorman,
  Alston

Doreen Mercer, Fulwood

Carole, Laurence and Edward
  Brown, Grimsargh

Ian and Stephanie Murray,
  Hoghton

Michael Feeley, Grimsargh

Bill Hough, Grimsargh

Mrs Joanne Smith, Grimsargh

Claire Rice, Grimsargh

Mr and Mrs D. Smith,
  Grimsargh

Andrew G. Brown, Grimsargh

Mr and Mrs Wilfred Gornall,
  Haighton

Miss E. O. Simm, Longridge

Mr and Mrs Unsworth,
  Grimsargh

Mrs Hannah Fisher, Grimsargh

Mrs Glenda Thomas, Grimsargh

David G. Williams, Grimsargh

Mrs S. F. Taylor, Grimsargh

Mrs Lilian Ibison, Grimsargh

Mrs Hazel Plum, Haighton

Caroline Trigg, Grimsargh

Kate Wilkinson, Grimsargh

Mrs C. Holland, Grimsargh

Mr and Mrs T. M. Pattinson,
  Grimsargh

Mrs A. Etherington, Grimsargh

Mrs E. Simpson, Longridge

Brian and Christine Dodding,
  Ingol

Diane M. Maier, Longton

Mrs F. Potter, Grimsargh

Mrs E. Best, Grimsargh

Joyce Chessell, Grimsargh

Jonathan and Jane Heaton,
  Grimsargh

Anne and David Barker,
  Grimsargh

Mr James Ashcroft, Grimsargh

John Mark Robinson, Ashton

Mrs Gladys M. Hundziak,
  Grimsargh

Mr Douglas Killip, Grimsargh

Grimsargh

THE STORY OF A
LANCASHIRE VILLAGE

List of Subscribers

Neil and Claire Bamber, Algarve
Aidan Turner-Bishop, Preston
Lee and Victoria Barker,
    Grimsargh
Mrs V. A. Wilson, Grimsargh
Mrs Ella Lewis, Grimsargh
Nigel Morgan, Fulwood
J. and T. Embley, Grimsargh
Mr G. Buckley, Lostock Hall
Mike and Gill Feeley, Preston
Jane and Paul Beckford,
    Longridge
Robert D. S. Wilson, Blackburn
Edward Norcross, Longridge
Brian Simm, Grimsargh
Eileen and Steve Murray,
    Grimsargh
Mrs T. Platt, Grimsargh
Mr K. R. Saunders, Grimsargh
Raymond and Hazel Taylor,
    Grimsargh
Mark and Pam Lamberty,
    Grimsargh
The Naudet Family, Grimsargh
Violet Mary Hitchin, Grimsargh
Mr and Mrs E. H. Clarkson,
    Grimsargh
Mr J. Wiley, Grimsargh
Miss W. P. Baines, Grimsargh
Mr and Mrs Duckworth,
    Grimsargh
David Kerr, Grimsargh
Sheila Gridley, Longridge
M. J. Jones, Grimsargh
Bako North Western Ltd.,
    Preston
Gavin John Brooks,
    Grimsargh
Mr J. M. Terry, Grimsargh
David Edward Buck, Longridge

Mr and Mrs D. G. McNamara,
    Grimsargh
Joseph Grimbaldeston, Grimsargh
Jane Hill, Haighton
Mr and Mrs G. I. Richmond,
    Haighton
B. Boyes, Grimsargh
Richard Simpson, Grimsargh
Eileen M. Parker, Grimsargh
Mr and Mrs R. Woollam,
    Grimsargh
Lynn Pickup, Grimsargh
Mr and Mrs N. Hindle,
    Grimsargh
Mr and Mrs M. Parker, New
    Longton
Ms B. Woollam, Clayton Green
Mr and Mrs R. Swan, Longridge
Canon and Mrs F. H. Levick,
    Beckingham
Beverley Whalley, Grimsargh
Val Conn, Grimsargh
Mr and Mrs C. Hindle,
    Hoghton
Anthony A. Cross, Tiverton,
    Devon
Alan Wilding, Peebles
Mrs Marian Roberts,
    Wymondham
Mr Gareth Lazell and Caroline,
    Isle of Dogs
Grimsargh House Rest Home,
    Grimsargh
Nigel Morgan, Fulwood
Gail Wright for a much loved
    father, Don Wright
Mrs Nora Houghton (née
    Isherwood), Grimsargh
Dr and Mrs Houghton and
    Family